MARS AND SEX

The Secrets of Sexual Astrology

TRISH MACGREGOR

CITADEL PRESS
Kensington Publishing Corp.
www.kensingtonbooks.com

In memory of Renie Wiley,
extraordinary astrologer, friend, mentor,
and a true Sagittarian right to the end.
1938–2002

And with special thanks to Kate Duffy,
the Aquarian visionary

CITADEL PRESS BOOKS are published by

Kensington Publishing Corp.
850 Third Avenue
New York, NY 10022

All Kensington titles, imprints, and distributed lines are available at special quantity discounts for bulk purchases for sales promotions, premiums, fundraising, educational, or institutional use. Special book excerpts or customized printings can also be created to fit specific needs. For details, write or phone the office of the Kensington special sales manager: Kensington Publishing Corp., 850 Third Avenue, New York, NY 10022, attn: Special Sales Department; phone 1-800-221-2647.

CITADEL PRESS and the Citadel logo are Reg. U.S. Pat. & TM Off.

First printing: January 2004

10 9 8 7 6 5 4 3 2 1

Printed in the United States of America

Library of Congress Control Number: 2003108624

ISBN 0-8065-2529-0

Contents

Introduction: Your Sexual Blueprint

*T*hink of a blueprint, the kind an architect creates before the first brick is laid or the concrete floor is poured. It represents *potential*, an ideal. The building will have so many rooms, doors here, windows there, a wooden staircase, skylights. But until something is actually built, only the blueprint exists, the raw potential, the possibilities.

A birth horoscope is also a blueprint. It describes your potential, the possibilities with which you're born. When you drew your first breath, the planets were at particular positions in the sky. Perhaps the Sun was in Taurus, the Moon in Cancer, Mercury in Aquarius, and on through the solar-system lineup, right on out to Pluto. Each sign that each planet occupied when you were born represents an archetypal energy that is your potential. Nothing in that potential is predetermined. How the various energies manifest themselves throughout your life depends on only one thing—your free will. In other words, *you* are in charge.

Your Sun sign symbolizes your primary archetypal energy, your ego, your individuality—everything that allows you to meet challenges and expand your life. To some extent, it symbolizes your creative abilities, authority, and personal power. The sign that Mars was in when you were born symbolizes your physical energy, stamina, and endurance, your thrust to individualize yourself, your capacity for aggression and action, and your sexuality. For a woman, the sign of natal Mars often describes what she's looking for in a mate and how she expresses her sexuality. For a man, it can describe his ability to form close bonds with other men and how he's likely to express his sexuality. The combination of the planetary energies of the Sun and Mars describes your sexual blueprint.

This blueprint reveals your sexual strengths and insecurities: whether you tend toward monogamy or promiscuity, whether you're essentially experimental or inhibited; your capacity for sexual gratification and the role that your sexuality plays in your adult life, your physical energy and stamina and your awareness of your own body, and your capacity for committed relationships. It can reveal whether you're jealous or possessive, how sexually intuitive you are, and the overall patterns inherent in your sexuality.

Each of us, of course, is influenced by the generation into which we're born. Baby Boomers who came of age during the sixties blew apart their parents' sexual mores by advocating an unprecedented openness about sexuality. Kids who are coming of age now, in the early part of the twenty-first century, are influenced by the sexual mores of *their* generation. But in this book, we're talking about a specific combination of planetary energies that constitute your personal sexual blueprint regardless of when you were born.

A FEW SPECIFICS

Advertisers know that sexuality lies at the heart of many choices we make. It influences which products we buy, from books to movies, and even the motels we choose to stay in when we travel. There's a funny ad running on TV now that shows a man and a woman in bed, in a motel. The man is ready to have sex. But the woman is so taken with the comfort of the bed that she isn't interested in sex. She just wants to sink into the sensuous feel of the sheets, the soft-ness of the pillow, and sleep. The couple never speak; they don't have to. The message is clear: the beds in *this* motel are so divine, they're better than sex.

Our sexuality manifests itself in our hobbies, our creative in-terests, our politics, our worldview. Most of the time, we don't think about sexuality in those terms. We think about it in terms of, well, sex. Sexual attraction. Sexual chemistry. Sexual com-patibility. Sexual preferences. Physical appetites. Or we think about it in terms of romance and love, as in Bogie and Bacall or Taylor and Burton. But regardless of how we think about it, when we are comfortable with our own sexuality, we are more comfortable about who we are and better able to achieve our po-tential.

Sexuality for a person with Mars in Gemini, for example, be-gins in the mind. Attraction is based on communication, lan-guage, an exchange of ideas. Aggression and action are based on language and creative expression. F. Scott and Zelda Fitzgerald both had Mars in Gemini, which was undoubtedly part of their fatal attraction. But whereas Fitzgerald became famous, Zelda went mad. This is where the Sun sign comes in. Fitzgerald had a Libra Sun, Zelda had a Leo Sun. He sought a balance that always eluded him and she had a deep need to be the center of atten-tion. Since she couldn't shine as a person in her own right, her creativity—and her sexuality—found expression in madness.

There are 144 Sun/Mars combinations, and each combina-tion is expressed uniquely and in a variety of ways. Take a woman with a Leo Sun and Mars in Taurus. This combination may not spell out the specific products she buys or the titles of the books she reads. But it certainly tells us the woman craves the spotlight and is likely to be attracted to people who play second fiddle to her. She has tremendous sexual and physical stamina, is sensual, with an inclination toward exhibitionism and a flamboyance that may border on the extreme. She has the relentlessness to achieve her ambitions. Madonna fits that ticket.

Cheryl Crane, the daughter of actress Lana Turner and her second husband, Stephen Crane, also has that same Sun/Mars combination. But the expression has been quite different. When she was fifteen, Crane stabbed her mother's lover with a butcher knife, killing him. She went to prison, attempted suicide several times, and was in and out of rehab. She eventually wrote a book about her bizarre and unhappy childhood, revealing that one of Turner's eight husbands had raped her repeatedly between the ages of ten and thirteen, experiences that ultimately shaped her sexuality.

In the event that you have a Leo Sun and Mars in Taurus, it doesn't mean you'll be the next Madonna or experience the horrors that were Crane's. These two examples are extremes and, let's face it, most of us fall somewhere in between. Even if you are Madonna's "astral twin"—born at the same moment, place, and date as Madonna—it's no guarantee that your life will be like hers. This is where free will comes in.

In researching this book, I started off by looking for people who have the same Sun/Mars combination that I do (Sun in Gemini, Mars in Taurus) and found dozens. But four caught my attention: John F. Kennedy, Nelson Rockefeller, Salman Rushdie, and Whitley Strieber. Hearsay and rumors about JFK aside, I don't know anything about these men's sex lives, and on the surface, there don't seem to be any similarities between them and me. I'm not a politician and will never be president; I'm not wealthy; I'm not a

Muslim; and I've never been paid a million dollars for writing about my abduction experiences. However, like Rushdie and Strieber, I'm a writer. Like Strieber, I have an interest in UFOs and things that go bump in the night.

The similarities have more do with how this Sun/Mars combination uses energy. Strieber, for instance, pursued his writing against tremendous odds. His book *Communion* was rejected by at least a dozen publishers, and he was told to forget the idea and stick to fiction. People thought he was nuts. He persevered, William Morrow eventually bought the book for a million dollars, and it was made into a movie with Christopher Walken. *Communion* launched Strieber on his life's work as an investigator of the weird and the strange.

This illustrates the need of the Gemini Sun to communicate combined with the persistence and fortitude of Mars in Taurus to do the work necessary to get to where you want to be.

But the Sun and Mars are just two pieces of the astrological hologram. In a natal chart, there are seven other planets and the Moon that must be taken into account, as well as the angles these planets make to one another, the placement of the planets in the houses, and factors like asteroids, midpoints . . . All of these details are important in your sexual blueprint. So if you want the full picture about yourself go to *www.astro.com* and click on "Free Charts" and enter your birth data in the form to view and print out your natal chart for free. If you don't have a computer, head over to the library and access this website.

If you discover that your Sun and Mars are holding hands in the fifth house or that they're opponents slugging it out across 180 degrees of separation and you don't have a clue what it means, then you've got several choices. Take an astrology course, buy some books and study it on your own, or find an astrologer

who can explain your chart to you. But one way or another, figure it out. After all, this is your *sexuality* we're talking about, and
it doesn't get much more personal than that.

LOVE & SEX

Ideally, love and sex should go together. But in astrology, they
don't. Venus is the babe of the zodiac, the representative of love
and romance. She symbolizes our capacity to love and be loved,
governs our ability to attract people with whom we're compatible,
expresses how we relate to people in intimate relationships, and determines our spontaneous attractions to others.

For a woman, Venus symbolizes her ability to form close bonds
with other women and often indicates the qualities she's looking
for in a mate. For a man, Venus symbolizes the kind of woman he
seeks. When two people share Venus/Mars or Venus/Sun contacts, the potential is great for a sexually satisfying, loving relationship. But even when they don't share these contacts,
compatibility factors often come into play through the elements
and qualities of the respective signs.

So even though this book is primarily about the interactions
between Mars and your Sun, there's a section on the role that
Venus plays in your sexual blueprint.

How to Use This Book

 verything you need to use this book and get the most out of it is included. The material is arranged by sun signs, with the Mars combinations described under each sign.

At the beginning of part two, there's an inventory of your physical and sexual energy. I strongly encourage you to read through it and see which of the statements apply to you. You'll find a similar inventory at the beginning of part three. At the end of the first inventory, you're asked to compose three questions about your physical and sexual energy. Throughout the course of the book, you'll be answering these questions.

In the appendix, there are ephemeres for Venus and Mars that cover the years from 1940–2010 and list the dates that Venus and Mars entered a particular sign. Simply locate the range in which your birthday falls to find out the appropriate sign for each planet. Turn to the Appendix and look up the sign Mars was in when you were born, then do the same with Venus. Then let's get started.

PART ONE

The Players

"Why were the aliens in older science fiction movies always from Mars?"

— Megan MacGregor

I

Apollo and Friends: The Sun and Planets

To the ancient Greeks and Romans, Apollo was the god of light, responsible for the ripening of fruit and the blossoming of the land. He was also considered to be the god of music, mathematics, healing, and of divination and prophecy. He had many sanctuaries and shrines where men could consult him about their own destinies through his priestess intermediaries, but the most famous was the oracle of Delphi. A busy guy, this Apollo, the all-around god, good at everything he did.

Since many astrological meanings evolved from mythology, it's not too surprising that Apollo is associated with the Sun. As the foundation of everything you embody in this lifetime, your Sun sign is the Apollo in your corner of the universe. It's where you shine in your own life.

Let's get specific. Let's say you're an Aquarius. What, exactly, does that mean? Your approach to life is primarily *mental*. You *think* your way through life. Your mind never shuts up. Internal chatter is your constant companion no matter where you are—on a date, at a funeral, at work, in your car, on vacation, asleep. But it isn't idle chatter. Not for Aquarius. This is the voice of your most intimate and private self; refuse to listen at your own peril.

As the visionary of the zodiac, you're forever dissatisfied with the status quo and constantly seek to break through outmoded ways of thinking. Where another sign sees an obstacle, you spot opportunity and challenge. However, you can be utterly rigid about your beliefs and blind to your own rigidity. *Me, rigid? Don't be absurd. I'm right, you're wrong, end of discussion.* You rarely doubt the validity of your own beliefs, and this resoluteness is your Apollo.

The nature of Aquarius—and every other sign—is influenced by its *element* and its *quality*. The first classification reads like an elementary-school science lesson: fire, earth, air, and water. Three signs are assigned to each element, and to some extent this classification helps explain why signs are compatible or incompatible sexually. The second classification describes how a sign uses energy: cardinal, fixed, or mutable. Four signs are assigned to each quality, one from each of the element groupings. This classification helps explain why there can be sexual chemistry between two signs who don't seem to have much in common.

ELEMENTS

The *fire* signs—Aries, Leo, and Sagittarius—tend to be impulsive and impatient, enthusiastic and dynamic. They're the doers of the zodiac, action-oriented, usually aggressive in some way. They live spontaneously, may be sexually precocious, and are rarely shy about telling you what's on their mind. You usually will know exactly where you stand with a fire sign. Boredom is anathema for these people; when they're bored, they walk away without regrets or apologies.

The *earth* signs—Taurus, Virgo, and Capricorn—are the pragmatists. They are grounded, stable, and dependable; the ones who finish the job that the fire signs started. In this grouping fall the planners and strategists, people who are in for the long haul. They're the architects of the zodiac, who build everything from houses to novels to companies and vast fortunes. They can be deeply sensual and are usually loyal and committed to any relationship in which they get involved.

The *air* signs—Gemini, Libra, and Aquarius—live in the mental realm. They're consummate communicators, sociable, curious, and collect information the way other signs collect art or rare books. For them, sexual attraction begins in the mind. A potential lover may look like a Greek god or goddess, but if that person doesn't communicate well, then air signs simply aren't interested.

The *water* signs—Cancer, Scorpio, and Pisces—feel and intuit their way through life. They're nurturers, and possess great compassion and terrific imaginations. They can be as sexually precocious as fire signs, but for different reasons. Where a fire sign is likely to follow the sexual whim of the moment, a water sign must be seduced emotionally. They're among the most secretive of signs, these three, but once you win their trust, you are welcomed into their private, most intimate circles.

QUALITIES

Cardinal signs—Aries, Cancer, Libra, and Capricorn—are self-directed individuals. Many of them have a singular vision that prevails in their lives, and they pursue it with a focused, dogged determination. They're often initiators who break new ground.

They can be intensely passionate, but that passion is influenced by the sign's element. Fiery Aries is usually more passionate than a watery Cancer. But Cancer is more emotional and intuitive. When cardinal signs get caught up in whirlwind sexual affairs, they live as frenetically as their emotions allow.

Fixed signs—Taurus, Leo, Scorpio, and Aquarius—are persistent, with firm opinions and beliefs, and have an unshakable certainty in their own worth as individuals. Never argue with a fixed sign. They are notoriously stubborn and never give up a belief or an opinion without a fight.

They can be profoundly sensuous, but their sensuality isn't confined to sex. It extends throughout their physical world, through an appreciation for everything the physical world has to offer. In relationships, they usually play for keeps, but when things don't work out, they get out and keep moving forward.

Mutable signs—Gemini, Virgo, Sagittarius, and Pisces—are known for their adaptability. It's their primary survival tool. They often are seekers of one kind or another, but don't always know what they're looking for. That's okay, too. They're flexible and go with the flow.

Their sexuality is often predicated on variety and diversity. That doesn't mean they're more promiscuous than other signs, only that routine is as anathema to them as boredom is to an Aries.

THEMES

Recently, a divorced friend who is also an astrologer signed up for one of the Internet matchmaking services. She filled out an exhaustive profile about herself—likes, dislikes, job, marital status, children, aspirations, date of birth. When interested parties contact her, one of the first things she asks for is the man's specific birth information: date, time, and place of birth. Then she draws up the man's birth chart and compares it to her own. She's a Leo, so she knows that on a Sun-sign level, she's most compatible with another fire sign or with an air sign. But because she's also an astrologer, she looks for other points of contact, beginning with Mars and Venus, and then calls me and we commiserate.

"I don't know about this," she says. "The chart says he's a workaholic."

"But look at that Venus. This guy's a true romantic. And hey, his Mars hits your Venus. It doesn't get any better than that."

"But he's a Scorpio," she moans. "They're so secretive. He's probably got four other women on the side."

And this is where Sun-sign themes come in. Astrologers often use keywords or themes for the signs that help to define their broad patterns. If one of my clients asks me to look for creative elements in her birth chart, then I use Sun-sign themes that are tailored for creativity. If a client asks me to look for intuitive or psychic elements in his chart, the theme addresses that. This kind of variety is possible with Sun signs precisely because they are our primary archetypes.

In terms of creativity, Aries is a pioneer; in terms of sexuality, Aries is The Initiator. Take a look at this table to find your sign's sexual theme.

TABLE OF SEXUAL THEMES		
Sun Sign	**Date**	**Sexual Theme**
Aries ♈	March 21–April 19	The Initiator
Taurus ♉	April 20–May 20	The Sensualist
Gemini ♊	May 21–June 21	The Chameleon
Cancer ♋	June 22–July 22	The Intuitive
Leo ♌	July 23–August 22	The Creative
Virgo ♍	August 23–September 22	The Analyst
Libra ♎	September 23–October 22	The Romantic
Scorpio ♏	October 23–November 21	The Powerful
Sagittarius ♐	November 22–December 21	The Optimist

Sun Sign	Date	Sexual Theme
Capricorn ♑	December 22–January 19	The Achiever
Aquarius ♒	January 20–February 18	The Individualist
Pisces ♓	February 19–March 20	The Empath

RULERSHIPS

Midnight Express was both a book and a movie about what happens to a young American man in the sixties who is busted for drugs in Turkey, lives through the horrors of a Turkish prison, and ultimately breaks out and rides to freedom on the Midnight Express.

What I remember most about this movie is that I came away from it understanding what an astrological rulership means. In the broadest sense, this is a story about addiction (Neptune) and its consequences (Saturn) in a foreign country (Jupiter). The violence (Mars) is counteracted by the power of an individual's desire for freedom at any cost (Uranus).

Ever since, the connection between story and astrology is the first thing I recognize when I read a book, watch a movie, or listen to someone relate an experience. It's the first thing I recognize when I experience something I know I'll remember.

Here's the scene: My husband, daughter, and I are on our way into Atlanta on I-20 in mid-July. It's a family vacation; we're going to visit my sister and my dad. We've got our dog and bird with us, a laptop, a huge cooler, pillows—too much stuff. We can't seem to travel light.

Suddenly, the van—a 1998 Windstar—sounds like it has a chronic and possibly fatal disease. *Goop* is smeared across the rear window. The dog abruptly sits up, attentive, apparently aware that something *not good* is going on. The bird begins to squawk. My husband, who is driving, pulls off to the shoulder of the road.

A nasty smell now permeates the air inside the van. I really hate the sound the engine makes when he turns it off.

There is a surreal moment when no one speaks, when we just look at each other, the engine ticking in the silence. I glance back at all our *stuff*, and cringe. We are seventy miles from Atlanta, it's the height of rush hour traffic; and trucks—very large trucks—are whizzing past us so fast that the van shakes and shudders. It's 103 degrees outside. We have a cell phone, great. We have a triple-A card, double great. Get busy.

Forty minutes later, help is on the way.

Two hours later, help arrives.

The verdict sure isn't good. Way down deep in the heart of the engine, the aorta exploded. Transmission blew. And the nearest place we can be towed is twenty miles back, a rural spot no larger than a punctuation mark on the map. The bird, now traumatized, crawls into the little hut in her cage and goes to sleep. The dog growls as she sits between Megan and me in the back seat of the tow truck.

We finally arrive at my sister's place around nine that night. I'm hungry enough to start gnawing on the floor. We don't have a car. We're supposed to be in North Carolina in two days.

The next day, we learn what a new transmission will cost. We learn that when you're in a town no larger than a punctuation mark, the part that you need won't arrive until you're already due home. The van is, as they say, a lost cause, a corpse. We have to buy another car. We learn that you're not in a good bargaining position when your van is towed into CarMax with transmission oil smeared across the rear window.

The good news about this story is that we were able to finish our vacation and both the dog and the bird survived the trauma. In astrological terms, this story is all about Mars (spewed oil, a blown transmission). But it also involves other planets—Mercury (a car trip), in which the unexpected happens (Uranus) to the engine, resulting in a blown transmission, and the purchase of another car.

Practically any event you can imagine, any object, disease, or emotion is ruled by a planet. And so is every sign. The nature of the ruling planet heavily influences the nature of the astrological sign. Take Aquarians. One of the reasons they are visionary individualists is because their sign is ruled by Uranus, the planet that symbolizes genius, sudden and unexpected events, rebellion, eccentricity, and originality. Ever wondered about the temper of an Aries? Blame its ruler, Mars, which governs not only sexuality, but war, the military, and fire.

Rulerships have changed over the centuries. Up until the late 1700s, Saturn was believed to be the outermost planet in the solar system. This presented a thorny issue in terms of rulerships. With only seven planets and twelve signs, there weren't enough planets to go around, so some planets were assigned rulership to two signs. Then in 1781, British astronomer William Herschel discovered Uranus and the neat, closed system that astrologers had worked with for centuries was blown apart.

Herschel called the planet George's Star, in honor of the king, but mythology won out. The planet became Uranus, son of Gaea, Mother Earth, and astrologers scrambled to figure out where Uranus fit in the cosmic theme of things. By the mid-1800s, they still hadn't figured it out and along came the discovery of Neptune. Then, in 1930, astronomer Clyde Tombaugh discovered Pluto, another wrench in the astrological works.

Tombaugh was actually looking for Planet X, which he and other astronomers believed existed because of the unexplained fluctuations in the orbits of Uranus and Neptune. He never found Planet X and data from the Voyager 2 proves that it never existed. Instead, we got Pluto, a planet whose light is so dim that it seems almost etheric.

These three planets are called transpersonal. They are invisible to the naked eye and because they move so slowly, they affect large numbers of people. Uranus takes seven years to move through a single sign, Neptune takes fourteen. Pluto, the snail of the zodiac, can take as long as thirty. An entire generation, then, may be born under the same sign of Pluto.

With the discovery of this unlikely trio, the rulerships were rearranged. Uranus was assigned rulership of Aquarius, Neptune was given rulership over Pisces, and Pluto was assigned to Scorpio. Now, however, astrologers may be facing another thorn, another dichotomy: the discovery of yet another planet.

Beginning in the 1980s, computer simulations of the solar system's early formation suggested that a string of debris, called the Kuiper Belt, might exist beyond Neptune. In 1992, astronomers discovered an object 150 miles wide that they named 1992QB1. Since then, nearly 600 objects have been spotted in the Kuiper Belt. In June 2002, two astronomers discovered an object that is 800 miles in diameter and about half the size of Pluto, lending fuel to the debate about whether Pluto is really even a planet. This new discovery, called Quaoar in honor of the creation god of the Tongva tribe, is about a billion miles from Pluto and four billion miles from Earth. It's the most distant object yet discovered in our solar system.

Whether it's a planet or not is almost beside the point. As telescopes become more powerful, it seems possible that more objects will be found in the Kuiper Belt and one or some of them may be proven to be actual planets. Many astrologers already work with a hypothetical planet called Transpluto—beyond Pluto—that is believed to influence human affairs in much the same way as Pluto.

The bottom line? Astrology, like man, is still evolving.

In the table that follows, the primary ruler of a sign is listed first. When you understand something about the planet that rules your Sun sign, the nature of the sign becomes much clearer.

NATAL VERSUS TRANSITS

When I started studying astrology, in the dark ages before the Internet, there weren't many books on the topic. The fact that I was an American living in South America further limited my choices. Our school library carried one book on astrology and the only American bookstore in Caracas didn't do much better. Once we moved back to the U.S., things improved but only marginally. It seemed that the few books I ran across were written for other astrologers, in a language no more comprehensible to me than Greek.

Today, of course, you can peg the word astrology into any search engine and come up with thousands of entries. Some are technical, some are not. Some are informative, others confuse. Even though there are only two broad concepts of astrology—Western and Eastern—there are many subcategories. In this book, we're dealing with a narrow focus of natal astrology and are concerned with only two planets—the Sun and Mars—and the signs they were in when you were born. When I refer to a sexuality blueprint, I'm referring to your Sun/Mars combination.

A newspaper horoscope is predictive astrology. It's based on the daily movement of the planets, their transits, and how they affect your Sun sign. But when an astrologer makes predictions for a client, the transits are interpreted for the entire natal chart, not just the Sun sign. So even though your Sun in Aries and your Mars in Sagittarius give you passion and fire, that doesn't mean your passion and fire are always hot.

As the Sun and Mars move through your natal horoscope, new

TABLE OF PLANETARY RULERS

Sign	Planetary Ruler	Keywords for Planets
Aries ♈	Mars ♂	physical and sexual energy, aggression, war, individualism, action, the military, fires, fevers, passion, rage, surgery
Taurus ♉	Venus ♀	love, romance, women, the arts and artists, sense of touch, pleasure, music, musicians, and musical instruments
Gemini ♊	Mercury ☿	communication, conscious mind, siblings, messages, short-distance travel, contracts, education and teachers, writers
Cancer ♋	Moon ☽	emotions, intuition, mother or the nurturing parent, the feminine, yin, prophecy, water, oceans, tides, the holistic mind
Leo ♌	Sun ☉	ego, self, father or authoritarian parent, children, vitality, power, fame, willpower, prosperity
Virgo ♍	Mercury ☿	same as Gemini section
Libra ♎	Venus ♀	same as Taurus section
Scorpio ♏	Pluto ♇, Mars ♂	transformation, regeneration, death, rebirth, afterlife, redemption, atomic energy, detectives, pseudonyms, the collective mind
Sagittarius ♐	Jupiter ♃	expansion, luck, success, higher mind, foreign (travel, countries, people), spiritual beliefs, worldview, excess
Capricorn ♑	Saturn ♄	responsibility, discipline, limitations, physical life, karma, authority, father, ambitions, serious outlooks on life
Aquarius ♒	Uranus ♅, Saturn ♄	individuality, genius, rebellion, disruption, sudden and unexpected change, freedom, inventions and inventors, explosives and explosions
Pisces ♓	Neptune ♆, Jupiter ♃	illusion, the visionary self, psychic, the unconscious, inspiration, escapism, addictions, journeys by water, telepathy and other psychic abilities

energies are born. Your natal Mars in Sagittarius may be hit by transiting Pluto in Sagittarius. Your Sun is hit by transiting Mercury in Libra. Your Venus is hit by transiting Jupiter in Virgo. Each of these hits means something. Each transiting planet acts upon the natal blueprint in some way and is manifested as an experience: your car breaks down, you get a new pet, you fall in love, you have a one-night fling with a stranger, you win the lottery, your marriage collapses, your son leaves home. These transits unfold in a particular way and a story emerges.

Then there's prediction by progression, by solar returns and lunar returns, and by eclipses and . . . You get the idea. Even though your fundamental sexuality blueprint remains, it isn't static. Between January 1, 2004 and January 1, 2005, for example, Mars will move through nine of the twelve signs. Each of these transits will impact your natal chart in some way and alter your sexual impulses and needs. You can look up these various transits of Mars and then read the appropriate entries in your Sun sign chapter to find out how a particular Mars transit will effect you. Even though the combinations refer to natal planets, the definitions of the transits are basically the same, but last only for the duration of the transit.

Many astrology websites list the daily transits. One of the best sites for daily astrological information and an all-around positive take on astrology generally is www.moonvalleyastrologer.com. Astrologer Celeste Teal posts Mars transits on the site. Another good site for general information is www.12house.com.

2

Mars, Risings, Houses

Mars has been a part of our collective imagination and of popular culture for more than a century, beginning with H.G. Wells's *War of the Worlds* in 1898. The story idea is simple. Mars is dying and the Martians flee their world and plan to take over Earth and all its resources. They attack London first and their powerful weapons—a heat ray and a toxic black smoke—seem to ensure their victory. But they're defeated by germs. Earth germs.

In 1911, Edgar Rice Burroughs wrote *A Princess on Mars*, the first of eleven novels about the red planet. In the books, the protagonist, John Carter, is a Confederate Army Civil War veteran who ends up being transported to Mars and, over the course of the novels, settles into a life there. He marries, gets involved in Martian politics, and fights for what's right.

In 1951, in Ray Bradbury's *Martian Chronicles*, "invader" is given a new twist. Human settlers arrive on Mars and the Martians are killed by the bacteria that the humans bring with them. But we care deeply about the Martians in Bradbury's classic because they are beautiful people of an ancient civilization.

In 1961, along came Robert Heinlein with *Stranger in a Strange Land*, about a human born on Mars, the only survivor of the first manned space mission to the planet. The protagonist, Valentine Michael Smith, is raised and educated by Martians, then is returned to Earth when he's a young man—with the sensibilities of a human, the perspective of an alien, and incredible psychic powers.

In terms of TV, there was *My Favorite Martian* and in film, a host of many forgettable movies. An exception was *Total Recall*, based on a Philip K. Dick short story, in which Arnold Schwarzenegger plays a man haunted by suppressed memories—specifically, journeys to Mars. The story has all the complex hallmarks of Philip K. Dick—paranoia, duplicity, deep and powerful secrets, and plenty of corrupt bad guys. The ending takes place on Mars, when atmospheric gases and water are freed from deep within the planet's rocks.

Part of our fascination with Mars is that it bears some similarities to Earth and may have been habitable at one time in the past—and may be in the future. Its surface has been dramatically changed by volcanism, impacts by asteroids and meteors and other celestial bodies, violent movements in its crust, and great cyclonic dust storms that frequently swallow the entire planet. Its polar ice caps grow and recede, like ours, with the change of seasons. Near the poles, the layered soil indicates that the planet's climate has changed more than once. Its ancient volcanoes, once powered from the heat of the Martian core, rise against the starkness with a kind of fierce purity. The largest volcano, Olympus Mons, is seventeen miles high and may be the largest in the solar system. There's also a titanic canyon about the size of the distance between New York and L.A.

Thanks to the Mars Odyssey spacecraft, it's now believed that billions of years ago, Mars was inundated by the largest floods in the solar system. No one knows where all that water went, but the Mars Odyssey detected substantial quantities of water mixed into the soil about three feet below the surface, near the Martian south pole.

So far, the mystery about water on Mars hasn't been solved. How much is frozen in the polar ice caps? How much of it may be locked in ice beneath the red surface? The answers may hold vital information not only about the Martian past, but about the formation of Earth and other planets in the solar system.

On a clear night at certain times of the year, you can walk outside after dark and glimpse Mars in the sky, a speck of rose-tinted light between 56,000,000 and 399,000,000 kilometers from Earth. Its diameter is a little more than half that of Earth, the length of a Martian day is 24.6 Earth hours, a Martian year is 1.88 Earth years, and gravity on the surface is about a third of Earth's. The atmosphere is unbreathable. Ninety-five percent of it consists of carbon dioxide. It has two moons, both so small that they may not be moons at all, just rock that has gotten trapped in the planet's gravitational pull. They are named after the two squires who served Ares, the Greek god of war: Phobos—which means fear, and Deimos—panic.

MARS IN ASTROLOGY

To the ancient Greeks, he was Ares, a savage god who was little more than a bloodthirsty son of a bitch. In the *Iliad*, Zeus says it like he sees it, that he finds Ares, his son, completely odious because he enjoys nothing but "strife, war, and battles." And on Olympus, he was intensely disliked for his blind violence and brutality.

This theme is beautifully illustrated in the movie *Gladiator*. Times are brutal in the Roman Empire, and brute strength is held in such high esteem that the populace turns out to watch men kill each other in the colosseum. Not surprisingly, Aries Russell Crowe won an Oscar for that performance. Now skip ahead a couple thousand years. In *Running Man*, one of the novellas that Stephen King wrote as Richard Bachman, this same theme is repeated, but now the protagonist (Arnold Schwarzenegger) is running for his life on national TV and surviving by his wits and brute strength. Same theme, different century.

But aggression, survival, and war are only one side of Mars. The Greek side. On the Roman side, he was called by the name we know him by—Mars. He was first and foremost the god of agriculture, the protector of cattle, and the preserver of corn. He was associated with the woodpecker, the horse, and the wolf. As the husband of Rhea Silvia, a vestal virgin, he fathered Romulus and Remus, who were suckled by a wolf.

The connection between Mars and sex probably came about as a result of Ares's affair with the goddess Aphrodite. She was married to a cripple, Hephaestus, and compared to him, Ares was handsome, dashing, courageous, all the things the Olympians looked for in a mate. Ares, of course, took advantage of the situation, and their lustful encounters on the "marriage couch" became well known to the other gods when Hephaestus ensnared the adulterous couple in an invisible net.

Since we are complex beings, our sexual blueprints are usually a mix of energies. Movies like *9½ Weeks*, *Last Tango in Paris*, and *Henry and June*, Anais Nin's take on her relationship with both Henry Miller and his wife, are a blend of Mars and Pluto (obsession). Erotic fiction, such as *Too Much Temptation* or *Never Too Much* by Lori Foster, or romantic fiction, like *Behind Closed Doors* by Shannon McKenna, are a blend of Mars and Venus.

However, the blend of Mars and the Sun, as your primary archetype, describes the details of your sexual blueprint: your physical energy; your survival instincts; your sexual insecurities and strengths; your capacity for intimacy and gratification, for sensuality and commitment; and how you use your emotional energy in sex and to pursue what you want in life. Let's see how this works in practice.

Magician and escape artist Harry Houdini was an Aries Sun/ Taurus Mars combination. Born Ehrich Weiss in Hungary in 1874, he was the middle son of five boys. His family moved to America to flee anti-Semitism and eventually settled in New York by way of Milwaukee. He had three loves in his life: magic, his mother, and his wife, Bess.

Houdini met Bess while performing at a children's party when he was twenty and she was just sixteen. Bess, the story goes, was infatuated with Houdini and approached him after the performance and told him that she liked him. His response: "Enough to marry me?" They were married several weeks later and the marriage endured for thirty-two years, until Houdini's death. According to Houdini's biographer, there's speculation that the marriage was never consummated because Houdini had placed Bess on a pedestal. Given Houdini's Sun/Moon combination, I find this difficult to believe.

The Aries Sun/Taurus Mars combination is sensual and passionate, with a capacity for great intimacy and commitment. It confers enormous physical endurance and energy, a pioneering spirit, profound survival instincts, and an iron will. We know that Houdini certainly was a pioneer as an escape artist and magician, that he was athletic from a young age, and that he was a perfectionist in his work. He exhibited patience and great attention to detail in planning his acts. Houdini's preoccupation with death is also well known. His survival instincts were so profound that he seemed to think if he could defy death often enough in his acts, he ultimately would defeat it.

What we know of Houdini's life and personality seems so attuned to the energy of his Sun/Mars combination that it strikes me as highly unlikely he would deviate from that energy in expressing his sexuality.

USING THE COMBINATIONS

The 144 Sun/Mars combinations in the next section pertain to natal signs. If you're comparing your combinations to another person's to find out how compatible you might be, keep a couple of basics in mind. The elements play a large part in sexual and romantic compatibility. If you have a Leo Sun/Virgo Mars (fire/earth) combination and your significant other has a Libra Sun/Pisces Mars (air/water) combination, then you should be sexually compatible because the elements in the combination are compatible. Elements that are the same work well together, too, such as two Suns in water signs, for example.

If your Suns are compatible in terms of elements, but your respective Mars signs are not, the relationship isn't doomed! It simply means that you have different approaches to sex. Liz Taylor and Richard Burton are an interesting example of this. She has a Pisces Sun and a Mars in Pisces; Burton had a Scorpio Sun and a Mars in Libra. Their Mars signs were at odds, but both their Suns were in water signs.

If you're looking for an indicator of overall romantic and sexual compatibility, then check out the Venus signs, too. If you're a man, then look for the sign of the other person's Venus; if you're a woman, pay attention to the sign of his Mars. The same rules apply in terms of elements. If the woman's Mars and the man's Venus are compatible, then sparks fly, according to the nature of the respective signs. Another compatible pairing occurs when the man's Venus is compatible with the woman's Sun, or the woman's

Mars is compatible with the man's Sun. Actress Susan Sarandon, for example, has a Libra Sun; her significant other, Tim Robbins, has Venus in Libra.

These contacts are important, but are only part of the picture. When an astrologer is looking for points of compatibility between two people, the entire horoscopes come into play. Some of the best and most passionate relationships I have encountered as an astrologer sometimes don't have the contacts you would expect between the Sun and the Moon, the Sun and Mars or Venus, or between Venus and Mars. There are other equally significant contacts that illustrate the deeper, soul purpose in the relationship. One of these contacts involves the Ascendant, the sign that was rising when you were born.

YOUR RISING SIGN

A horoscope is divided into twelve unequal pieces called houses. Each house has a particular significance and the placement of your Sun and Mars within those houses adds another layer to your sexual blueprint.

The sign of each house is calculated according to the sign that was rising at the exact time that you were born, your rising sign or Ascendant. There are many different ways to estimate your Ascendant, but the only accurate way is to have your chart done. Use one of the Internet sites mentioned earlier in the book or find an astrologer who can provide you with a computerized birth chart. Many New Age bookstores offer a computerized chart service for about $5 a chart, without interpretations.

Once you have your rising sign, jot it down on the chart on the next page, on the horizontal line just above house 1. If your rising sign is Aries, it's also the cusp of your first house. Then, moving through the zodiac, Taurus would go on the cusp of the second

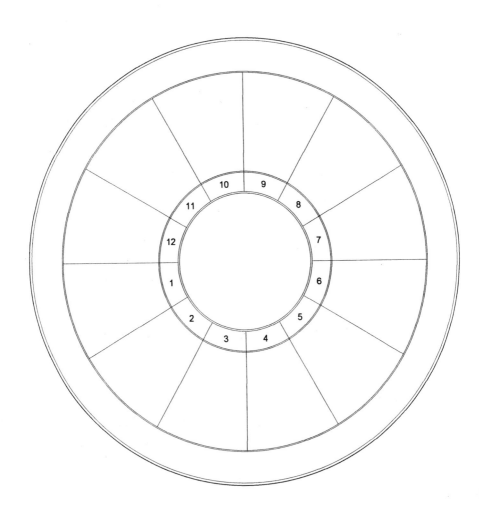

This wheel is intentionally blank!

house (the line between houses 1 and 2), Gemini would go on the cusp of the third, and on around until you end up with Pisces on the cusp of the twelfth house. If your rising is Taurus, then that's the cusp of your first house, Gemini would be the cusp of your second, and on around the horoscope to Aries on the cusp of the twelfth.

Once you set up the signs on each of the house cusps, you're ready to place your Sun and Mars in their respective houses. If you have a Gemini ascendant, a Sun in Gemini, and Mars in Libra, then the Sun goes just below the ascendant, in the first house and Mars in Libra goes in your fifth house because Libra is on the cusp of that house.

Each house, just like each sign, has its own associations. The expression of a planet's energy in your natal chart involves both its sign and its house. Next, we look at the descriptions of the Sun and Mars in each of the twelve houses. Each description includes names of well-known people who have the same house placement in their natal charts.

MARS & SUN IN THE HOUSES

First House: The Self

Mars: You have exceptionally strong self-confidence and sexual energy. You're competitive, assertive, headstrong, aggressive. You need to dominate your immediate environment. You have good leadership ability, but can lack direction. You may be accident-prone.

Examples: Linda Blair (*The Exorcist*), writer Truman Capote (*In Cold Blood*), Nicholas Cage, the Dalai Lama

Sun: You have initiative, personal warmth, excellent physical vitality. Your self-expression is important to you. Your leadership abilities are excellent.

Examples: George Lucas, humorist Erma Bombeck, Harry Houdini, Eva Peron

Second House: Finances and Personal Values

Mars: You are aggressive about earning money. Your sexual power may be mixed up with money issues. You're usually the dominant partner in a relationship.

Examples: Kurt Cobain, J. Paul Getty, actress Linda Lovelace (*Deep Throat*)

Sun: You're lucky with money. You have a knack for being in the right place at the right time for financial opportunities. Your personal values are molded by the men in your life.

Examples: Albert Camus, Robert De Niro, Ellen Burstyn

Third House: Communication and Siblings

Mars: You can be aggressive in the way you communicate. You may regard sex or sexual issues as a method of communicating. You want a lover who is experienced and you have very definite ideas about your sexual likes and dislikes. There can be discord with siblings, relatives or neighbors.

Examples: Herman Hesse, Ansel Adams, Jorge Luis Borges, Adele Davis

Sun: You shine as a communicator and that communication can take any form. You may have a preference for older partners in sexual relationships.

Examples: Paul Cézanne, Hans Christian Anderson, Walt Disney, Winston Churchill

Fourth House: The Home and the Nurturing Parent

Mars: You probably have an active sex life. You value independence in your partner and are looking for love, loyalty, and a partner whose background and roots are similar to yours. You have strong emotions related to early childhood. Mars here usually indicates a very competitive person.

Examples: Wilt Chamberlain, Greg Allman, Chris Evert, Vanessa Redgrave

Sun: You value self-expression and encourage everyone in your home to communicate their feelings and thoughts. You dominate your domestic scene. Your own childhood was probably happy and you have a strong relationship with one of your parents.

Examples: Woody Allen, Neil Armstrong, Amelia Earhart, Julia Roberts

Fifth House: Creativity, Children, and Pleasure

Mars: You pursue romance and sexual pleasure aggressively. You or your partner may value competitive sports and athletics. Your passions are sensuous. In a woman's chart, this placement can indicate difficult childbirth. Your creativity is important to you and you pursue it with passion.

Examples: David Brinkley, model Naomi Campbell, William Faulkner

Sun: This is a powerful placement for creativity. You actively pursue sex for pleasure and this pursuit may be intimately connected to your creative drive. You are good with children, who may play into your creativity in some way.

Examples: Joni Mitchell, Anais Nin, Louis Armstrong, Leonardo da Vinci

Sixth House: Health and Work

Mars: You have many sexual contacts through work. You're looking for a partner with whom you can share daily work routines, perhaps through a business you run or own together. Much of your physical energy goes into your daily work routine. You may run high fevers when ill.

Examples: Jodie Foster, presidential candidate Gary Hart, David Copperfield, F. Lee Bailey

Sun: You need to have your mate recognize your expertise in the work area. Your health is connected to the satisfaction you feel about your daily work. Your creative work *is* your daily work regardless of whether or not you make your living at it.

Examples: Antonio Banderas, Jean Auel, Samuel Beckett, Carl Jung

Seventh House: Partnerships and Marriage

Mars: Sex is vital to your committed relationships or marriage. You're seeking loyalty, monogamy, and equality in a partnership. This placement can indicate underlying tensions in a partnership that are diffused by a satisfying sexual relationship. You can be argumentative and will argue your point until you either win or the other person walks away.

Examples: Maya Angelou, Frederick Chopin, Brian De Palma, Michael J. Fox, physicist Fritjof Capra

Sun: Your self-expression is connected to your most intimate relationships. If you're sexually happy and satisfied in your partnership, your creative expression reflects it. Your partner is either in business with you or fully supports your creative endeavors. You're able to make friends of any potential enemies.

Examples: Ray Bradbury, Gordon Cooper, Gus Grissom, Katharine Hepburn, Ezra Pound

Eighth House: Sex and Shared Resources

Mars: You're looking for an intimate relationship that has it all: great sex, understanding, intimacy, and a sharing of common resources. If you can't have that, then you're really not interested.

All or nothing, in other words. You seek deeper meaning in everything.

Examples: Drew Barrymore, Shirley MacLaine, George Gershwin, Ellen Goodman

Sun: You have excellent intuition. Your financial prosperity increases after marriage. Your father or the men in your life are helpful to you financially. You could inherit money or some other legacy from your father's side of the family. You're attracted to offbeat topics: reincarnation, life after death, UFOs, ghosts. You share your resources readily with others.

Examples: Psychic and author Sylvia Browne, Deepak Chopra, Edgar Cayce, Betty Ford, Sean Penn

Ninth House: Higher Mind

Mars: The ideal partner shares your worldview, love of travel, and educational background. When your spiritual beliefs are in sync with your partner's, your sexuality is heightened. Foreign cultures and people figure prominently in your life.

Examples: Richard Bach, Philip K. Dick, Al Gore, Jackie Onassis, Carl Schultz

Sun: You're fascinated by foreign cultures and people. Your partner may be foreign-born or you may meet this person while traveling in a foreign country. You and your partner share a similar worldview.

Examples: José Feliciano, abductee Betty Hill, D.H. Lawrence, alternative health guru Andrew Weil

Tenth House: Profession and Career

Mars: You may be so busy making a name for yourself professionally that your sexuality is repressed. Or, your sexuality may be intrinsic to your professional achievements. Regardless of how this energy manifests itself in your life, one thing is for sure: Mars in the tenth house is a powerful placement for achieving what you seek professionally.

Examples: Ray Bradbury, Bob Guccione, M.C. Escher, Jimi Hendrix, Alison Lurie

Sun: You achieve success in your chosen profession. You have a great thrust for power and could be drawn into the public eye. Father figures and older men are helpful. Your sexuality may be tied up somehow with power issues.

Examples: Kathy Bates, Art Bell, Lizzie Borden, Johann von Goethe

Eleventh House: Wishes and Dreams, Group Associations

Mars: Friendship is a prerequisite to a sexual relationship. You may meet your partner through groups you belong to or through friends. You want to share common dreams and hopes with your sexual partners.

Examples: Eccentric artist Salvador Dali, author Jeffrey Archer, Helen Gurley Brown, Harrison Ford, Billy Joel

Sun: You're looking for a partner who shares your ideals and humanitarian concerns. Your friends are usually warm and generous people and are important to you. You benefit through your group associations and, in fact, may meet your partner through one of these groups.

Examples: Cher, Johnny Depp, Timothy Leary

Twelfth House: Personal Unconscious, Institutions, Karma

Mars: Repressed anger may make your sexual relationships difficult. You need time for solitude and reflection and should consider some sort of physical/spiritual discipline as a way of dealing with this anger. Alcohol or drug usage can be excesive. Yoga, tai chi, or meditation would be beneficial. You're prone to secret romances and affairs and your sexual energy may be channeled somehow into institutions and things that happen behind the scenes. You're exceptionally proficient at working behind the scenes.

Examples: Former first lady and founder of an institute for substance abuse Betty Ford, Anne Archer, O. Henry, Bo Derek

Sun: You work well behind the scenes and value your privacy. There can be unresolved issues with the father or with authority in general. You're able to reach deep within yourself for intuitive guidance. Your sexuality is *your* business, no one else's.

Examples: Cleveland Amory, Pearl Bailey, Billy Crystal, Harrison Ford

MARS AND PLANETARY MOTION

Every planet except the Sun and the Moon turn retrograde—an apparent backward movement through the zodiac. When a planet is retrograde in a birth chart, its energy is directed inward, creating greater tension and stress. The release of this tension is usually worked out according to the sign and house placement.

A retrograde Mars in Libra in the third house might indicate someone whose sexuality is expressed through some type of communication behind the scenes, in private. An example might be someone who writes romance or erotic fiction novels under a pseudonym. Although Libra is usually a social sign, with a retrograde planet in Libra, the individual is more interested in understanding himself than he is others and may be something of a loner.

The most powerful Mars placement is when Mars is stationary in the birth horoscope, which means it stalls as it's about to turn direct or retrograde. This intensifies the planet's energy. The direct (forward) motion of Mars is the most common.

In the Mars appendix, SD means that Mars is stationary and

about to turn direct and SR means that Mars is stationary and about to turn retrograde. If you look at the entry for January 19, 1952, you'll see that Mars was in Scorpio on that date. On March 25, 1952, the Mars position is indicated as SR, meaning that Mars is still in Scorpio, but is about to turn retrograde. On June 9, 1952, the Mars position is SD in Scorpio, meaning that it's now turning direct again. So if you were born between March 26, 1952 and June 8, 1952, then your Mars is retrograde in Scorpio. Translated, this means that a lot of your energy is directed inward, toward understanding your own motives and ambitions. Whatever you tackle, you do so with an awareness of how it expands your understanding of yourself.

PART TWO

The Sun/Mars Combinations

"... our sexual energy and our creative energy
are very closely intertwined."

—JULIA CAMERON,
from *Walking in this World*

INVENTORY OF YOUR
PHYSICAL AND SEXUAL ENERGY

*B*efore you look up your Sun/ Mars combination, go through the checklist below and check the items that apply to you *most* of the time. Then see how your answers stack up against the descriptions of your planetary energies.

PHYSICAL ENERGY

1. My physical energy is excellent _____ usually good _____ not very good _____
2. I exercise regularly _____ sporadically _____ not at all _____
3. I practice yoga, tai chi, or something similar _____
4. I enjoy _____ play _____ competitive sports
5. I play competitive sports professionally _____
6. I don't need more than 5–6 hours of sleep at night _____
7. I need at least 8–10 hours of sleep a night _____
8. I'm aggressive professionally _____ in my personal life _____
9. I enjoy activities that carry an element of physical risk (parachuting, sky diving, scuba diving, etc.) _____
10. I pursue what I want relentlessly _____
11. I plan and strategize in the pursuit of my goals or dreams _____
12. I seize opportunities and run with them _____

13. I act first and worry about the consequences later _____
14. I'm blunt and outspoken _____
15. I'm a quiet or shy person _____
16. I consider myself to be a participant rather than an observer
    _____
17. I consider myself to be an observer rather than a participant
    _____
18. I'm goal-oriented _____
19. I'm intuitive _____
20. I consider myself creative _____ not creative _____
21. I anger easily _____
22. It takes a lot to get me mad _____
23. I'm patient _____ impatient _____
24. My ideal form of entertainment/pleasure is:
    a concert _____
    watching a video at home _____
    working at what I love _____
    shopping _____
    spending the evening with my significant other _____
    eating at a gourmet restaurant _____
    foreign travel _____
    reading _____
    being with my family/kids _____
    going to a movie _____
    doing volunteer work _____
    brainstorming with friends _____
    partying _____
    having an adventure _____
    other (state) _____

SEXUAL ENERGY

1. I'm comfortable with my sexuality _____
2. I'm usually the aggressor in sexual situations _____
3. I have a strong sex drive _____
4. Sex: I can take it or leave it _____
5. I prefer being involved in a relationship before I sleep with someone _____
6. In a committed relationship, I'm monogamous _____
7. I'm a flirt _____
8. In some of my relationships, my significant other has been unfaithful _____
9. I'm rather passive about sex _____
10. I want a relationship that is all-encompassing—mind, body, soul, emotions—the whole package _____
11. I want to be courted and seduced _____
12. When things are going well in my sexual relationship, my whole life works better _____
13. When I'm in love with someone, I want to live with that person _____ or legalize the relationship by getting married _____
14. Name 7 things that are essential to you for a great relationship:

    _____
    _____
    _____
15. I find it easy _____ difficult _____ to separate my emotions from sex
16. Before I sleep with someone, I have to feel an intuitive connection _____ chemistry _____ emotionally secure in the relationship _____ just a raw physical attraction _____

17. I'm promiscuous and enjoy it _____
18. I'm aware of how powerful an affect my sexuality has on other people _____
19. My sexuality is completely separate from the rest of my life
    _____
20. I expect to be sexually active all of my life _____

BRAINSTORMING

List three questions about your sexuality and love life. These can cover anything. What do you really want in a sexual partner or significant other? Why haven't you found the right partner? Are you happy with the partner you have? What would you change about your own sexuality or that of your partner? How can you improve your love life? Are you happiest alone? Why do you feel you need to be half of a couple?

The idea here is to be honest with yourself and not worry about the answers. Just ask the questions. Throughout the course of the book, you'll be answering them.

MY QUESTIONS

1. _____
2. _____
3. _____

3

Sun in Aries ☉♈

THE INITIATOR
Cardinal Fire

"My way or the highway."

Strengths: Independent, resourceful, fearless, leadership qualities, pioneering, entrepreneurial
Weaknesses: May not follow through, extreme impatience and
restlessness, intolerance for slowpokes
Sexual Blueprint: Experience is everything.

The spirit of the Aries Sun is that of a trailblazer, a pioneer, an
entrepreneur, someone who initiates and makes things happen.
You tackle everything with courage and certainty and often exhibit a resourcefulness that surprises you. *Where'd that come from?*
you wonder. *How'd I do that?*

You rarely mull over what you want in life—that is, you aren't
a planner, an analyst. But, somehow, you're very clear about what

you want and need and how you're going to get it. In a crisis situ-ation, you may not be the calmest person around and you may not have a clue what you're going to do. You just do it. You act instinctively. You're a survivor.

Aries individuals are often the ones to break new ground in the arts, scientific research, space exploration, computers, what-ever seizes their passions or rises out of their personal experi-ences. Aries Joseph Campbell brought the power and scope of mythology to ordinary people. Aries Betty Ford founded one of the first and probably the most well-known centers for alcohol and drug abuse.

You're passionate and aggressive, reckless and impulsive. Life with you is rarely boring. You're usually quite comfortable with your sexuality, and even if you aren't, you wouldn't admit it to yourself or anyone else. If your ardor isn't reciprocated, you're not the type who sticks around, hoping for a second chance. You're *gone* and on to newer and better things.

SUN IN ARIES AND . . .

MARS IN ARIES ♂ ♈

Your commanding presence is like a force of nature. When you enter a room, people don't just notice; they stare. You enjoy hav-ing this effect on others. You like being noticed. But too much of it bores you just as quickly as not enough of it, and there's noth-ing in the world you hate more than boredom.

Your restlessness and impatience are extreme. You act hastily and impulsively, and once something bores you—a project, a re-lationship, your life, whatever it might be—you walk away with-out regrets or apologies.

You have a terrible temper and blow up at the slightest provocation. Once you've blown, it's over. Life is too short to hold grudges. Your survival instincts are excellent. You're fearless, intent on doing things your own way, and pursue whatever you desire with passion and an unerring belief in yourself.

Competitive sports interest you or you're involved in some way with them. You have natural athletic ability and enjoy risky pursuits—rock climbing, bungee jumping, parachuting. When you're the one competing, you compete to win and may be a sore loser.

As a double fire combination, you have a powerful sex drive. You're headstrong, rash, and impulsive about sex. You don't hesitate to seize the initiative and are clear about what you like and dislike sexually. Your capacity for intimacy may be stunted somewhat by your impatience and rashness unless you have a planet like Venus or the Moon in a water or earth sign.

You can be sensuous, particularly if you trust your partner implicitly and he or she realizes how important your ego is to you. You're deeply emotional and rarely mince words in a relationship. Despite your love of independence, you thrive in a fulfilling relationship that's built on respect, mutual interests, and a satisfying sexual intimacy. However, your impulsiveness often propels you into relationships and sexual liaisons with people who may bring out the worst in you. The adage "Look before you leap" applies to this combination.

Once love enters the picture, you prefer monogamy and place your trust implicitly in your partner. If your partner violates this trust, your shock is considerable and your wounds, deep. The good news? You aren't the type to pine away and feel sorry for yourself. When you get over the initial hurt, you move on.

Best Matches: Sparks fly with a partner whose Venus is in Aries or another fire sign. Mars or the Sun in a fire sign works, too. Any Aries combination is volatile, passionate, and unpredictable, but never boring.

Examples: David Letterman, Joseph Campbell, actor James Woods, Danish writer Isak Dinesen, feminist Gloria Steinem

MARS IN TAURUS♂ ☿

You approach everything with a measured patience and usually finish what you start. You're rarely defeated by obstacles. Thanks to your incredible determination and will, you're able to plow through nearly any obstacle or challenge that life throws your way.

You definitely have a temper. Anger is most likely to sweep through you, a rushing flow like lava that scorches and destroys everything in its path. Then the rage burns itself out and that's it. A purging.

You like and need stability in your life and once you have it, you build on it. You're acquisitive and the items you acquire hold a special aesthetic quality—rare books, art, music, perhaps memorabilia of a particular age. If you're involved in the arts, you perfect your craft in a methodical way, building on each of your creations.

There's a mystic in you, someone drawn to the deeper mysteries in life, the cosmic X-Files. You may not talk about it, but anything that smacks of the weird and the strange intrigues you.

You're sensuous and have a powerful sex drive. But it isn't just sex that appeals to your sensuality. You're the type who can walk into an autumn woods on a misty morning and *see* the smells, *hear* the colors, *taste* the sounds. At moments like this, you're filled with the majesty and grandeur of nature and you feel it throughout your body, a sensuality that is bone-deep.

When you experience this kind of sensuality in a relationship, you're willing to explore the terrain and see where it leads. If this requires commitment and monogamy, that's fine. Your capacity for intimacy and honest communication flourish in a committed relationship and may involve some sort of artistic or creative endeavor or a particular worldview or spiritual camaraderie that you share with your partner.

You have physical stamina and strength. You may push yourself too hard at times so that burnout is a possibility unless you follow the dictates of your body, for which you have great respect. You take care of it, exercise, eat right, and if you have any habits that aren't healthy, you should be able to break them by doing nothing more than making a decision to do so.

Your body can be a conduit to intuitive knowledge. It may happen when you're with a lover and suddenly *know* that you and this person have been together before in other lives. Or you may touch an object and *feel* its history. Or you may be off alone somewhere when your flesh suddenly crawls and you're absolutely certain that the dead are watching you. With practice, through disciplines like yoga or tai chi or meditation, your body can become a psychic conduit, capable of gleaning information from nonordinary sources.

Other people may consider you to be selfish, egocentric, and stubborn, but these attributes are actually integral to your survival instincts. You never give up. You never surrender. How can that be bad?

Best Matches: A partner with a Venus in Taurus will be sexual, sensual, and loving. A partner with a Venus in Aries will be sexual, sometimes jealous, but will usually give you space and independence.

Examples: Funnyman Charlie Chaplin, Marilyn Ferguson (*The Aquarian Conspiracy*), Celine Dion, actress Patricia Arquette

MARS IN GEMINI♂Ⅱ

Everything begins in your mind. You enjoy spirited discourse and rarely back down from an argument where you're trying to prove that you're right. You're so deft at expressing yourself that you can talk circles around most people. When you come up against someone who confronts you about not having all the facts, you may stretch the truth to make your viewpoint fit. It isn't that you're a liar; you simply don't like to lose an argument.

Your mental restlessness begs for a creative outlet. Without one, you spend a lot of your energy locked in petty arguments. You have writing and communication ability and should develop those abilities. You enjoy travel, the newness and excitement of the road, and may be able to combine this enjoyment with your natural communication abilities to create a professional niche for yourself. You collect facts as well as a gossip, but are able to turn these traits into a professional or personal advantage.

You're so restless you may drive the people around you crazy with your need to be doing, moving, talking, communicating. You benefit by taking time to simply sit back and chill. Read a book, watch TV, *relax*.

Sexually, variety is the name of the game. You won't be pinned down, penned in, or restricted in any way. You're forthright about what you like, who you are, and are probably quite comfortable with your sexuality. For you, there are no taboos. You value humor in a partner. *Amuse me. Make me laugh.* In return, you can be just as funny and animated as a standup comic, but beneath that mask lies the passion of the Aries Sun that whispers, *Show me how much you love me. Adore me, be loyal to me.*

When you're in the middle of some all-consuming project—professional or personal; the distinction often doesn't matter as long as it's consuming—your sexuality is temporarily pushed aside.

It's nothing personal. It's simply that all your energy is poured into whatever you're doing or creating.

If your partner communicates as well as you do, then your capacity for intimacy is infinite. If he or she is the strong, silent type, the relationship won't be long-term regardless of how great the sex is. Your urge and need for honest communication is paramount to a satisfying relationship.

Monogamy and commitment are problematic when you're younger. There're so many people to meet, so many relationships to sample. But if you're still uncommitted by the time you reach your late twenties, commitment begins to look better and more feasible. While you still value your independence and need diversity, you're looking for a partner who will love and satisfy you no matter what. A tall order, but for the Aries/Gemini combination, nothing is impossible, nothing is an obstacle.

Sensuality, like most things in your life, begins in your mind. It sounds odd, that something we associate with physical touch begins with a thought, an idea, but that's how it is for you. In your relationships, your mind must be courted. You must be seduced intellectually. If the mental camaraderie isn't there, there's no sexual chemistry for you.

Best Matches: Look for a partner with Venus in Gemini or an air sign, Venus in Aries or another fire sign, Sun in a fire sign, Mars in an air sign. All combinations work, but any combination with Gemini will be more mental and communicative.

Examples: Astrologer and author Linda Goodman, biographer Kitty Kelly (*Jackie Oh!*), author Erica Jong, singer Diana Ross

MARS IN CANCER ♂ ♋

Your energy is intuitive and emotional. You don't necessarily wear your heart on your sleeve, but you're apt to take everything personally. As a double cardinal sign, you're tenacious when you want something and don't hesitate to pursue it with all the passion and emotion that you possess. But if, at any point in that pursuit, your heart is no longer in it, then you back off and find some new goal, adventure, or relationship.

You're not a control freak, but control issues may figure prominently in your life. These issues usually focus on your home life and your immediate personal environment. Guests who arrive without warning, professional snafus that bleed over into your personal life, not being able to do *what* you want *when* you want; these kinds of things push your buttons.

You're a private person who has hobbies and passions that are yours and yours alone. You don't lack for friends and are always eager for a good time and an adventure. But when your private time is squeezed out, your energy is rapidly depleted.

There can be discord in your home and family. The discord is pronounced when you insist on controlling your significant others, your partners, your kids. Your great ambition and singular purpose work in your professional life, but may not be welcome at home.

Security is a dominant issue in your sexuality and can overshadow your sexual activity. Despite the Aries Sun need for independence, your greatest sense of sexual freedom happens in a monogamous relationship where you are loved and respected. As long as you temper your need to control your immediate environment and the people in it, a mutually loving relationship mitigates domestic discord.

Your instincts and intuition flourish in a loving sexual relationship. You sense what your partner likes and dislikes and have excellent insight into his or her personality. Your capacity for intimacy in this kind of relationship is profound and vitally important to you. However, the nature of Cancer is to sidestep sticky emotional issues, to move the way the crab moves when confronted, so you may not be as forthcoming about your own emotions as you expect your partner to be about his or hers. You can get away with this kind of evasion for a while, but it eventually undermines the relationship and you'll be forced to deal with it.

When your intuition is in high gear and you feel a deep connection to your partner, your sensuality is profound. These perfect moments create mental snapshots that remain with you in great detail for years. Although you're highly intuitive, that quality isn't reliable in relationships because you read into it what you want the most. This can lead to major mistakes in sexual relationships where you're looking for love and satisfaction with impossible partners.

Your sexuality can be erratic. You go through periods where you're celibate and feel just fine about it. Or you may go through periods where sex is paramount in your life. It always boils down to your feelings about yourself, your partner, your overall satisfaction with your life. You're a tactile person, though, so when you're in the mood, your partner definitely knows it.

Best Matches: A partner with a Venus in Cancer or another water sign is probably the best match for you. But Mars in another water sign, or Sun in Leo or Sagittarius would work, too. With someone whose Venus is in Cancer, the relationship is intuitive and nurturing; with a Scorpio Venus, the relationship is intense and sexual; with a Pisces, the relationship is gentle, compassionate, and kind.

Examples: Haley Mills, William Shatner, Eddie Murphy

MARS IN LEO ♂ ♌

This double fire combination is, like the double Aries combo, a powerhouse of energy. But the Aries/Leo combination has greater warmth and personal charisma and is a true people magnet. You're an inspiration to other people, who look up to you as a model of leadership abilities and a will of iron.

Your physical vitality is strong and keeps you moving long after the competition has gone home for the day. You're willing to work hard and tirelessly for what you want and always have a contingent of friends and supporters who are willing to work on your behalf. You're the decisive type, able to think on your feet, and even if you don't have all the answers, other people think you do.

You're a proud person, with a strong sense of right and wrong, what's fair and what's not, and you can always be counted on when someone is depending on you. You're deeply stubborn, insisting on your right to live your life *your* way, to uncover and define your own beliefs. This is great. Nothing develops self-reliance faster than to make your own choices, right or wrong, and live the consequences.

Your restlessness and need for physical activity benefit through a daily exercise routine of some kind. The discipline not only keeps you in top physical shape, but keeps your mind focused on essentials and burns off some of your energy.

You aren't a power monger and aren't interested in controlling or manipulating others. But you do want to exert control over your own life and that control is functioning best when you work at something you enjoy.

Your sexuality is about self-expression. How this manifests itself in your life depends to a large extent on deeper issues—the degree of your self-confidence, the depth of your need for recognition and love, and what you're looking for in a sexual partner.

As a double fire sign, you tend to be direct about sex and when you're in the mood, that means you're in the mood now, not tomorrow. The fact that you can be demanding may put some peo-

ple off, but hey, that's how it is and why should you change? Man
or woman, you have tremendous sex appeal and are usually well
aware of its impact on other people. You're courageous, but un-
like the double Aries, you're rarely reckless and typically aren't
interested in thrills just for the sake of thrills. It's as true for sex as
anything else.

When you need to, you play the sexual game well. The actor
or actress in you plays whatever role the situation requires and
carries off an Oscar-winning performance. The problem is that
you really don't like playing games and when you do it too often,
the line between illusion and reality blurs and your partner or significant other is confused by your mixed signals.

Your capacity for intimacy is especially strong when you're
with a partner who is as direct about sexuality and relationships
as you are. However, you want to be the center of your partner's
attention, to be appreciated. And when you're not, the relationship probably doesn't last.

Best Matches: Venus in Leo or another fire sign is best. It
brings passion and excitement to the relationship. Mars in an air
sign or Sun in a fire or air sign would add intellectual camaraderie.

Examples: Hans Christian Anderson, Al Gore, Ram Dass,
Quentin Tarantino

MARS IN VIRGO♂♍

This earth/fire combination can be difficult. Virgo Mars makes
you careful and diligent in everything you do, and this runs up
against the Aries impulsiveness and recklessness. In much the
same way that an engine is fine-tuned periodically, you need to
make continual minor adjustments in your life to get the most
from this combination.

You try not to rush into anything. It's tough to resist sometimes, though, with that Aries energy jerking you around. Rushing leaves you feeling unprepared, and few things worry you more than that. When this combination functions smoothly, your energy is expressed in a practical, efficient way, with an acute attention to detail. You're self-disciplined, unselfish, and generally enjoy helping other people. Perhaps that's one of the reasons Mars in Virgo is often attracted to the health or medical fields and the healing arts.

Professionally, you'll pioneer something new and entirely different by paying attention to details, gathering the facts, and studying them for how they can be used pragmatically and to help others. The more independent you are in your work, the happier you'll be. This combination is excellent for writing—*if* you can make your Aries Sun sit still long enough.

Your strong sense of responsibility and duty make you prone to criticizing others who don't meet your standards. This only alienates people. You can't be judge and jury about any life except your own. Even self-criticism is best to avoid; it only undermines your confidence.

This combination isn't very physically active. You'll walk a mile if the mood hits, but regular, disciplined exercise doesn't interest you. Your survival instincts center around your intellect, your communication abilities, and your intuitive grasp of what makes people tick.

You're discreet and discriminating when it comes to sex and sexual partners. This isn't surprising, given your propensity for caution in other areas of your life. That said, you do like variety every bit as much as Mars in Gemini (also a mutable sign), but only as long as variety spells relationships rather than one-night stands. You just aren't frivolous where sex is concerned. Monogamy is your preference.

In a committed relationship, your capacity for intimacy, communication, and spontaneity flourish. You like having a solid personal base from which to build the rest of your life and things actually unfold more smoothly for you when you have that base. It's as if a solid relationship frees you to pour your energies into some other area because the personal stuff is taken care of.

You're flexible and adaptable when it suits you, but you won't bend over backward in a sexual relationship to make things work. Your gift for analysis provides you with a firm grasp on your own boundaries and bottom lines. You're so capable of taking note of details in every facet of your life that the smallest nuances are the most telling for you. This is certainly true in terms of your sexual blueprint. A smile, a joke, an unexpected courtesy or confidence can trigger an electrifying attraction.

Your sensuality begins in the mind, just as it does for Gemini. But with you, there's a twist. Your sensuality is awakened through one-to-one communication, a baring of the souls, rather than just by ideas.

Best Matches: For sparks and chemistry, look for Venus in Aries or Virgo. Aries would bring more passion and excitement and Virgo would be more grounded. Venus in an earth sign or Sun in a fire sign are electric, too.

Examples: Betty Ford, William Holden, actress Elizabeth Montgomery, Pearl Bailey

MARS IN LIBRA ♂ ♎

Fire and air are compatible, but Aries and Libra are in opposition—180 degrees apart. That means they'll never see eye to eye on much of anything. If these opposing energies are galvanized somehow, brought to bear against a single goal or issue, then there aren't any limits to what you can accomplish within the area of human relationships.

You seek to understand the dynamics of relationships, both in your own life and in the lives of others. You crave balance, harmony, peace. These attributes may elude you in your own relationships because you're often too willing to compromise just to keep the peace.

You enjoy the arts, music, beauty in all its guises. You have considerable creative talent and numerous friends and acquaintances in the arts. The law, politics, and the judicial process interest you. Professionally, your options are wide open and you'll trailblaze and pioneer regardless of where you end up.

You're a bundle of contradictions—fiery but soft-spoken, determined but ambivalent in affairs of the heart, clear about your purpose in life, but muddled about how to attain what you want. A challenge, no matter how you look at it. But your aesthetic appreciation of life is unparalleled in the zodiac.

You're romantic, passionate, sensual, with a powerful sex drive. And yes, your emotions get in the way. Or they pave the way. It depends on which side of the Libra fence you favor. A part of you craves companionship. Another part of you abhors it. No easy answers on that score.

Sexually, you initiate. But because you can't bear the thought of hurting anyone, you flunk the course on ending a relationship. This can lead you into a kind of duplicity where you carry on simultaneous relationships or flirtations. If these small deceptions catch up to you, there's hell to pay.

Other than the peace and harmony bit and the fact that you prefer moonlit beaches and candlelit dinners to noisy nightclubs, you're uncertain of your parameters and bottom lines. You, like the Borgs in *Star Trek*, tend to merge with your partner's likes and dislikes. Big mistake. You need to draw on the strength of your Aries Sun for independence in thought and beliefs and leave your

Libra Mars back on the beach. Your life, sexually and otherwise, will work only when you know who *you* are.

You enjoy intimacy, companionship, and a partner with common interests. When you're courted and seduced romantically—moonlit dinners, good music, a slice of paradise—you awaken sensually. The main problem you have with commitment is a fear that romance will dry up. You can't imagine a life without romance. But romance works two ways and if you do your part, your partner will do the same.

Your survival instincts center around relationships. You can make a friend of anyone and often win over your enemies.

Best Matches: Venus in Aries or an air sign; the Sun in a fire or air sign. With a Venus in Aries, the relationship is passionate. A Venus in Leo may require too much fawning from you to be viable. A Venus in Sagittarius would be daring and fun.

Examples: Steve Martin, Dudley Moore, Herb Alpert

MARS IN SCORPIO ♂ ♏

Fire and water. Any grade-school kid can tell you what happens when these elements meet. The intensity of Scorpio seeks to squash the passions of Mars. But before you begin to wish you were born under a different combination, look at the positive aspects.

You're a born detective, able to ferret out secrets, hidden motives and agendas, and to get to the heart of any mystery, human or otherwise. Research and psychiatry may appeal to you. Or surgery. Or a dozen of other professions in which you have to probe to find answers. Your energy revolves around issues dealing with power, understanding things, and sexuality, not necessarily in that order. Your persistence and determination are legendary and may even surpass that of Mars in Taurus.

Although intensely emotional, you rarely show it. To do so would be to sacrifice control and surrender your power. Even your anger remains hidden, simmering and bubbling until it's expressed as biting sarcasm. You're deeply intuitive, often psychic, and unusually aware of the deeper interconnections among people and events. You understand that a single thought, positive or negative, is tremendously powerful. If you're spiritually aware, then you know to use this ability with utmost caution and to focus on the positive, the upbeat.

You're rarely neutral or ambivalent about anything, and compromise is a challenge. But your strong opinions, likes and dislikes, are definite professional assets. Your survival instincts rest on your intuition and your ability to penetrate to the truth.

This combination defines the term *strong will*. When you bring the full power of your will against anything or anyone, mountains move, empires topple, and sexual relationships are forged or collapse.

In your scheme of things, sex is a conduit to deeper understanding and communication. That's really what you're after—not the act itself, but the deeper, intuitive level of whomever you're with. Through the physical contact, you want to get to the heart and soul. Yet there are times when sex either doesn't interest you or you repress your desires out of some moralistic stance that stems back to your childhood.

You have charisma, a smoldering sexuality that attracts the opposite sex in droves. Whether you act on these attractions depends, to a large extent, on the rest of the package. Is the person funny? Fun? Are there common interests?

In the sexual arena, as well as in the rest of your life, you never forget a slight. In some individuals, this can be summed up as: *Don't get mad. Get even.* The repercussions from this belief can be severe.

Like Mars in Taurus, your sensuality can be aroused through nature. A sunlit beach with the warm sand against your feet and the scent of salt in the air can be as sensual as a sexual encounter that meets all your emotional criteria. The degree of your aggression, both sexually and physically, is always tied to how badly you want something or someone.

Best Matches: Stick to basic science. A Venus in Aries is passionate but a Venus in Scorpio would be emotionally intense. Stick to compatible elements.

Examples: Howard Cossell

MARS IN SAGITTARIUS♂ ♐

You're passionate about your ideals, and bring all your double fire energy into putting those ideals into action. Patience definitely isn't your strong suit, but when an ideal is at stake, you do whatever it takes—even cultivate patience—to make it happen.

You have abundant physical vitality that keeps you running from sunrise to sunset. But there's always purpose behind what you do. You can't tolerate wasting your energy on things that don't matter to you. Your best bet is to be self-employed, working at something you love, calling your own shots. This gives you the freedom so necessary to who you are. Unless you're fortunate enough to stumble over your passions right out of the womb, it's likely you'll have more than one professional pursuit in your life. Entrepreneur to actor, actor to artist, artist to adventure writer. Something along those lines.

You may have athletic talents, but if it requires teamwork, you won't be interested in a long-term commitment. You're more the solitary, outdoors type, happy to hike, swim, camp, rock-climb, and jump out of planes all on your own. A sort of James Bond of the zodiac.

Your sense of right and wrong is well developed and your ideals prevent you from ever giving anyone else a raw deal. Your survival instincts are based on your personal philosophy and spiritual beliefs.

Sexually, you want the same freedom from restrictions that you seek in the rest of your life. *If it feels good, do it.*

Your natural optimism is a kind of safeguard against disaster, so that even when things in the sexual and relationship department don't turn out the way you would like, you manage to put a positive spin on the experience. However, you're impulsive and reckless at times in your choice of partners and would benefit from some forethought before you leap into an experience you might regret. It behooves you to get to know your partner first. Does he or she share your idealism and philosophies? Do you have mutual interests? You know the drill.

Your intuition is terrific, but you often prefer not to listen and go your own merry way, certain you have all the angles figured. You're blunt in sexual matters, aren't much of a game player, and do best becoming lovers with someone who is first your friend.

You can be sensual, especially when your partner enjoys honest communication. Intimacy is important to you in a committed relationship, but getting you to commit is something else altogether. To remain in a monogamous, committed relationship, your heart and soul must be on fire.

Best Matches: Venus in Sagittarius or another fire sign means passion and fire; Venus in an air sign or Mars in an air sign means a free-flow of communication; Sun in fire or air signs creates good energy.

Examples: Billy Carter, Doris Day, Billy Dee Williams

MARS IN CAPRICORN♂♑

The family of a friend who has this combination used to joke that within minutes of being born, she was planning her career. That about sums up this position. Ambition, careful planning, hard work, and pragmatism; these are your hallmarks. You want to be recognized for your achievements.

When you find your niche, you become singular in your dedication, pouring enormous energy into that particular path. You're a builder who puts her career together one piece at a time, always with an eye on the larger concept, the bigger picture, the future. Whatever you do, though, must be practical, grounded, and useful.

The inner tensions you experience usually involve a clash of wills between Aries and Capricorn. Aries wants to rush and move ahead; Capricorn wants to plan and strategize. Both energies are needed when you're up against a challenge or obstacle. Sometimes you plow through the challenge, Aries style. Other times you attack it Capricorn style, through careful planning. The method that works the best is the one backed by the power of your passions.

Your organization skills are extraordinary—but only when Aries doesn't rush in and make a mess of things. You do well in any profession or line of work where you can use your organization skills, logic, and ability to plan. Your survival instincts revolve around these same abilities.

Your sexuality is filled with contradictions. On the one hand, you want the entire package—fireworks, whirlwind seduction, the earth moving. Preferably, this happens within the context of commitment and marriage. On the other side, you keep a tight rein on your sexual impulses and desires. Over the course of your life, you may fluctuate between these two extremes until you find a happy medium.

Your sensuality is strongest when you release your control over your emotions and simply go with the flow. This is also when your capacity for intimacy is at its height. You do want companionship and equality in a partner, but on your own terms. Perhaps that attitude lies at the root of your sexual challenge. Learn to accept people as they are, the good with the bad, and don't make the mistake of thinking you'll change the person.

Aggression and assertiveness work in two ways with this combination. Either you're assertive about everything, sexual issues included, and insist on running the show, or you attract people who act out that role in your life. In the first instance, you have to learn that you don't always have all the answers and when you don't, you should step aside. In the second instance, the lesson is to reclaim your power.

Your anger is often mixed up with your natural aggression. If you don't deal with it, you attract situations that force you to deal not only with the anger, but with its cause. Best to do it the other way around; get at the origin, resolve it, and move on.

Best Matches: Venus in Capricorn or in Aries, Sun in an earth sign, or Mars in an earth sign.

Examples: Francis Ford Coppola, Washington Irving, musician Henry Mancini

MARS IN AQUARIUS♂︎♒︎

Your energy expresses itself through innovation, reform, independence, and "the family of man." Like Mars in Sagittarius, you love your freedom and independence and chafe at any restrictions that are imposed upon you. You have no great love for authority and do your best professional work when you're self-employed or you're the boss.

You're an innovative thinker whose survival instincts revolve around the intellect and finding new ways of doing things. There's a lot of the idealist and humanitarian in you and these ideals often push you in your life's direction. You want to benefit the larger world in which you live and these benefits may evolve out of some personal concern or project.

You aren't particularly adaptable to change, but once you set your sights on something, you go for it with determination and persistence. You're assertive by nature rather than by design, and rarely hesitate to say what you think and believe and why. You have fixed opinions and the groups you associate with support your opinions, interests, and ideals. In fact, you're great at working with groups that form around a common cause. Although you understand the power of the masses, you also understand that a single individual can change the world.

You have an unemotional approach to sex. Whether this is good or bad depends on other elements in your birth horoscope, but it gives you a certain power in that when a relationship ends, your life doesn't fall apart. You assimilate the lesson and move on.

The biggest turn-on for you is the intellect and, specifically, ideals that are like your own. Your partner may be someone you knew and loved first as a friend, whom you met through one of the groups to which you belong. Your relationship may not be passionate by other people's standards, but you don't live by other people's standards anyway, so who cares? You're most interested in a soul connection.

This combination has its share of tensions. You don't want to need anyone in a sexual relationship, yet you enjoy companionship and sex with the right person. You don't want to be trapped or forced to conform, so you sample what's out there and invariably find something lacking. For you, as with Gemini, intimacy begins in the mind. The essential difference between the two signs, however, is that you demand originality, freedom, and innovation in your partner.

Best Matches: Venus in Aquarius, Venus in Aries or another fire sign, Venus in an air sign, Mars in a fire sign, Sun in a fire or air sign.

Examples: Ellen Goodman, Hugh Hefner, Anne McCaffrey, Paul Theroux, Julie Christie

MARS IN PISCES ♂ ♓

Your energy, like that of Mars in Cancer, is emotional and intuitive, inward-driven. You're always on the lookout for the unifying truth, the larger picture, the outer limits of the imagination. Your spiritual or religious views are essential to your well-being.

This is another fire/water combination, difficult to navigate even under the best of circumstances. Your concerns about the external world are secondary to what goes on inside of you. This is part of what makes you a master at dream recall, the interpretation of oracles, symbols, and intuitive experiences. Through your imagination and intuition, you're able to tap into cutting-edge trends in fashion, design, and anything in the arts.

Your conflicts center around the inner-driven nature of Mars in Pisces and the externally focused Sun in Aries. You aren't very assertive, even when a situation calls for it and Aries is screaming in your ear. Under the influence of alcohol or drugs, your self-confidence shines, which may be one of the reasons Mars in Pisces is prone to addictions.

People figure you for a pushover and take advantage of your generous nature. The best way to break this pattern is to realize you have as much right as anyone else to state your opinion and to make a conscious effort to do so. Nowhere is it written that anyone has to be a victim.

In sexual matters, your bottom line is simple: it's all or nothing. So forget casual sex, casual encounters, casual anything in this area.

You're rarely the aggressor in a sexual relationship, either because you're too unsure of yourself or because you're terrified of rejection. But when you get involved, you commit deeply.

Your compassion for others is so profound that it can act like a magnet for people who need to be saved from themselves. You hate to see anyone in emotional pain so, of course, you're there to help. And the other person grabs onto you like a dying man seizing a life preserver. Down you both go in a spiral of complex needs and desires and your personality is subsumed. You love to be needed, but who needs this?

Sometimes, these kinds of experiences propel you on to the path where you're supposed to be—as a counselor on addictions, writing speculative fiction, who knows? Your life is riddled with possibilities.

Your patience in all things is admirable and when you do connect with your soul mate (because nothing less than that will suffice), you're a loving, committed partner finally living the ideal.

Best Matches: Venus in Pisces or a water sign, Venus in Aries, Mars in a water sign. It's best to stick to Venus or Mars in a water sign, so there's an easy, smoother emotional flow.

Examples: Oleg Cassini, Erich Fromm, Pierre-August Renoir, Steve McQueen, Spencer Tracy

SENSE-MEMORY EXERCISE FOR SUN IN ARIES

Mars represents our physical senses and each of us has at least one sense that is stronger than the others. Maybe you have an incred-

ible sense of taste or touch. Perhaps your hearing is acute. Whichever sense is your strongest is your most reliable conduit for
understanding something about yourself or others, your environment, and your personal world.

In the space below, you're going to describe an instance where
one of your physical senses played a vital role. When I did this activity at a workshop, one woman described her first sight of the
Amazon River. A man in the group described the taste of the best
Cuban coffee he'd ever had. Another man described the music
that was playing in the background of a nursing home the day his
father died. In each description, everyone else was drawn so fully
into the moment that we were *seeing* the Amazon, *tasting* that
coffee, *hearing* that music. That's the kind of presence you should
bring to this activity.

In your description, be detailed and specific. Be fully *there*.

_____

_____

_____

_____

_____

_____

Now look back at the three questions you asked in the inventory at the beginning of part two. The description you've just
written pertains to your second question. The Aries woman who
described her first sight of the Amazon River, for instance, had
asked what she was really looking for in a partner. She realized
from her description that she was seeking not only a traveling
companion, but someone who would share her love of the exotic,
the utterly foreign, the mysterious, and the extraordinary.

4

Sun in Taurus ☉ ♉

THE SENSUALIST
Fixed Earth

"I persevere."

Strengths: Stable, grounded, stubborn, persistent, earth-centered, deeply mystical (but won't admit it), reticent, security-oriented, endurance, pragmatic, patient, sensual, inherently creative

Weaknesses: Generally inflexible, stubborn, fixed opinions, not particularly aggressive unless angry

Sexual Blueprint: Charismatic and sensual lover.

You're a cultivator. You take the ideas that Aries has initiated (and perhaps walked away from) and make them real, practical, stable, and useful. You have such firm opinions and beliefs that when someone is trying to get you to change your mind about something, you need to be convinced of its validity. *Prove it to me*, says Taurus.

You love beautiful surroundings, whether in nature or in your own home. You love art, music, good food, and may have talent in any of those areas yourself. You have enormous patience and persistence. You may not be the speediest worker around, but you nearly always finish what you start.

You need material security, but also enjoy spending money. You're very adept at handling other people's money as a banker or a trust attorney, or even using a copy of Quicken® to handle your own investments and finances.

Your senses of touch and taste are highly developed and your sexuality is earthy, romantic. A lot goes on under the surface. You tend to be subtle and quiet about your feelings concerning sex and your sexual relationships. However, once you fall for someone, you fall hard. You're a sensual lover, a committed partner, and your romantic attachments—the good ones, anyway—ground and stabilize your life.

SUN IN TAURUS AND . . .

MARS IN ARIES♂♈

No two ways about it; this combination isn't easy to live with. There are times when you feel as if your body is inhabited by two separate souls, each one with needs, desires, and an agenda. The trick is to coax the two to work together by honoring their individual needs.

The patience of your Taurus Sun is constantly at war with the impatience of your Mars in Aries. At times, it feels like some medieval torture device. Even so, your energy is best expressed through spontaneity and taking the kinds of risks that will drive your Taurus Sun crazy. These risks are in the area of finances, security, the cultivation of long-range goals, and your personal values. When you feel an impulse to do something in one of these areas, follow it. Your world will expand in direct proportion to the degree of your risk.

Your physical energy level is nothing short of incredible. You probably don't need much sleep and are able to hum right along, shouldering more than your share of responsibilities and activities without faltering. But when you do falter, when you need to chill out, you dive into solitude and head for nature. It's likely that you enjoy camping—we're talking the rustic sort, a sleeping bag on the ground versus a forty-foot trailer with a satellite dish and a microwave oven—and losing yourself in some mystical connection with the cosmos that no one else understands.

You may never admit it, but you're a romantic. It's not that you need the external trappings, flowers and moonlit beaches; you're looking for the deeper connections, the brushing of souls, the inexplicable chemistry, the sense that you and your significant other are *in the groove*.

Just what, exactly, is this groove? It's a knowing, an intuitive certainty, that you and your significant other are co-conspirators who came together to complete some spiritual contract in this life. Complicated? Yes. Difficult? Probably. Committed? Absolutely. But even if you haven't met that person yet, everything you experience in terms of your sexuality is a steppingstone toward that single relationship, that bonding.

Despite your impatience and restlessness, you have a marvelous capacity for intimacy if only—and here's the zinger—you can release your preconceived notions about how things are *supposed* to be. Sink in to every moment. Be present.

You're comfortable with your sexuality, feel at home in your body, and instinctively sense which partners are right or wrong for you. But you may not listen to those instincts when you should because the Aries part of you is so impatient. It's likely that you're the aggressor sexually, and when you aren't, it isn't due to a lack of self-confidence.

You have a keen sense of timing in life that is connected to your awareness of higher forces and power, to patterns and symbols. You have a knack for being in the right place at the right time. You honor and appreciate other people's individuality and need for freedom and independence. You can be outrageously stubborn about your opinions and beliefs, but this stubbornness also makes you a loyal mate and loving partner.

Best Matches: Venus in Aries or another fire sign, Venus in Taurus, Sun in Taurus or another earth sign, Mars in a fire sign.

Examples: Hedda Hopper, Jessica Lange, baseball player Billy Martin

MARS IN TAURUS♂♉

Sensuality permeates your life. This doesn't mean that sex is uppermost in your mind all the time—although it can be—but it *does* mean you're a tactile individual whose senses are highly developed. A walk on the beach, listening to music, a hike in the woods, a gourmet meal; any of these pursuits will renew your spirit and replenish your soul.

As a double Taurus and a double earth sign, you're grounded, stable, stubborn, and security-conscious. You may be acquisitive, too. You're physically strong, take care of your body, and probably have some sort of regular exercise routine that you follow. You enjoy good food and could be something of a culinary expert yourself.

You have an artistic bent born of your deep aesthetic appreciation for everything and anything beautiful, and probably have talent in music, dance, writing, or a similar area. You could enjoy gardening, too. Faced with a barren yard, for instance, you can see the finished product in your mind and, following that blue-print, are able to turn the barrenness into something breathtaking.

You're very much a craftsman, eager to perfect your profes-sional and creative skills, and have the patience to follow through on anything you tackle. Your persistence is legendary among the people who know you well. You feel committed and responsible for anything you begin and nearly always finish what you start, even if your heart isn't in it.

You're mystically inclined and, in some way, it influences many of your choices in life, including your sexual and romantic part-ners. You're a sensual romantic, but you don't think of yourself that way. When you're in the middle of a relationship, you gener-ally don't analyze or dissect what you're doing; you just live it, fully there, fully present, in a Zen sort of way. Sexual chemistry is a priority and once you feel it, other things assume importance—mutual interests, a common appreciation of the arts, music, nature, and the mysterious and unknown. Quite often, sex is a conduit to recognizing people you've known in other lives.

You're independent and usually give your significant other as much freedom as he or she wants. Sometimes with this combina-tion, there's an element of possessiveness. Due to your love of beauty, you like your sexual partner to be physically attractive and to express appreciation for everything that you are.

When you're hurt in a relationship, the wounds run deep, and, all too often, anger is what purges the hurt and allows you to move on. As a double Taurus, you may have the "bull's rush": anger that is slow to build, but which, once it explodes, can be a blinding rage.

Bottom line? You love to be loved, sexually, emotionally, and spiritually, and shouldn't settle for anything less.

Best Matches: Venus in Taurus, Mars in an earth sign, Sun in an earth or water sign. Venus in Taurus would be the most romantic and sensual choice. Mars in an earth sign would indicate a practical, earthy relationship, with deep loyalty.

Examples: Glen Campbell, Salvador Dali, Shirley MacLaine, Billy Joel

MARS IN GEMINI ♂ ♊

Your energy finds its best expression through some form of communication. Whatever form it takes, you're in it for the long haul. Your Taurus Sun gives you persistence and the ability to move steadily forward, and your Mars in Gemini gives you intellectual agility, quickness, and a sense of humor. Taurus stabilizes the Gemini tendency to scatter its energy.

The Gemini part of this equation often finds expression in duality: two marriages or significant relationships, two separate and distinct careers, or two personalities—public and private, for instance, or the passive observer and the activist. It also makes you not only an avid conversationalist, but a good listener as well.

You probably take care of your physical self through proper exercise, diet, and all the other things the experts say contribute to longevity and good health. It's likely that an equal amount of energy goes into the development and expression of your intellect through education, workshops, and travel. Whether your talent is the spoken or the written word, you're an excellent communicator, able to get your ideas across with clarity and panache. You aren't a quitter and the word "surrender" probably doesn't exist in your vocabulary.

That said, there's a restlessness to your mentality. You're an intellectual nomad, a person always in search of new ideas and concepts, new ways of doing things. Your antennae go up, you find the flow, and you leap in with both feet.

You may feel a certain urgency about your creative abilities, a need to act now, to seize the opportunities. Listen to that inner voice. It's usually right. Besides, you're a creative individual, intellectually flexible, and have the staying power to get to wherever you want to go.

In terms of your sexuality, you're an intellectual sensualist. You find the sound, flow, and texture of language to be sensual. Before any kind of physical relationship exists for you, your mind has to be courted and seduced, and there has to be a clear channel of communication between you and your partner. Once that exists, there're no barriers to intimacy and commitment.

The emphasis on your intellectual pursuits can sometimes serve as your defense against being rejected or getting hurt. You sublimate your sexuality so that you can't be tempted to get involved with anyone. While this is an effective protection for an interim period, it's not something you'll be able to continue indefinitely. You thrive on physical contact and your innate curiosity in people and in the world pushes you out among people again. Your nature, after all, is to answer the five interrogatives: what, why, where, when, and how. One way or another, those questions get answered through your relationships with others.

You're usually comfortable with your sexuality and, as long as your communication needs are met, you prefer a committed and monogamous relationship.

Best Matches: Venus in Gemini or another air sign, Venus in Taurus, or another air sign, Mars in an earth sign, Sun in an earth sign. With a Venus in Gemini, the relationship is based on communication and shared intellectual interests.

Examples: Charlotte Brontë, Robert Browning, Barbra Streisand, Sue Grafton, Uma Thurman

MARS IN CANCER ♂ ♋

You're so in tune with your inner self that you're constantly able to muster the energy and vitality to achieve anything. You're mindful of other people's feelings and your achievements are never accomplished at someone else's expense. The energy of this earth/water combination is expressed in a stable, reliable way through intuition and emotions.

You respect other people for their talents and abilities and cheer them on, something that endears you to your family, friends, and partners. If your daughter says she would like to be a screen-writer when she grows up, you don't dampen her spirits with the usual thing you hear from parents—it's too competitive, it takes years to make a living doing that, and why doesn't she become a doctor or a teacher instead? You encourage her to seize her dream.

Your sensitivity extends into all areas of your life. You have a deep love and respect for animals, both in the wild and as companions, and try to nurture wounded souls, animal or human, in any way you can. Intuitive and psychic ability often accompany this combination.

As with the double Taurus combination, your sexuality has a deeply spiritual component. It's not as if you have to have a spiritual connection with every one of your partners, but the only relationships that matter are those in which the connection exists. Your definition of spiritual, of course, is intrinsic to this equation, so it's to your benefit to understand what constitutes spiritual for you.

The trimmings are important, too: the initial chemistry, the synchronicities involved in how you meet this other person and how the relationship unfolds, and how well you and this other person can communicate your feelings and discuss these events.

More often than not, your sensuality is linked to your sense of deeper connections and possibilities.

Usually, Mars in Cancer takes everything so personally that feelings get hurt before things even get off the ground. Your Taurus Sun mitigates this somewhat because Taurus can be tough as nails when it comes to emotions and emotional defenses. But if the other person really gets under your skin and worms his or her way down deep inside your heart and the sex is great besides, then you may take some casual remark much too personally and blow it out of proportion. The basic issue here is that Mars is external energy, not usually associated with emotions, but Cancer is pure emotion. It's like expecting a fish to walk on land and breathe air.

The good news is that none of these things is insurmountable. Once you understand the fundamentals of what make you tick, you can be alert for certain patterns in yourself and take steps to prevent misunderstandings. For you, self-awareness is key to everything.

Best Matches: Venus in Cancer, Venus in a water sign, Mars in a water or earth sign, Sun in an earth or water sign. With a Venus in Cancer, romance and love are as important as sex.

Examples: Coretta Scott King, George Lucas, Frank Capra, Joe Cocker, Audrey Hepburn

MARS IN LEO♂♌

You think big, live big, and excel at creative work. This earth/fire combination makes you proud, stubborn, and fixed in your opinions and beliefs. Your independence and the depth of your creative drive is best used in self-employment or in a profession where you have the freedom to call your own shots.

Your leadership abilities are evident in anything you take on, but really shine when you're involved in something about which you feel passionate. Whether it's a creative project or a personal mission, your passion stokes excitement in other people and garners support. You would make an excellent teacher, especially if the subject is something near and dear to your heart.

Your personal warmth and generosity toward others means you never lack for friends or lovers. Your Taurus Sun, though, may like a bit more privacy than your Mars in Leo, so there can be conflicts in that area. Despite Leo's thrust toward the limelight, Taurus isn't always comfortable in that role.

You have a temper, but it takes a lot to set you off. When you do explode, it's major. You aren't the type to hold grudges or cling to your anger, so once you've blown, it's over.

You're a physically active person who, like most Tauruses, is conscious of your body and your health. You may enjoy workouts at the gym, yoga, tai chi, and perhaps even meditation, *if* you can convince the Mars in Leo to sit still long enough. Due to your highly developed sense of touch, you enjoy back rubs, massages, chiropractic treatments, and anything else that involves manipulation of joints and muscles. You probably don't get sick very often, but when you do, you seek out alternative therapies that can be used alone or in conjunction with more traditional medicine.

Your highly attuned sense of touch makes you an ardent and passionate lover. You don't have to be in a committed relationship to enjoy sex. For you, it's pleasurable and creative regardless of the structure of the relationship. However, when you're in a committed relationship, your passion, pleasure, and creative drive are taken to new levels and often have a spiritual component.

Your capacity for intimate communication is at its greatest when your partner shares your creative and spiritual interests. It's then that you become co-conspirators, co-adventurers, co-creators of whatever you're building together. You're supportive of your partner's needs, goals, and dreams, and find that the more you give in that respect, the more you get in return. In times of crisis, your survival instincts are sharp, your compassion is deep, and you go the extra mile to help whoever needs it.

Best Matches: Sparks fly with a Venus in Leo or another fire sign or with a Mars in a fire sign. For stability, look for a partner with Venus, Mars, or Sun in Taurus.

Examples: Cher, Ulysses Grant, writer Vladimir Nabokov

MARS IN VIRGO ♂ ♍

Details, please. Okay: double earth, stability, precision, problem-solving, and a search for perfection through an attention to details and service to others. Before you get all bent out of shape about that last part, it simply means that you enjoy using your talents and abilities to help other people. There's no implication here about victim or goody two-shoes or little Miss Priss, sitting on the sidelines, wishing she were as popular as the blond bombshell next door.

Now that we got through that part, here's the real scoop. There's no better analyst in the zodiac than Virgo. With Mars in this sign, you probably approach most everything in your life with one eye on how the pieces fit together to form a comprehensive whole.

For instance, when you ask *why*, you want a detailed answer, and this is true whether you're asking about a work-related issue or a relationship issue. And then you mull over that answer, dissecting it, picking it apart and putting it back together again until you understand what it really means. This process makes you a consummate communicator, and whether it's through the written or the spoken word, music, or some other art form, you're able to express your ideas clearly and precisely. This combination sometimes indicates mystical underpinnings in creative abilities and endeavors.

Taurus usually doesn't suffer from feelings of inadequacy, but Virgo sometimes does. With this combination, self-criticism and criticism of others won't be as caustic as a double Virgo combination, for example, but it may surface from time to time. You may find yourself becoming judgmental in your most intimate relationships, a part of you standing back and sizing up your partner for what's wrong with him rather than what's right. It's the quickest way to dampen whatever chemistry you feel.

Even when you're not in a critical mode, you're cautious about your sexuality. You carry on endless dialogue with yourself that boils down to one question: should you or shouldn't you? And while you're doing all this, the sensualist in you is chafing at the bit. While the Taurus Sun can have sex anywhere, anyplace, at any time, and doesn't have to be committed to do it, Mars in Virgo would rather play by the rules.

Communication and chemistry are prerequisites to a sexual relationship for you. Unless both are present, you just aren't interested. Truth be told, you would rather work within the parameters of a committed relationship. It doesn't have to be marriage, but it does need to be a mutual commitment. Only then do you really let your emotions shine.

If you can somehow pour your critiquing into a creative venue or into solving problems for other people, you and everyone else around you will be happier and more productive. Your intuition and general creativity will flourish, too.

Best Matches: Venus in Virgo or Taurus, Mars in an earth or water sign, Sun in an earth sign. Venus in Virgo could make for a judgmental relationship in unaware people, but otherwise both individuals would excel at communication. Venus in Taurus would be the most sensible choice.

Examples: Peter Frampton, Willie Nelson, Mike Wallace, Stevie Wonder

MARS IN LIBRA ♂ ♎

Social butterfly, party animal, defender of justice: true, true, and true. But it's not the full picture. This combination begs for an adjustment in attitude. Yes, you're great with people. You're a people person, eager to listen to others' stories and to learn from them. Yes, you enjoy being around people and probably have a network of acquaintances that circumnavigates the globe. Yes, you're always seeking the ideal balance, the perfect peace, a kind of divine diplomacy and idealism. But, once again, it's not the whole story.

You're a paradox, a contradiction, even to the people who know you the best. The problem is that Taurus is an earth sign and Libra, air. A part of you craves a stable, predictable life, where events and experiences unfold along the lines of what is known, visible, comprehensible. But another, deeper part of you is a social adventurer, quick to make friends because you cut through the masks and pretensions and get right down to the heart of the matter, whatever it may be.

You love being surrounded by beauty, and your home and workplace reflect this. You create an atmosphere of peace and harmony in your personal environment and may collect art or rare books or a certain type of music.

You're immensely creative, with possible talent in music, acting, the arts, or in the communication field. Since you're able to see the many sides of a given issue, you would make a terrific counselor or psychologist. Once you decide on your professional path, you pursue it with diligence and patience.

You're a romantic sensualist. You want a moonlit walk on a

perfect beach, beautiful music, a garden of roses. Toss in an exchange of ideas about people, society, and relationships over a gourmet meal and you've got your ideal. On a practical, day-to-day level, intimate communication and commitment are integral to your well-being.

Although most of the time you prefer monogamy and commitment, you don't need commitment to enjoy sex. You dislike hurting anyone's feelings, so sometimes when you're dissatisfied in a relationship, you may clam up and move on, distancing yourself without the other person realizing it. Then, suddenly, you find yourself involved in simultaneous relationships and have to keep your lies straight so that neither of your significant others is hurt. This duplicity is rarely intentional, but the repercussions are the same either way. Everyone gets hurt and the balance you desire in your life goes south.

There can be a didactic quality to this combination at times. Sigmund Freud, for instance, was so determined that his theories on sexuality were correct that he simply couldn't accept that Carl Jung disagreed. Their friendship ended because of it.

Best Matches: A Venus in Libra or in Taurus would be ideal, but you would also do well with a partner who has Mars in an earth sign or the Sun in an earth or air sign.

Examples: Sigmund Freud, actor Doug McClure

MARS IN SCORPIO ♂ ♏

This combination is best described as two little peas in a pod. Mars is considered to be coruler of Scorpio, so the planet is comfortable here. Its water element fits nicely with Taurus's earth. Even though the two signs are opposite each other in the zodiac, the combination forms a kind of fulcrum, one providing what the other lacks. Both are fixed signs; this makes you deeply stubborn.

You insist on doing things *your* way or not at all. Black or white, good or bad, up or down: your life may be one of extremes.

You're a reticent and often secretive person who would make a great researcher, detective, psychologist, or psychiatrist. You also would excel in the medical field as a physician or surgeon. Whatever you do, you are methodical, thorough, and no detail is overlooked. However, you're so headstrong and insistent on doing things your way that you may get into power struggles with bosses. Your best venue is self-employment or working in a job where you have a lot of freedom.

You're exceptionally intuitive, with penetrating insight into other people's motives and inner workings. This is a bonus in both your professional and personal life, and is certainly a plus in your most intimate relationships—when you use it. One of the most obvious manifestations of your intuition is through synchronicities or feelings of dejà vu. If you pay attention to them and listen to your inner guidance, then the extremes that you might experience over the course of your life are either illuminated or mitigated.

Your sexual blueprint is intense, powerful, and sensuous. The all-or-nothing attitude of Mars in Scorpio is softened by the earthy romanticism of Taurus, so that you eventually realize that sexual relationships, like many other facets of life, exist in shades of gray as well. If you deny yourself experiences that don't fit into your rigid demands, *you* lose. It may be necessary for you to enter that gray area at times to get to the core of the real issues and to expand your capacity for intimacy.

There's tremendous potential with this combination for genuine intimacy, trust, communication, and companionship, but only if you can open yourself to uncertainty. By doing that, you may feel as if you're losing some of your iron control over your life— and your heart—but if you don't do so consciously, then events will do it for you. We're here to *experience* life and part of that experience for each of us involves opening ourselves to the unknown.

Power issues always will be a big deal for you—control over yourself, over others, over your environment. But your challenge is to direct your need for power in a way that allows you to fulfill your potential.

Best Matches: Venus in Scorpio, Venus in Taurus, Mars in a water sign, Sun in an earth or a water sign. Venus in Scorpio would mean an emotionally intense, sexual relationship. Venus in Taurus would be more romantic and sensual.

Examples: David Bryne, author Richard Wilhelm (the man who brought the I Ching to the Western world), Madeleine Albright

MARS IN SAGITTARIUS♂ ♐

Optimistic, freedom-loving, philosophical, and spiritual: all these adjectives fit you. The energy of this fire/earth combination finds expression in orating, publishing, crusading, and traveling in search of larger truths.

Your spontaneity sweeps you into situations and relationships that look great for about two seconds, then you get that tightness in the pit of your stomach and all you want to do is get out. This pattern may repeat itself many times over the course of your life until you learn to think before you leap, to take a few deep breaths before you blurt out what's on your mind.

You're physically energetic, probably don't need much sleep, and should have a regular exercise routine to keep you in shape and help burn off some of that energy. You're acutely aware of your physical body, how you feel and look. Even though you may not care how other people see you, you're aware of it.

With your fun-loving nature and numerous and varied interests, you're a people magnet with no shortage of acquaintances, friends, and potential lovers. You enjoy variety in your relationships and sexual encounters, and have no qualms about one-night stands. Your challenge is commitment. The very word makes you uneasy. This pattern changes only when someone comes along who either matches or surpasses your freedom-loving tendencies. When this happens, your capacity for intimacy and communication deepen appreciably, and you mine a whole new dimension of your own psyche.

Your sensuality is triggered when you and a significant other are in sync in terms of your worldviews, philosophies, and spiritual beliefs. This commonality can be the very thing that prompts you to commit.

You excel in communicating your ideas. However, there's sometimes a tendency to become so myopic about what *you* believe that you become evangelical about getting the message out. You become a person *with a mission* and find yourself locked in religious or political arguments where there are no winners.

You enjoy travel, often to far-flung outposts of the world, and pride yourself on being able to pick up and go on a moment's notice with nothing more than a backpack and an ATM card for emergencies. Your travels often have a deeper purpose, a spiritual searching intimately connected with the development of your worldview and spiritual beliefs. Some of your sexual relationships will occur overseas or with foreign-born individuals.

Strong intuition usually accompanies this combination. You may be especially adept at reading patterns in predictive systems—astrology, the tarot, the *I Ching*. The challenge is being able to read these patterns for yourself with the same ease that you're able to read them for other people. Mythology may be one way of doing this. Perhaps, at the root of your spiritual search, lies an unconscious need to uncover your personal mythology.

Best Matches: Venus in Sagittarius, Venus in Taurus, Mars in a fire sign.

Examples: Comedian George Carlin, golfer Jack Nicolaus, science-fiction writer Roger Zelazny

MARS IN CAPRICORN ♂ ♑

You're a builder, someone who works steadily and dependably toward a goal, a dream, or an achievement. Even when you're young, you assume responsibility and aren't afraid to work hard to get what you want. This impeccable work ethic sustains and drives you for most of your life. The word "workaholic" probably fits you.

Capricorn is known for its singular vision, always moving forward and perhaps uphill as well, like a horse wearing blinders; Taurus is known for its reliability and for getting the job done. Put the two together, and you have a powerful force. You may not move with the speed of a roller coaster, but you nearly always get where you're going.

Your sexual blueprint is a curious amalgam of sensuality and caution. You have a powerful sex drive, but control it until you trust the other person. Your trust, however, is a difficult thing to win. You have specific rules that have to be met first. This rule business is connected to Capricorn's need for structure, parameters, and borders. You're adept at compartmentalizing your emotions, so it's easy for you to enjoy sex without commitment and, in some respects, it keeps your life uncluttered. No messy emotional entanglements. No need to discuss differences. No need to sit around waiting for the phone to ring. During times like this in your life, sex is just another need to be met.

Once your trust is won and your emotions enter the picture,

your warmth, passion, and capacity for intimacy rise to whole new levels, surprising even you. You find that you like having the stability of a relationship and that it frees your energy, allowing you to pursue personal and professional goals. You're as supportive of your partner's goals and dreams as he or she is of yours. Yet even in this kind of relationship, you expect your personal space to be respected in the same way that you respect other people's personal space. It's not so much a matter of privacy as it is one of your *requirements*. If that rule (or any of your other rules) is violated, your anger can be extreme.

With this combination, anger isn't a volatile explosion. It's a kind of seething, silent resentment that grows and festers and manifests as an Arctic cold until the point where something small and innocuous sets you off. Then the explosion is like a purge, sweeping everything out of your system. It leads either to estrangement or to deeper levels of communication.

Best Matches: Venus in Capricorn or Taurus, Mars in an earth or water sign, Sun in an earth sign. With either Capricorn or Venus, the relationship would be grounded, ambitious, security-minded, and sensuous.

Examples: Judy Collins, novelist Daphne du Maurier, president James Madison, Katharine Hepburn

MARS IN AQUARIUS ♂ ☵

You're all about intellectual pursuits, groups and causes, and anything that ignites your mind. Despite the emphasis on intellect with this combination, you have intuitive skills that are often remarkable. You may not listen to your intuitive voice as often as you should, but when you do, your life unfolds on track.

Your friends and the groups to which you belong are important to you, especially groups that share your worldview and interests, and support your goals and dreams. You may feel conflicted at times because you also value your privacy and solitude as well.

Mars in Aquarius has a visionary quality that actually supports Taurus's mystical streak. In that sense, this earth and air combination get along. You tune into cutting-edge and futuristic trends, and your work may involve something in that area. Leonardo da Vinci drew airplanes three hundred years before they were invented. Author Harper Lee tuned into racial discrimination in her Pulitzer prize–winning book, *To Kill a Mockingbird*, then never published anything else, and, true to her Taurus sun, protects her privacy.

As a double fixed sign, you're fiercely independent and deeply stubborn. It's unlikely that anyone can talk you out of doing something you've already decided to do unless they present a very convincing argument.

Your sexual blueprint is idiosyncratic. Whereas your Taurus Sun makes you a sensual romantic, your Mars in Aquarius demands that your mind be courted and won over. You're perfectly capable of enjoying sex without commitment, but you probably won't be interested unless you and a prospective partner share some deeper intuitive link. You're looking for the Spock mind-meld from the original *Star Trek* series.

Once you have that, your capacity for intimacy deepens and the rest of your life bursts wide open. Suddenly, you realize you can still be independent, still have all your causes and missions, your passions and avocations, and maintain a committed relationship, too. Your physical energy increases. Your creativity veers into new directions. This doesn't mean that a mind-meld is going to solve every relationship problem you encounter, but it will make certain things much easier.

This combination creates a strange and profound compassion, strange because the focus is supposed to be on the intellect, and yet the heart is often drawn in as well. You can't stand to see anyone suffering. Whether it's the homeless family on the street or the stray cat that comes to your door every morning mewing for food, you have something to give. Money, time, effort, a network of aid—you make it happen.

Best Matches: Venus in Aquarius or an air sign, Venus in Taurus, Mars in an air sign, Sun in an earth sign.

Examples: Leonardo da Vinci, Ryan O'Neal, author Harper Lee

MARS IN PISCES ♂ ♓

This energy often finds its best expression in idealism, compassion, intuition, and a profound imagination. Even though Mars is uncomfortable in Pisces, this earth/water mix works surprisingly well as long as you keep a few things in mind.

Your natural tendency to plunder the depths of your imagination is fine *if* you can prevent it from becoming an escape outlet, and put it to creative use. The way to do this is to draw on the practicality of your Taurus Sun, which is a master at taking the abstract and making it tangible. There can be something of a martyr/victim syndrome with Mars in Pisces, so when you get involved in relationships, don't think of yourself as the other person's savior. Don't martyr yourself for love or sex, or anything else, for that matter. Your intuition should provide reliable guidance in this area. Just listen to it.

In a committed relationship where you and your partner are equals and are able to communicate honestly, your capacity for intimacy flourishes, and you feel you can be exactly who you are.

Within those parameters, you thrive on intimacy, and the deeper your mutual trust, the better the relationship.

In a sexual but uncommitted relationship, you may get along just fine for a while, convincing yourself that you can live with no expectations and keep things just on a sexual basis. But then something shifts—an internal shift usually triggered by an event—and you realize you're deluding yourself. This is usually true for both men and women who have this combination.

Quite often with this combination, friendship develops into something deeper when you realize you both have something vital in common. It may be something as simple as a love of books or movies, or something as complex as an ideal or a spiritual philosophy. In instances like this, the transition from friend to sexual partner is apt to be rather sudden—the right place and right person at the right time.

Your Mars in Pisces allows you to imagine *what might be*. In any kind of relationship, these imaginings propel you to seek either the ideal or the totally unrealistic. However, if you allow your Taurus Sun to ground your expectations, then you'll be in a much stronger position to manifest what you really want in a relationship.

Once you're in a relationship that satisfies you on every level, your loyalty, love, and trust are unshakable. The relationship frees you to pursue the many other things that seize your passion: your ideals, humanitarianism, and innate creativity.

Best Matches: Venus in Pisces or a water sign, Venus in Taurus, Mars in a water or earth sign, Sun in a water or earth sign. Venus in Pisces softens the relationship and Venus in Scorpio intensifies it.

Examples: Martha Graham, Michelle Pfeiffer, Ronald Reagan, Che Guevara

SENSE-MEMORY EXERCISE FOR SUN IN TAURUS

Mars represents our physical senses and each of us has at least one sense that is stronger than the others. Maybe you have an incredible sense of taste or touch. Perhaps your hearing is acute. Whichever sense is your strongest is your most reliable conduit for understanding something about yourself or others, your environment, and your personal world.

In the space below, describe an instance where one of your physical senses played a vital role. Perhaps you visited the pyramids and were overpowered by their sheer majesty. Maybe while you were at a friend's house, you tried a new kind of food and found it completely disgusting, the sort of disgust where you surreptitiously slip the food into your napkin. This experience can be positive or negative or anything in between. The point is to be detailed and specific.

_____

_____

_____

_____

_____

The incident or situation you've just described pertains to the second of the three questions you created in the inventory at the beginning of part two. If the connection isn't immediately apparent, look for the metaphor. One Taurus client described an experience he had with a bear while he was out camping. Although he wasn't physically injured, the bear had been outside his tent for part of the night, ravaging his cooler, knocking things around, making an awful racket. He had lain inside his tent, too terrified to move, the noise echoing around him. He had been acutely aware of the softness of his down sleeping bag, of the chill against his face, of how numb his hands were, of how full his bladder was. He had confronted his own mortality by making a mental list of the things he wanted to do before he died.

His second question? *What do I really want to do with my life?* He made the list that night.

5

Sun in Gemini ☉ ♊

THE CHAMELEON
Mutable Air

"Change is the only constant."

Strengths: Adaptable, flexible, innovative, a networker, quick-witted, excellent communicator, logical yet has strong intuition, innovative

Weaknesses: Can be too adaptable and flexible, great restlessness, mentally changeable, scattered energy

Sexual Blueprint: It all starts in the mind.

In many astrology books, Geminis are described as flighty, scattered, and about as competent as a one-winged bird. Don't believe a word of it. You're the networker of the zodiac, the consummate communicator who is driven by a profound curiosity about everything.

You collect facts—a piece here, a piece there—and suddenly,

something clicks and you understand how to bring the facts together into a comprehensible whole. You do the same thing with your networks of friends and acquaintances, bringing together people from vastly different backgrounds, connecting them through some thread of commonality that only you really understand. You do all this twice as fast as anyone else because there are "two" of you. Your sign is symbolized by twins, which is why Geminis are often said to be of two minds, two moods, almost as if they are two people.

You have the gift of gab, a way with words, with language. You would be excellent at sales, writing, oratory, or songwriting. You probably have considerable creative talent, and your challenge is to figure out which talent to nurture and develop. Yes, your energy can be scattered at times, particularly when you have a dozen projects going on simultaneously and you spread yourself too thin. But when you focus your lightning-quick mind on a single talent, goal, or project, you unleash the full scope of your energy and achieve whatever you desire.

Physically, Geminis are usually thin, wiry. It's all that nervous energy you have, which burns up fat before it gets settled in. Sexually, you enjoy variety. This doesn't necessarily mean multiple partners, but a partner who is as curious and versatile in interests as you are. Chemistry for you begins in the mind, in communication, in an exchange of ideas and philosophies, of personal histories. If that mental chemistry doesn't exist, then you aren't interested.

SUN IN GEMINI AND . . .

MARS IN ARIES ♂ ♈

Your energy is best expressed through action and communication. You have an abundance of ideas, diverse talents, and the energy to make it all happen. However, you may be involved in so many pursuits that your energy is scattered and you find it difficult, if not impossible, to do any one thing well. The trick is to take the one passion that is the most important to you and pour all of your energy and creative drive into it.

This is much easier said that done. After all, so many things interest you, and whenever you're excited about something—an idea, a project, a relationship, a place—you just have to experience it to the fullest. Only by continually flitting from one interest to another do you keep your nemesis—boredom—out of your life.

Or so you believe.

The truth comes back to that single passion, whatever it is. Since introspection isn't your strong point, you have to rely on your intuition, your impulses, and your gut feelings to find the passion. Once you find it, you have to nurture it, develop it, wrap your energy and talent around it, and make it happen. And you'll never be bored throughout this process.

Boredom can be a major problem for you in your relationships. Things might be humming along just fine, then suddenly the person you're with does or says something that triggers panic. *Oh my God,* you think. *There goes my independence, my solitude. I'm outta here.* And off you run, leaving your partner gasping in the dust and wondering what happened. The challenge—and let's be blunt here—is to think before you leap into bed with someone. As corny as it may sound, follow your mother's advice: get to know the person first. Do his or her interests and passions coincide with yours? Does the person have the kind of curiosity that you do? Is he or she eager to learn new things and to embrace all kinds of experience? Does he or she enjoy spirited debate?

Once you find the right person, your sexuality shifts to an entirely new level. Sex is no longer just a physical act, but a way to connect emotionally and spiritually, too. You discover that you don't have to sacrifice your independence for commitment and that the two, in fact, can complement each other. The more committed you are, the more independent you are and the greater the energy you free up for other pursuits.

Simple, right?

Best Matches: Venus in Aries, Gemini, or a fire sign, Mars in a fire or an air sign, Sun in an air or fire sign. Venus in Aries would spell excitement and passion; Venus in Gemini would mean lots of talk and common intellectual interests.

Examples: Clint Eastwood, Angelina Jolie, Prince, Jack Kevorkian

MARS IN TAURUS ♂ ♉

You use energy in a stable, grounded way, working methodically toward the achievement of a particular goal. Thanks to the versatility of your Gemini Sun, that goal may involve some facet of communication, teaching, traveling, business, or the arts. It's likely that you'll have more than one profession or career in your life, but when you find your niche, the thing you love more than anything else, you'll stick to it and work as long and hard as it takes to get what you want.

You aren't the volatile type. Gemini is generally upbeat and optimistic and Mars in Taurus is somewhat laid-back. But if you're pushed into a corner, if someone makes unreasonable demands on you, if one of your buttons are pushed (and you probably have a number of buttons), you may see red and your temper leaps away from you at the speed of light. On a positive note, though, you don't usually hold grudges. Oh, you may mull the incident over for a long time and have serious second thoughts about the person who triggered the incident, but eventually you release the whole thing and move on.

Gemini lives mostly in her head; Taurus lives mostly in the body. Put them together and you have a curious mix. You know exactly what you have to do to take care of yourself, to live long and prosper, as Mr. Spock would say. But when your creative urges call, when you have five million things to do that should have been done yesterday, your exercise, sleep, and nutrition may be the first things to bite the dust. The solution? Crop the five million to two, sleep an extra half-hour, cut your exercise routine in half, and add another ten or fifteen minutes to both preparing your food and eating.

Your senses of touch and sight should be pretty well developed. Through these senses, you're able to assess people with a fair degree of accuracy. The big question, naturally, is what you're really looking for. Your Gemini Sun is all over the place in that regard, fickle and flirtatious, often carrying on two relationships at once. But your Mars in Taurus is looking for stability, commitment, a partner with whom you can enjoy not only sex but every other area of your life, too.

You have a genuine and profound need for a deep, spiritual connection with a significant other. That connection usually has to happen before anything sexual develops, although, given your Gemini Sun, everything is open to change, even that. But you're happiest when you know the connection exists. And then your capacity for intimacy and commitment flourish to a degree that astonishes you.

While Gemini is social and Taurus something of a loner, a compromise can be reached in terms of your sexuality. If, for instance, you're involved in a relationship that is sexual but uncommitted and that suits both you and your partner, then take it for what it is and look for other treasures in the relationship. No experience is ever lost on this combination. You can learn from anyone, anything, anywhere, at any time. And you'll take what you learn with you into the future, where it will serve to deepen your capacity for intimacy and commitment of your heart and soul.

Best Matches: Venus in Taurus or Gemini, Mars in an earth sign, Sun in Gemini or Taurus.

Examples: Dutch artist M.C. Escher; novelist, talk shot host, and UFO investigator Whitley Strieber; Salman Rushdie

MARS IN GEMINI♂Ⅱ

You're a whirlwind of nervous energy, flitting from one thing to another at a speed that dizzies lesser mortals. Your energy is best expressed through communication of all types, from writing and art to sales and public speaking to acting and politics. Whatever profession you choose, your Gemini Sun will make sure that your output is prolific and that you always feel pressed for time.

You're probably a trivia expert, one of those people who collects information and facts without even thinking about it. All these bits of trivia are filed away in that steel-trap mind of yours and enable you to talk about virtually anything with anyone and sound like an expert, even if you aren't. You also collect stories, gossip, and minutia about movies, books, websites. You're a walking encyclopedia of interesting tidbits. When you bring your considerable intellect to bear on any single area, your success is assured.

Even though you have many friends and a network of acquaintances, the people you feel closest to are those who share your immense curiosity and your major interests. This is especially true in sexual relationships. With most Gemini Sun individuals, seduction begins with the mind, in an exchange of ideas and philosophies. But when it's a double Gemini combination, that deeper intellectual connection has to exist before anything can develop.

This combination can be sexually precocious when younger and somewhat experimental. But you're not all that interested in sex just for sex; for you, sex is a conduit to deeper communication. Since air represents the mind and intellect, you're able to compartmentalize or rationalize your emotions, so you don't have much trouble with uncommitted relationships. In fact, when you're younger, every relationship for you is the uncommitted kind: no rules, no expectations. But as you get older, the lure of this kind of relationship begins to wear thin and you're hungry for something deeper and more lasting. When you find it, your capacity for intimacy and commitment flourish. You're an excellent communicator regardless of what kind of relationship you're involved in, but when commitment, love, and mutual intellectual respect enter the picture, you pour out your deepest thoughts.

Your curiosity extends to everything around you—people, events, situations, the mysterious, animals, businesses, popular culture. A part of you is fascinated by things that go bump in the night and at some point in your life you may delve more deeply into this area, investigating and exploring it for answers to larger questions.

With such an abundance of nervous energy, it's important that you care for your body in the same way that you care for your mind. Find some activity that you enjoy and can do regularly. Food usually isn't a big deal for you—you eat what's in front of you. But because you're always in such a hurry, you tend to eat on the run. Slow down, take a deep breath, and eat foods that are good for your nerves and for your lungs, which are the weakest part of your body.

Best Matches: Venus in Gemini or an air sign indicates excellent communication; Mars in an air or fire sign, Sun in an air or fire sign adds passion and sexuality.

Examples: French artist Henri Rousseau, Bill Moyers, Bruce Dern, author T.H. White, astrologer Grant Lewi

MARS IN CANCER ♂♋

All the things you read about Gemini still hold true—communicator, networker, social butterfly—but with Mars in Cancer, these facets of your personality are expressed in an intuitive, nurturing way.

You're a gregarious sort, with numerous acquaintances and contacts from every walk of life. You're a warm, compassionate person who, once you find your niche, is able to nurture that ability or talent throughout the course of your life and use it to benefit everyone. Jacques Cousteau, for instance, discovered that he loved to explore the world beneath the sea, and eventually his personal passion became something much larger. He became a crusader for the ocean environment and brought its wonders into our living rooms.

You may live near water (or wish that you did) or enjoy water sports. Swimming is an excellent exercise routine for you and the more regularly you do it, the longer your muscles hold their firmness and tone. Even though eating and food aren't the areas around which a Gemini's life usually revolves, Mars in Cancer often brings a much different consciousness to food. You may enjoy cooking or have a particular food that you absolutely love.

Sexually, you can be elusive—and evasive. When you meet someone, you immediately have some left-brain questions: Is the person worth your time? Is there chemistry? Are you in the mood for a relationship right now? And—bottom line—is this someone

with whom you can connect on a deeper level? Your intuitive an-
tenna immediately twitches and starts gathering information to
answer those left-brain questions.

Although Gemini can get sexually involved and keep emotions out of it, Cancer has a tougher time doing that, because the
sign is all about emotions. This presents one of the quintessential
dilemmas of your life, and how it plays out depends on other
facets of your natal chart. Although you may be successful for a
time in keeping your emotions out of a sexual relationship, that
probably will change. Asking Cancer not to feel is like asking the
rest of us not to breathe.

Your have a tremendous capacity for intimacy *if* your criteria
are met: genuine communication, mutual compassion and emotional involvement, and a deep intuitive link that has more to do
with Cancer's needs than with Gemini's. Once you find someone
who fits the bill, you're happier, healthier, and it seems that every
aspect of your life unfolds more smoothly.

Best Matches: A Venus in Cancer or Gemini is best. But consider a Sun in an air sign for excellent communication and a
Venus or Mars in a water sign for an intuitive and imaginative
touch.

Examples: Jacques Cousteau, Joyce Carol Oates, Nicole Kid-
man, former JFK press secretary Pierre Salinger

MARS IN LEO ♂ ♌

Your energy is expressed through dramatic events, situations, and
people. You love being on stage and the center of attention wherever you are. And when someone or something steals your limelight, you either withdraw to pout—or you try harder. Your Gemini
Sun doesn't mind sharing some of the limelight that your Leo
Mars invariably grabs. But Gemini is generally more interested in

networking, and when your energy is moving in that direction—in other words, away from you—Leo shoves toward center stage. When Leo tries too hard, the result can be embarrassing for you and everyone around you.

A lot of personal warmth and generosity accompany this combination, so you don't have a shortage of friends and acquaintances. But the friends to whom you are closest are those who share your creative interests. You probably have talent in drama, the arts, music, or communication, and should strive to home in on the one talent about which you are passionate. Once you decide on a goal, you go after it with a fixed, single-minded purpose and usually achieve it. But before you get to that point, you probably will have a variety of jobs or even several professions. Everything you learn during this time is fodder for your creativity.

You have considerable willpower and may have a quick temper—not explosive, not violent—just quick, like a brilliant burst of lightning. Once you let off steam, that's usually the end of it.

Your sexuality has at least one constant—the need to be appreciated. But you're not looking for ordinary appreciation. You want outward demonstrations of appreciation and affection. Flowers. A surprise hot-air balloon ride. Tickets for a Caribbean cruise. You want to be courted and seduced in showy, flashy ways that tell the rest of the world that your partner adores you.

Sexually, you aren't looking for just anyone. You want the romance that sweeps you away, the partner who has style and panache, and knows how to use it to make you feel special. Okay, so maybe we all want this at some level, right? Maybe it's our secret wish. Well, the difference is that you're up-front about it. *Adore me.* Perhaps this is why acting is such a magnet for people with this combination. They can pretend when they act. They can zip themselves into the skin of another character.

All of this aside, you're able to enjoy sex without commitment or expectations as long as the person you're with acknowledges and recognizes your uniqueness. You have sex appeal, personality, creative talents. So get on with your life!

Best Matches: Venus in Leo or another fire sign creates sparks. Venus in Gemini or another air sign is good, too.

Examples: Michael J. Fox, Donald Trump, Boy George, Anne Frank, Paul Gauguin, Paul McCartney

MARS IN VIRGO♂♍

Your energy is best expressed through an exacting attention to detail in the fields of communication, teaching, medicine, computers, or the arts. You have very definite ideas about what you're doing and where you're going. You can be exceptionally intuitive when you need information immediately and don't have time to do the research. But you also make a great researcher, digging for details with startling precision.

This combination produces writers. If you write nonfiction, you do so with the skill of a craftsman. If you write fiction, your attention to detail is so good that you're able to create a credible world with compelling characters.

You have a lot of nervous energy. If you don't burn it off through regular physical activity, then you probably lay awake at night, worrying and fretting about every little thing that's gone wrong in your life. You can be extremely critical, both of yourself and others, and the only way to avoid this habit is to become aware of it. The next time you catch yourself turning that analytical eye on yourself or someone else, deflect it into your creativity, where it will serve you far better.

Your reasoning abilities are sound and practical, but not infallible when it comes to sexual and romantic matters. Sexually, you're discreet and often cautious. You can also be indifferent when you're involved in creative work that takes up a lot of your time. You figure if you can't be with the right person, why bother? You're looking for nothing less than the perfect mate, the perfection of an ideal, a mental communion with a partner who fits your exacting criteria.

Sometimes, your criteria for a partner is a defense against getting hurt. Then you're apt to be detached, observant, and must be lured out of your protective shell. Hidden deep within you, though, is a romantic whose mind must be courted, seduced, and won before commitment ever happens. You're looking for a partner with whom you can communicate on every level.

Once the communication exists, the romantic in you really blossoms. You enjoy getting flowers, love poems, books, art. You enjoy being surprised with tickets to a museum, a concert, or some far-flung corner of the globe. But you're just as content to picnic in the mountains or haunt some favorite bookshop all afternoon.

When your partner can communicate as well as you do, everything else unfolds according to the needs of the heart.

Best Matches: Venus or Sun in Virgo heighten mutual interests and Sun in Taurus or a Venus in Gemini bring practical communication skills. Don't dismiss Mars or the Sun in an earth sign.

Examples: Helen Hunt, Stevie Nicks, F. Lee Bailey, Johnny Depp, Latino musician Paquito D'Rivera.

MARS IN LIBRA ♂ ♎

Your energy is best expressed in the sphere of human relationships and partnerships, and in the arts and music. You have a terrific sense of fairness and are able to see the many sides of a given issue. As a result, you probably find yourself mediating disputes and arguments within your own family and among your friends and coworkers. They trust you and your opinions.

This double air combination creates a wired intellect that literally hums with ideas and mental energy. You have a lot of creative talent that begs to be nurtured and developed. You nurture your creative self through art galleries, concerts, good books, and through your relationships with others.

You're very much a social person, with a wide and complex network of friends and acquaintances. You genuinely enjoy people and discovering who they are and what motivates them. Their stories fascinate you and you often file the most interesting ones away in the back of your steel-trap mind. You seek harmony and balance in your life, and even when these qualities prove elusive, you're adept at helping other people find these qualities in their lives.

You probably don't have any long list of criteria that has to be met before you get involved in a sexual relationship; you can be as detached about sex as you need to be. In fact, you may carry on simultaneous relationships, juggling them the way the rest of us juggle the demands of daily life. It's not that you're intentionally duplicitous, only that you don't like to hurt anyone. In relationships that are purely sexual, your motto is "No expectations." That means you're free to leave whenever you want, without anyone getting hurt.

But when it comes to committed relationships, you have your priorities. Although the Gemini Sun isn't particularly romantic, your Mars in Libra definitely is, and you want a partner who instinctively recognizes and courts that part of you: flowers, a romantic cruise to the Caribbean—someone who shares your artistic and musical interests. Your capacity for intimacy is as strong as the commitment you make to a relationship.

You would excel in anything related to the arts, counseling, and the law. You're savvy enough to find a professional niche for your passions, and there's no telling where that might lead. With your innate grace and charm and your gift for the spoken word, you probably can talk your way into just about anything, anywhere, at any time.

Best Matches: Venus or Sun in Libra means a network of artistic friends; Venus or the Sun in Gemini or in another air sign or Mars in an air sign heightens mutual communication.

Examples: Peggy Lee, gangster John Dillinger, author Francoise Sagan

MARS IN SCORPIO♂︎♏︎

Mars co-rules Scorpio, so this is a comfortable position for the planet. But it may not feel so comfortable to you because air (Gemini) and water (Scorpio) don't have much in common. Where Gemini zips around, collecting facts and trivia, Scorpio probes, digs, researches, and usually unearths whatever it's looking for. Where Gemini is satisfied with superficial knowledge, Scorpio needs to know the absolute bottom line, the final, unvarnished truth. This dilemma has no easy solution. But if you can learn to work with this combined energy instead of constantly pushing against it, there's little that you can't achieve.

With this combination, what you see is never all you get. If you ask the people who know you best to describe you, they'll barely skim the surface. And that's because even your family and most intimate friends are fooled by that sociable Gemini Sun and fail to realize that beneath that happy-go-lucky exterior lies an investigator, a detective, a philosopher, a mystic or a psychic, a person who is secretive and basically distrustful of others.

You excel in any profession that allows you to research and investigate. You may have talent in music, acting, athletics, or the arts. The challenge is to find your singular passion and pursue it. As you're en route to wherever you're going, keep in mind that people are rarely indifferent to you. They either like you or dislike you. The chemistry is there or it isn't. There doesn't seem to be much middle ground.

Sexually, you're a complete enigma. Even you don't understand your sexual impulses, needs, and compulsions. Sometimes you're indifferent to sex, and other times it's all you think about. You certainly don't need commitment to have sex, and there are many times in your life when you prefer to remain unfettered. However, when someone comes along who penetrates your defenses, who actually perceives the truth behind your many facades, then your trust is won and you invite the person into your private sanctuary. And if things continue to go well and the person proves to be genuinely worthy, you let him or her in on all your secrets. Then sex is taken to a more truthful, piercing level and ceases to be something you can walk away from without emotion.

When you're in a mutually committed relationship, you don't have any trouble being faithful. This is true for both men and women with this combination. Male or female, you will defend and stand by your significant other with absolute loyalty. Of course, you also expect the same thing in return. You do have a jealous and possessive streak which may need watching. However, a committed relationship grounds you and frees you to investigate and research to your heart's content.

Your challenge is to learn how to release the past, to forgive, and to embrace change. It may sound like a tall order, but each time you do it, the process gets easier.

Best Matches: A Venus or Sun in Scorpio means passion; Venus in any water sign brings deeper emotions; Sun in Gemini or another air sign highlights mutual communication.

Examples: Sally Kellerman, novelists Colleen McCullough and Harriet Beecher Stowe, existentialist and writer Jean-Paul Sartre, Liam Neeson

MARS IN SAGITTARIUS ♂ ♐

You see the best in everything. Your natural optimism and buoyancy are infectious and people love being around you. You're the life of every party—unless you get into an argument about politics or religious beliefs, and leap onto your soapbox to make your point.

This air/fire combination is inherently restless. You're always on the move, searching for the larger picture, the bigger truth. Travel is probably one of your passions, and the farther and more exotic it is, the better. Your travels always have a purpose beyond seeing whatever there is to see. Perhaps you're searching for mythologies and folklore of foreign cultures. Maybe you're on a UFO hunt or researching material for a novel or screenplay. Whatever your purpose, you take away valuable insight from these trips.

Your bluntness often catches people off guard. Just when they're expecting some superficial, amusing remark, you come out with a sharply honest observation that leaves them speechless. Your way with language, written or spoken, is remarkable, and when used to defend the underdog or to go to bat for some cause about which you're passionate, language is one of your most powerful weapons. But when you use it to beat other people over the head with *your* philosophies and beliefs, *your* politics or religious agenda, you undermine your own authority. You became the person every-one avoids.

You're a natural flirt, genuinely interested in other people and their stories. Your warmth and sensuality are such an intimate part of you that you couldn't disguise or hide these qualities even if you wanted to. You tend to be up-front and blunt when you're interested in someone and are often the aggressor in a sexual rela-tionship. In an uncommitted relationship, you're looking for fun and diversion, variety and excitement, and your need for inde-pendence keeps you free of emotional entanglements. You aren't the jealous or possessive type and are probably pretty casual about sex.

That casualness changes when you find a partner who ignites your imagination, shares your worldview and your passions, and who gives you the freedom you demand. Then sex becomes a way to communicate and to connect at a spiritual and psychic level. Once you find a significant other, your capacity for intimacy is practically infinite and you bring all your flirtatiousness, curiosity, and warmth into the relationship.

You excel at everything you enjoy and would do fine in any career where you work with people or have the opportunity to express your knowledge—teaching, sales, publishing, the arts, athletics, communication. You would make a terrific inspirational or motivational speaker.

Best Matches: A Venus in Sagittarius, Leo, or Gemini, a Sun in Sagittarius or Aries, a Sun in Aquarius or Libra. Sparks fly with a Venus in Sagittarius, but neither of you may stick around long enough for a commitment.

Examples: Steffi Graf, Judy Garland, actor Gene Barry

MARS IN CAPRICORN♂♑

Oops, what happened here? You probably have wondered this more than once in your life, especially when your Gemini Sun is racing toward something and your Mars in Capricorn slams on the brakes. *Slow down,* demands Capricorn. Or, even worse: *I'm in charge here.* Welcome to the air/earth combination that can be challenging and frustrating, but ultimately rewarding if you follow a few simple rules: set goals and lay out a strategy for achieving them; pursue the things that you enjoy; don't trust smooth talkers; lighten up on yourself and learn to relax; develop variety in your life; forget status and go for whatever makes you feel good.

These rules are a mix of Gemini and Capricorn energies, fair and equal as these things go. But Mars in Capricorn wants everything *its* way and your Gemini Sun wants to be free to pursue whatever seizes *its* attention. Your challenge is to find the delicate balance between the two.

Power issues surface periodically in your life with bosses, partners, employees, children, cops, the government, and anyone else who has something to teach you. These issues involve how to claim the power that is yours and how to work with the power that others hold over you. In many instances, the central power issue has to do with your ambition.

Your sexuality has several personas. The Ice Queen comes into play when someone comes on to you who doesn't interest you in the slightest. The Boss takes over when you feel somewhat insecure in a sexual or romantic situation and feel more comfortable calling the shots. When The Boss is out to lunch, Chatty Cathy or Chatty Charles take over, masking insecurities through constant chatter.

When you finally get right down to the bottom line, though, you're looking for someone who complements you: the yin to your yang, the yang to your yin. Yes, you have certain parameters that must be met (but who doesn't?), and yes, you may be tougher than most when it comes to adhering to your parameters. But once the parameters are respected and the chemistry is sizzling, you discover that the rules you've established were just to protect your heart. To find sexual satisfaction, and an emotional and spiritual union, you have to open yourself to change and new possibilities. And then the other you emerges—Seductress—who can be sensual, intimate, and communicative.

If the sexual relationship develops into commitment, you aren't the type to stray unless the circumstances are extraordinary or your partner turns out to be something other than what you believed. And then you don't stray; you just terminate the relationship.

Best Matches: Venus in Capricorn, Gemini, or Taurus, or a Sun in Gemini, Libra, or Aquarius.

Examples: Environmentalist and writer Rachel Carson, actress Kathleen Turner, writers Thomas Mann and Lillian Hellman, John Wayne

MARS IN AQUARIUS ♂ ≋

Social and artistic visionary, communicator, paradigm-buster, radical thinker, futurist: all these adjectives can fit this combination. The energies of this double air combination work well until Aquarius gets stubborn and refuses to go along with the Gemini agenda. Then there can be tug of wars, internal arguments, rationalizations. It's all part of the intellectual thrust of this combo, where the mind is the temple.

You're an adamant individualist, independent and talented. You're able to imagine *what might be*, and you have the network of friends and acquaintances who will help make it happen. If you're in the arts, your gift is being able to bring out the best in other creative people, which in turn helps you to tap the best in yourself.

Since this combination is so mental, physical activity just for the sake of being physical doesn't appeal to you. But put it into an artistic context—dance, performing, acting—and you throw yourself into it. You benefit greatly from this kind of physical activity, but also need the other kind: the routine, boring kind that brings you down to earth and keeps you flexible and fit.

Your intuition is sound and often works through synchronicities—seemingly random encounters, experiences, and situations that turn out not to be random at all, but which address some issue in your life that needs attention.

You're comfortable with your sexuality and you're looking for a partner who is as different and unique as you are. First and foremost, that individual has to be able to communicate thoughts and feelings with equal ease. He or she must have enough varied interests to keep you interested, and should be involved, or at least interested, in humanitarian causes, just as you are. The person should also be idiosyncratic, maybe even eccentric, and as radical in thought as you are.

Until that partner appears, sex without strings isn't a problem for you. Your freedom is paramount to your happiness, and you prefer to get up and leave in the morning without having to account for where you're going or when, if ever, you'll be back. But when you find a partner who respects your freedom and also has the other qualities you seek in a partner (this may be someone you know first as a friend), then everything shifts. The mind link—becomes the connection to a deeper sexuality and emotional depth. In this kind of relationship, you're loyal and genuinely committed, and don't want to be anywhere else.

Best Matches: Venus in Aquarius or Gemini, Venus in Libra, Sun in Aquarius or another air sign. A little fire never hurt, either, but stick to the Sun in Leo or Sagittarius.

Examples: Isadora Duncan, composer Richard Wagner, actor Basil Rathbone

MARS IN PISCES ♂ ♓

The bad news is that Mars really isn't comfortable in the dreamy, imaginative world of Pisces. Mars, as the physically and sexually aggressive planet of the zodiac, doesn't know quite what to make of psychic, emotional Pisces. However, the combination with Gemini mitigates this somewhat because both signs are mutable. That is, both signs are exceptionally adaptable, able to adjust to rapid or erratic change. The flexibility of this combination defines your survival instincts.

It also defines your sexuality. When sex is available, great. When it's not, that's okay, too. You can adapt to any situation, but sometimes you're *too* adaptable, adjusting your opinions and beliefs to fit whomever you're with so that your own personality is subsumed. Sometimes the people you attract are wounded in some way, and you care for them, nurture them, and perhaps, deep down, see yourself as their savior. Your compassion, huge as it is, will get you into trouble with these types. You're better off channeling your compassion into your creativity, spiritual beliefs, and into the development of your innate psychic abilities.

When you're able to balance who you are with what you need, your most intimate partnerships may be with people whom you have known first as friends. Through friendship, you discover whether the other person is someone with whom you can share the entire package of emotional, spiritual, and physical intimacy and trust. Once you find that person, you're a loyal and loving partner. If you and your partner are involved in creative work together, your imaginations and creative abilities flourish.

Escapism is a theme with this combination. Sometimes it manifests as addiction—to alcohol, drugs, even sex. Its best and most useful expression is through creativity. In either case, the fundamental issue has to be addressed: What are you escaping from? What is it about reality that seems so harsh to you that you have to escape from it?

Intuition and psychic ability are usually well developed with this combination. At times, the ability is so powerful and accurate that it frightens you. You would benefit from taking workshops or seminars in psychic development or you may want to consider teaching others how to develop their own abilities. If you listen to your intuitive voice and follow its guidance, you save yourself considerable heartache in personal relationships. But you have to *really* listen because sometimes your needs dictate your perceptions.

Your intuitive ability allows you to access deep wells of inspiration, to dip into what psychologist Carl Jung called the collective unconscious. In this place, you're able to tap into archetypes and mythological knowledge that you can translate into a creative expression that appeals to all people.

Best Matches: Stay clear of people who have a Sun, Venus, or Mars in Capricorn or Scorpio. Their need for control will overwhelm you. Your best bet is someone with a Sun or Venus in gentle Cancer or sensual, earthy Taurus.

Examples: Marilyn Monroe, Allen Ginsberg, actress Annette Bening, writer Dashiell Hammett, Benny Goodman, Vincent Price

SENSE-MEMORY EXERCISE FOR SUN IN GEMINI

Mars represents our physical senses, and most of us have at least one sense that is stronger than the others. Maybe you have an incredible sense of taste or touch. Perhaps your hearing is acute. Your strongest sense brings you immediate and reliable information about yourself or others, your environment, and your personal world.

In the space below, describe an instance where one of your physical senses played a vital role. This experience can be positive or negative or anything in between. The point is to be detailed and specific.

_____

_____

_____

_____

_____

The incident or situation you've just described pertains to the second question of the three you created at the beginning of part two. If the connection isn't immediately apparent, look for the metaphor.

One Gemini friend has keen sight—not in the context of 20/20 vision (she wears glasses), but in that she notices everything within her personal environment. She described an incident that had happened one night while she was in bed reading. She noticed her cat crouched in the window, inordinately interested in something outside. Everything about the cat's body language suggested stealth. His tail flicked back and forth. His ears twitched. He seemed disturbed. He acted differently than he did when he was stalking a bird or a mouse. It alarmed her, so she got up and went to another part of the house and peered through the curtains. She saw a man outside, on his hands and knees, trying to peer through her bedroom window. She called the police and they caught the guy and discovered that he'd been living in the wooded area nearby.

Her second question was: *Why do I attract the wrong kind of men?* She interpreted her description to mean that there was some quality in her that attracted men who were predators. To break the pattern, she needed to understand what that quality was, and change it.

6

Sun in Cancer ☉♋

THE INTUITIVE
Cardinal Water

"I feel, therefore I am."

Strengths: Intuitive, nurturing, sensitive, imaginative, kind, gentle, security-conscious, enigmatic, elusive, single-minded

Weaknesses: Uncomfortable discussing emotions, moody, overly protective, secretive

Sexual Blueprint: Emotion ties everything together.

You definitely listen to a different drummer. That drummer lives within and whispers to you constantly, offering opinions and ideas that are largely intuitive and tied together by the subjective lens through which you view the world.

You're symbolized by the crab, that little creature whose sideways movement typifies the way you deal with emotional issues. You're a master at avoiding emotional confrontations and even discussing what you feel. Yet, you're the most feeling of people, in touch with the minute fluctuations of your inner self. Paradox often defines your world.

Roots and your home are important to you. Your home may be an actual house or it could be a tent, an RV, a converted van or bus. You can establish a life base anywhere. Whatever you call home, it's *your* space and is part of what makes you feel secure and grounded.

Sexually, you're often enigmatic and elusive. But this is mostly a facade that covers insecurity and a need for the whole package—not just sex, but sex with deep emotional, intuitive and spiritual connections as well.

SUN IN CANCER AND . . .

MARS IN ARIES ♂ ♈

Fire and water don't get along. But both Cancer and Aries are cardinal signs, and use energy in the same focused, directed fashion. The expression of this energy centers around your home and family, and the nurturing of a career, children, a spouse or significant other, as well as your creativity, intuition, passions, and interests.

In some way, you may break with the tradition defined by your heritage and family. It's a decision that comes as much from the heart as it does from a conscious awareness of what is most important to you. The Duke of Windsor, who had this combination, did exactly that when he abdicated the throne to marry Wallis Simpson.

You have what it takes to break new ground in your chosen profession, to pioneer new ideas or to find a new way of approaching things. You are probably happiest when you're working out of your home or when you're calling your own shots, either through self-employment or in a profession that allows you a great deal of latitude. Dr. Kubler Ross pioneered a new way of working with the dying when she wrote her seminal book, *On Death and Dying*, in 1969. She was the first to describe the five stages of dying. In the course of her long professional life, she worked with more than 20,000 people in the final stage of life. She *nurtured* (Cancer) and *pioneered* (Aries).

Sexually, this combination can feel uncomfortable at times. Your Cancer Sun craves the deepest connections with a partner, but tends to be cautious and measured about sex. Your Mars in Aries is passionate, spontaneous, and restless to cut to the chase. The challenge is to bridge these two energies, a process that requires some introspection and experience.

A bit of introspection helps you to define your boundaries and your bottom line. But there's no substitute for experience. So you can get along just fine for a while in a sexual relationship that has no strings, no expectations. Sooner rather than later, though, your heart will get mixed up in it and unless your partner feels as you do, you'll get burned. If you get burned often enough, you'll learn how to meld these two energies.

You have a tremendous capacity for intimacy and when it's reciprocated, your intuitive and spiritual connections to your partner deepen and flourish and take you places you haven't imagined. Although your Cancer Sun can be clingy and needy, your Mars in Aries will nip it in the bud before it can go too far. Trust your inner guidance.

Best Matches: Venus or Mars in Cancer, Venus in Aries, Sun in a water or earth sign. Venus or Mars in Cancer could be a clingy relationship, but very intuitive. Venus in Aries would be passionate.

Examples: Elizabeth Kubler-Ross, Geraldo Rivera, Prince Edward (Duke of Windsor)

MARS IN TAURUS♂︎♉︎

This earth/water combination is rather like two little peas in a pod. Their energies mesh smoothly most of the time. In whatever you do, you're in for the long haul. You're a builder, an architect of dreams, and once you commit to a particular path, you pursue it intuitively, building on each previous challenge and success with the patience of a saint.

Whatever your profession, you pursue it with great determination. You're not a quitter and don't recognize limitations imposed on you by an external authority. You are your own authority.

You're a sensual person, as easily moved by the touch and sight of money as you are by the sight of physical beauty, the sound of beautiful music, the taste of exquisitely prepared food, or the scent of some exotic flower. You find the mystical in nature and can be transported by nothing more than the softness of damp grass against your bare feet or the sight of stars strewn across a velvet night sky.

In terms of relationships, sexual or otherwise, you're a private, reticent person. You feel, but you don't have any great burning need to talk about it. *Feelings just are.* And you act on them. Your feelings are the most direct and immediate conduits to your intuition.

You're a romantic, nostalgic, one of those people who shows close friends pictures from your wedding that happened way back when and never mind that the marriage ended badly. You remember the good times like they were yesterday. You remember a caress, a kiss, the particularly poignant moments. This memory of yours makes it harder to release pain and anger and angst.

You want nothing short of union. With someone. Or with something—a mission, a dream, a cause, a creative path, a particular profession or career. You have a tremendous capacity for intimacy, as long as it doesn't require you to talk too deeply about what you feel. Maybe you hope that your partner will divine what's going on inside you. Maybe your partner is or will be one of those people with whom you share an almost telepathic union, so that a glance, a touch, is all you need to communicate. But if you don't have that kind of partner, you need to learn how to open up about what you're feeling.

You're comfortable with your sexuality and enjoy partners who are comfortable with *their* sexuality. Sometimes, your Cancer Sun is attracted to people who are psychologically wounded or who have sexual hang-ups of some kind. You figure you'll help them, save them, change them. But at the same time, your Mars in Taurus balks and doesn't want any part of the project. This is a possible challenge for the Cancer/Taurus combination that you can meet by letting your intuition guide you.

Best Matches: Venus in Taurus or Cancer, Mars in a water or earth sign, Sun in a water or earth sign. The first combination would be grounded, practical and the second would be intuitive and security-conscious.

Examples: Tom Cruise, Arthur Ashe, Franz Kafka, Ginger Rogers, Ross Perot, Red Skelton, Henry David Thoreau

MARS IN GEMINI ♂ ♊

You're an unusual combination of intuition and intellect, of emotion and mind, and your challenge is to draw upon both without compromising or sacrificing either one. A tall order, perhaps, but not impossible for someone with your raw talent and insight.

You're an excellent communicator, and this ability can manifest itself through the written or spoken word, music, the arts, drama, business—whatever you choose. You may have several careers over the course of your life, but once you find your singular passion, you commit to it fully, completely. If you act, you're able to merge yourself with the character you're portraying. If you write, you're able to sink into the soul of your characters. If you're a musician, you become the music that you play.

Your mind is your most sensual organ. Sounds odd, doesn't it? But for sexual chemistry to exist, you have to be seduced by the other person's intellect and that person, in turn, must be intrigued by how and what you think. Without that mental connection, you just aren't interested. This doesn't mean that every encounter you have must involve some heavy philosophical discussion and an exchange of ideas and personal histories. Your interest can be triggered by someone who is interested in what interests you. This may be enough for a while, but at some point it will begin to feel superficial to you and you will either make it clear that you want something more in the relationship—or you'll go elsewhere.

While your Mars in Gemini can detach from emotions, your Sun in Cancer can't. How you resolve this gaping difference between the two energies depends on your particular survival skills. One of those skills is that you can talk yourself into anything and, for a while, convince yourself to believe it. This works as well with relationships as it does with the rest of your life. Imagine it: You're cornered in a dark alley by thugs with knives. You don't have a cell phone or a black belt in karate. You're not even wearing shoes that are good for running. What do you do?

You start talking, seeking to establish a rapport. You convince yourself that you can talk your way out of this. You believe this so strongly that you act according to that belief, and your potential attackers react to your action. Your intuition kicks in (why was it silent when you walked into this alley, anyway?) and you emerge from the alley in one piece.

Fiction? Maybe. But the point is this: If you convince yourself that you believe something, that new belief can become so powerful that it transforms your life. It can release you from the past, from pain that you hold within, and from any situation or relationship that holds you captive.

Best Matches: Venus in Gemini or Cancer, Mars in an air sign, Sun in Cancer, Gemini, or another air sign. With Gemini, the relationship would be mental, based on common interests.

Examples: Carlos Santana, Richard Bach, Meryl Streep, Arlo Guthrie, UFO abductee Betty Hill

MARS IN CANCER ♂♋

You live in a world through which emotions run like some huge and powerful river. Everything in your life is viewed through a lens so subjective that you constantly read between the lines, looking for meaning in situations or in remarks where none exists or is intended.

You do best in a career where you can use your intuition. The options are unlimited, anything from medicine and the alternative health field to politics, acting, the arts, business. You pursue your goals in a focused, directed way, rarely wavering once you have decided what you want to do professionally. Since your emotions are a powerful force in your life, the profession that you select should be one in which you can use your emotions as a force for change.

Since both the Sun and Mars are in a cardinal water sign, everything that makes Cancer uniquely Cancer is emphasized: intuition, the importance of home, family, and security, emotions, great sensitivity and imagination. The focus of your life may be family—your parents and siblings, as well as your partner and any children you may have. But family can also mean an extended family—your neighborhood, community, state, or country. Your home is your castle; it's where you feel most secure.

Sexually, you can be elusive and as secretive as any combination that involves Scorpio. But where Scorpio is secretive from distrust, your secrecy stems from a fear of getting hurt and from a basic insecurity that can make you clingy and needy. *Will you love me in the morning? How much do you love me? Show me how much you love me. Please love me.* No wonder you consider sexual relationships to be risky. After all, it means you've allowed someone else into the private sanctuary of your life.

Your preference is for a committed and monogamous relationship in which you and your partner build a life together. Your creative abilities flourish in this kind of relationship and so does your capacity for intimacy, trust, honest communication, and sexual satisfaction. If you know that you're loved, there's no reason to feel insecure. If you aren't insecure, you aren't as likely to be clingy and needy. If you aren't clingy and needy, you free up energy that can be channeled into constructive pursuits.

Regardless of how your sexuality unfolds over the course of your life, your most powerful and reliable source of guidance remains your intuition. However, since it's difficult for a double Cancer to be truly objective about herself, it might behoove you to use a divination system that can confirm your intuitive knowledge. The *I Ching*, the tarot, or astrology may be a good place to start.

Best Matches: Venus in Cancer or another water sign, Mars in a water sign, Sun in Cancer or in an earth sign. With a Venus in Cancer, the relationship could spell too much mutual clinginess.

Examples: Natalie Wood, Robin Williams, short-story writer Ambrose Bierce, Calvin Coolidge, John Glenn

MARS IN LEO ♂ ♌

Mars is very much at home in fire sign Leo, where its energy truly shines. However, combined with water sign Cancer, you face several challenges that are worth mentioning. Where Leo demands center stage, Cancer tends toward shyness. Where Leo is direct about emotions, Cancer is evasive. Leo gets to the point about sex, but Cancer holds back. You get the idea here. This combination calls for adjustment to be able to use its energy to the fullest.

You're best in a profession that provides you with a public platform of some sort, but in which you can also use your intuition and your inherent creativity. If you can do this, you'll be happier, healthier, and far more productive than if you get trapped in a typical nine-to-five job. Part of the secret of navigating this combination seems to be to find your passion and pursue it with determination and purpose.

You're a motivated individual when it comes to things that interest you and projects in which you can strut your stuff and shine. But if a project or responsibility is thrust on you that fails to seize your interest, you'll procrastinate and drag your heels and eventually find someone else to do the job.

In the sexual arena, your Mars in Leo usually takes over, making you frank and direct about what you want, need, and what you're looking for. Your Cancer Sun will be jerking on your shirttail every second of the way, though, trying to shut you up. You enjoy being recognized and appreciated by your partner and nothing shows that appreciation faster than some flashy or dramatic exhibition of your partner's affections. But beneath the flash and the drama, there has to be some real substance that appeals to your intuitive and emotional side. Your Cancer Sun would love a surprise houseboat trip down some lazy, deserted river. But that isn't public enough for the Mars in Leo, who would prefer a surprise hot-air balloon ride at sunrise.

You're deeply passionate and sensual and this is true whether the relationship is committed or no strings attached. In a no-strings relationship, you probably won't allow the other person to see your flaws—or whatever you deem to be flaws—and you will strive to always be on top of things, in charge. You are, after all, a consummate actor when you need to be and this talent serves you well in everything you do. But in a committed relationship that fulfills all your needs, you feel free to be exactly who you are without apologies or regrets.

Best Matches: Venus in Leo or another fire sign, Mars or the Sun in Cancer or a water sign.

Examples: Ringo Starr, Harrison Ford, Willem DaFoe, Italian writer Oriani Fallaci, Buckminster Fuller

MARS IN VIRGO ♂ ♍

Cancer and Virgo, water and earth, complement each other. Your intuitive abilities flourish with this combination and your emotional extremes are tempered somewhat. When your energy is channeled into creativity, your penchant for details and perfection leaves no stone unturned and produces exemplary work. When this same energy is turned toward relationships, it can result in an internal dialogue that goes something like this:

Why is he looking at me like that? What's it mean? Why is she so quiet? Did I do something to make her angry? Well, it doesn't matter. I don't need her (or him). I don't need any of this. And so on. This dialogue helps you to place your emotions into perspective and can also serve as a defense mechanism. Carried to extremes, though, it can set up a wall of resistance to any kind of involvement.

Even if you're not aware of it, you have criteria that must be met in any kind of relationship. It's all part of your quest for perfection. But what this quest really concerns is the perfection of self. At some level, you consider yourself a work in progress, a diamond in the rough that must be hewn and polished. And that's fine, unless it's carried so far that you become hyper-self-critical or hypercritical of others. When you find yourself locked into a critical mode, try to detach somehow, step back, and allow your intuition to provide the information and perspective that you need.

You aren't the type to rush into a sexual relationship unless the chemistry is so strong that you throw your usual caution to the wind. Even then, you're discreet and private, the camera in your head snapping pictures of every detail, every nuance. Later, within your inner sanctum, you take each of these mental snapshots and dissect them, analyze them, and test them against some intuitive gauge to determine how genuine your partner is and whether the relationship has a future. You may not always be conscious of doing this, but at some level the process is ongoing. Each encounter with your partner provides more information and additional opportunity for reflection. It's as if you're feeding data about this relationship into your soul's hard drive.

You do this in every facet of your life, which is why you excel in any profession where your intuition and discriminating intellect can work together. Medicine, journalism, acting, some aspect of the law, the arts in general: all are good choices. Find what Abraham Maslow calls "your bliss." Then live it.

Best Matches: Venus in Virgo or Cancer or another earth or water sign, Mars in an earth sign, Sun in an earth sign.

Examples: Sylvester Stallone, Ernest Hemingway, Kathy Bates, Barbara Cartland, Dianne Feinstein, Alice Munro, Tokyo Rose

MARS IN LIBRA♂︎♎︎

As a double cardinal sign, you have focus and a singular vision that will take you wherever you want to go. You can usually see the many sides of a given issue, an ability that might be used in counseling, the law, or any facet of the arts. The intuitive part of this equation gives you excellent insight into other people—their motives and personalities, the whole canvas of who they are and what makes them tick.

One of the primary themes of your life concerns balance: how to create it, maintain it, and use it successfully in your life. Part of the challenge is that you are torn between your need for privacy (Cancer) and your need for socializing (Libra). Relationships are vital to you, but so is your privacy. Resolving this conflict takes effort, introspection, and the development of—here's that word again—balance!

You're a true romantic, one of those people who loves to be in love and who enjoys the excitement of a whirlwind romance. You want to be courted with flowers, poetry, art. You want your partner to appreciate you for your creative talents, your sense of fairness, your inner beauty, your sensitivity and imagination. You usually don't have trust issues, so you're willing to give these same things in return to the right partner.

However, sometimes you're much too willing to bend over backward to accommodate your partner's needs and your needs are subsumed in the process. Granted, in any relationship there has to be mutual cooperation, but what ends up happening in many of your relationships is that you do 80 percent of the cooperating. The next time you find yourself doing this, take steps to change your behavior. Your relationships—sexual and otherwise—will improve. You'll find that your capacity for intimacy will deepen, your channels of communication will open up, and your partner will pick up the slack so that cooperation is more equitable.

Your intuition is so strong at times that you're able to delve into the realm of archetypes and come up with the next big idea, innovation, or cutting-edge trend. You may have to set aside a few minutes every day to quiet your conscious mind so that your intuitive voice can speak, but you'll never regret the time required. You have visionary qualities.

Best Matches: Venus in Libra or Cancer, Venus in an air sign, Mars in an air sign, Sun in Cancer or another water sign.

Examples: Abigail Van Buren/Jeanne Phillips (Dear Abby), Nikola Tesla, Cat Stevens, Nelson Mandela, George Orwell

MARS IN SCORPIO ♂ ♏

Cancer and Scorpio are water siblings and work well together in this combination. The natural intuitive and imaginative qualities of your Cancer Sun are heightened by Mars in Scorpio.

You're an intense person, deeply emotional and extremely secretive. You don't extend your trust to just anyone. The people who are closest to you have had to earn your trust by proving they are worthy of your friendship, love, or support. Bottom line? You're a difficult person to get to know. You may also be something of a control freak—overprotective if you have kids, possessive with your significant other, and intent on controlling as much as you can in your personal environment. It's not that you seek to control people or situations just for the power; you simply want your personal environment to be fixed, predictable, steady.

Intense also defines your sexuality. Sex for you is never about just sex. It's an alchemy of the spirit, a soul connection, a meltdown at the most profound and transcendental levels. It won't be like that with everyone you're with, but that's really what you're looking for. And when you find that individual, it's likely that he or she is someone you have known in past lives. Intuitively, the fit will resonate for you, it will *feel* right. You will *recognize* each other.

In this ideal relationship, your passion is profound, your capacity for intimacy is untainted by distrust, and you're able to communicate your deepest needs and fears. In other words, this kind of relationship becomes an equal partnership in the truest sense of the word.

However, even if you get involved with someone you've known in other lives, it doesn't necessarily guarantee smooth sailing. After all, this combination can be one of extremes. Power will be (or is) an issue: who owns the power and who doesn't, how sex is used or not used in power struggles, how you both deal with power in the relationship. There's another, thorny issue that you may have to confront also: jealousy and possessiveness.

You're attracted to people who have claimed their own power and aren't afraid to use it judiciously, fairly, ethically. You seek this same quality in friends and professional associates. In terms of professions, you do well in any career where you can use your prodigious intuition to get to the bottom-line truth—researcher, detective, psychic, physician, actor, teacher. If you're self-employed, that's even better. You enjoy working out of your home and being your own boss and CEO.

Best Matches: Venus in Scorpio or Cancer, Mars in a water sign, Sun in a water sign. With a Venus in Scorpio, the relationship would be emotionally and sexually intense.

Examples: Yul Brynner, Dan Akroyd, inspirational speaker and writer Marianne Williamson, Bill Cosby

MARS IN SAGITTARIUS ♂ ♐

There are times in your life when this combination feels like an engine constantly in need of a tune-up. At other times, it's the blessing that catapults you out of whatever rut you've fallen into or the burning quest that forces you out of your comfort zone to embrace change. It's not a feel-good combination, but it's rarely boring.

Here's the central conflict: your Cancer Sun really yearns for roots, a place to call home. Your Mars in Sagittarius craves adventure and travel and values independence above almost everything else. How you resolve this conflict depends to a great extent on other facets of your natal chart, but one thing is certain: resolve it you must.

One of the ways to resolve this is through your profession. Get into something where you can use your intuition and imagination to grasp the larger picture, whatever that may be. Publishing, travel, the ministry, fashion, design, athletics, the arts, your own business: try to find a niche in the professional world where you can combine your passions with your needs. One man with this combination, for example, became a tour guide who specialized in putting together "homes away from home" in foreign locales. A woman with this combination started a publishing business in her home.

In the sexual arena, this combination may create conflict for you. Your Cancer Sun is cautious and reserved when it comes to sex, even somewhat mistrustful at times. But your Mars in Sagittarius has no qualms whatsoever in being blunt and direct about sex. Where your Cancer Sun has moods that change at the speed of light, your Mars in Sagittarius is generally optimistic and upbeat about everything, especially sex. Where your Cancer Sun wants commitment, your Mars in Sagittarius wants no strings, no expectations, and all the one-night stands it can get.

To bridge this dichotomy, allow your intuition to do its work when you meet someone to whom you're attracted. What does your inner voice say? How does your body feel in this person's presence—comfortable or uncomfortable? Are there any odd aches and pains that weren't present moments ago? Take your cues from what's going on around you. Is the scene tranquil or chaotic, noisy, quiet, or something in-between? Did anything odd or synchronistic happen to bring about this meeting? Learn to interpret the language of the unconscious—both within and without.

Whomever you get involved with—and here, we're talking about a committed relationship—should respect and understand your need for independence and freedom. In turn, however, you must be willing to respect your partner's needs, whatever they are. This is where Mars in Sagittarius sometimes falls short, but precisely where your Cancer Sun will remind you what your obligations are to the other person.

Best Matches: Venus in Sagittarius or another fire sign, Venus in Cancer, Mars or Sun in a water sign.

Examples: Pierre Cardin, Bill Blass, George McGovern, comedian Dan Rowan

MARS IN CAPRICORN ♂ ♑

The water and earth in this combination get along fine. But Mars in Capricorn is opposed to your Cancer Sun, which can make you argumentative and defensive. You know what you want and probably have laid out a strategy for attaining it. But you're a bit rough around the edges when it comes to your people skills and, as any good manager knows, your business achievements are only as good as your supporters and backers.

You're ambitious and willing to work long and hard for whatever it is you're striving to achieve. If you can find a profession or creative outlet in which you can blend your intuition with your solid work ethic (and work on your people skills in the process), you should be able to achieve virtually any goal that you set.

You push yourself so hard that other things in your life get shoved aside—relationships, relaxation, travel, your spirituality. Granted, you can't take any of that to the bank and they may not make you immortal, but without those things, life may not be much fun. Lighten up on yourself. Take a few days off. Take a vacation. Get in touch with the people you love. It will give you a whole new outlook on life.

So where does sex fit into this workaholic picture? Well, quite often it doesn't. Given your Cancer Sun's penchant for privacy and fear of getting hurt and your Mars in Capricorn's burning quest for success, sex is often the first thing that bites the dust. *Oops, got five million things to do. Can we reschedule for tomorrow night?* Okay, so it would be worse if you were a double Capricorn. But if you treat sex and your intimate relationships like a power lunch, your heart may turn arid and you'll learn the meaning of loneliness the hard way.

Given the right set of circumstances (relaxation, a vacation, a beach on some far-flung island with a partner who understands just who you are), sex becomes a release and then a means to deeper communication and intimacy. And it may even turn out to be a powerhouse of inspiration in which you discover that your partner is just as ambitious as you are. How about if you go into business together?

Despite all the ambitions of Mars in Capricorn, though, the emotional and intuitive nature of your Cancer Sun helps to keep you centered on what really matters. Every time you begin to stray, that soft voice inside of you begins to whisper and, if you're smart, you pay attention to what it says.

Best Matches: Venus in Capricorn or Cancer, Mars in an earth or water sign, Sun in Capricorn or an earth sign.

Examples: Actors Freddie Prinze and Barbara Stanwyck, folklore figure Lizzie Borden

MARS IN AQUARIUS ♂ ≈

The challenge with this combination is that you must learn to use your intuition in a way that complements all your mental energy. Quite often, this happens naturally over the course of your life. You may find yourself drawn, for example, to certain professions, groups, or situations in which your intuition flourishes. If you fight your intuitive voice—rationalize it, deny it, pretend it doesn't exist, then you're in for a world of heartache. If you can embrace it and learn to channel it constructively, it will never steer you wrong.

You're an individualist, a lover of freedom, a rebel, a paradigm-buster. You realize that one person can make a difference in the world and in some way, shape or form, you intend to make your contribution. You are also aware that we are all connected at some level, that humanity is the family of man, and what affects one affects many.

Where your Cancer Sun takes many things on faith, your Mars in Aquarius is more empirical. The possible conflict between these two can be resolved by becoming aware of an inner resonance that signals when something is right for you. Sometimes this may feel like an inner heat that spreads throughout your body, a comforting warmth. Other times, it may be a pure, undiluted *knowing*.

In relationships, you're looking for a partner whose intellect, interests, and passions match your own. You need a lot of freedom, but are also willing to give the same freedom in return. The conflict arises when your Cancer Sun wants to set down roots and establish a home and family, while your Mars in Aquarius is still eager to be on the road, having adventures, discovering the world, and fighting for various causes.

Your friends are vitally important to you and it's possible that when you get involved, it will be with someone you know first as a friend. Friendship is nonthreatening. Sex just for sex doesn't bother you, even though it may drive your Cancer Sun into therapy. But even in a relationship that is purely sexual, you need to feel mentally stimulated by your partner. If the relationship is ever going to move into commitment, that mental connection has got to be there. You, like your air-sign siblings, must be seduced first through your mind.

You excel in any profession that involves science, computers, communication or teaching, or cutting-edge thought. Even though your Cancer Sun has strong nurturing instincts, you probably aren't interested in nurturing anyone in the typical Cancer sense. You're more likely to nurture people's minds, creativity, and intellectual passions.

Best Matches: Venus in Aquarius or another air sign, Sun in Aquarius or another air sign.

Examples: Writer Pearl S. Buck

MARS IN PISCES ♂ ♓

This double water combination indicates an extraordinary imagination, deep compassion, creativity, and an emphasis on spirituality. Your sensitivity to your environment is so strong that you often absorb the feelings and moods of the people around you.

You're like a psychic sponge in this respect, so it's vital that you associate with people who are generally optimistic, upbeat, and positive in their philosophical views.

You may be something of a loner—not by choice so much as by nature. You need periods of solitude to replenish your energy and creativity, and benefit from pursuits like meditation, yoga, and tai chi. Professionally, the door is wide open. If you act, you're able to climb deep inside your characters; if you write, you do so from a profound spiritual or emotional base; if you're an artist, you become the medium through which you work. In other words, regardless of what you do to earn your living, you're able to immerse yourself in it completely.

Unless you have a lot of planets in Aries, Capricorn, or Scorpio, you probably aren't aggressive. In sexual matters, you either have a wait-and-see attitude or an attraction is triggered by an intuitive sensitivity to the other person. You aren't the type to get involved in a sexual relationship that has only sex as its basis. You want deeper ties, deeper communication, a soul connection. You're pretty much a homebody, so your ideal partner would have that same love of home and hearth and share your creative and spiritual interests. This relationship is the ideal for intimacy and an exploration of your mutual creative talents.

In the absence of this ideal, you may repress your sexual urges. You can go for long periods of time without sex, pouring that energy into creative or spiritual pursuits. But sooner or later you have to confront the absence of sex and intimacy in your life. Sometimes this combination comes with emotional baggage from childhood, issues that beg to be addressed and resolved. Therapy may be one solution. Another solution is to find an outlet where you help other people forget or solve their own problems.

When Mars in Pisces is combined with a water-sign Sun, a martyr/savior syndrome may be present. This usually comes about because you lack self-esteem or feel you're unworthy, or because you have been taught to believe you are a weak, needy person who should do anything to maintain a relationship. Think of it as a type of insidious brainwashing and do whatever you have to do to break the belief. You have a lot to offer. But only if you truly believe that you do.

Best Matches: Venus in Pisces or Cancer, Mars in a water or earth sign, Sun in a water or earth sign.

Examples: Novelist Herman Hesse, Tom Hanks, Eva Marie Saint

SENSE-MEMORY EXERCISE FOR SUN IN CANCER

Mars represents our physical senses and most of us have at least one sense that is stronger than the others. Maybe you have an exquisite sense of taste or touch, or can hear a pin drop a block away. Your strongest sense brings you immediate and reliable information about yourself or others, your environment, and your personal world.

In the space below, describe an instance where one of your physical senses played a vital role. This experience can be positive or negative or anything in between. Be detailed and specific.

_____

_____

_____

_____

_____

The incident or situation you've just described pertains to the second question you created in the inventory at the beginning of part two. If the connection isn't immediately apparent, look for the metaphor.

At a workshop, a man with his Sun in Cancer related a poignant story about his dog, a black lab who had been with him for ten years. He focused on the sense of touch, and described how he felt whenever he ran his fingers through the lab's fur at the end of the day. Just the feel of her fur at the end of a frazzled workday left him with a sense of peace and utter contentment. She apparently felt the same way because as he petted her, she periodically licked him, her warm, soft tongue sliding over the back of his hand like a caress. In this simple exchange between man and dog lay the expression of loyalty, love, and contentment.

His second question was: *What am I looking for in a partner?*

He interpreted his description to mean that he was looking for a partner with whom he could share loyalty, love, and contentment—and for someone who also loved dogs!

7

Sun in Leo ☉ ♌

THE CREATIVE
Fixed Fire

"I shine wherever I am."

Strengths: Loyal, dramatic, magnetic personality, optimistic, honorable, ambitious, generous, passionate, protective of children

Weaknesses: Stubborn, has to be center of attention, needs to be needed, egotistical, extravagant, arrogant

Sexual Blueprint: Romance me. Show me how much you love me. Then we'll talk about commitment.

When you enter a room, everyone knows it. And you don't even have to utter a word. Your personal charisma is one of your most powerful assets. You probably became aware of that when you were still young and learned early on to use it to your advantage. You exude confidence, have a flamboyant style, and life is your stage.

Professionally, you need to be in charge. A managerial position would be OK, but CEO would be your preference. Your talent is multifaceted and whatever you choose as a career should include work about which you feel passionate. You won't stick around in a job or profession that bores you or in which you can't shine. Your natural leadership abilities and your dramatic flair make you an ideal candidate for the dramatic arts.

You're a people magnet who never lacks for friends, acquaintances, and lovers. You're forthright and direct when it comes to sex and are sometimes disappointed when you discover that not everyone is as frank and honest as you are. You love flattery and often have a court of admirers. You enjoy being pursued and romanced and are a passionate lover with a terrific capacity for intimacy. You can be quite impulsive, however, and fixed in your opinions about how relationships and everything else in life should work.

LEO SUN AND . . .

MARS IN ARIES ♂♈

As with any combination involving Mars in Aries, there's a pioneering spirit that is never dormant. With this double fire combination, you're attracted to anything new and exciting and you're constantly on the move, seeking unexplored vistas.

You're courageous, spontaneous, independent, and will try anything at least once. You can be outrageously impulsive, doing things on the spur of the moment that may astonish or shock your more conservative acquaintances. But their shock isn't of any concern to you. In fact, the people who are shocked probably won't be your acquaintances for very long.

Physically, your hair is probably unusual in some way, thick and possibly curly. If you're a woman, you take great pride in your hair and if you're a man, you may be somewhat vain about your hair. Your probably have compelling eyes, too, that radiate emotion and your general joy of life. Your Mars in Aries should make you athletic or, at the very least, physically active. You benefit from a daily exercise regimen, preferably something aerobic that keeps your heart in shape.

In the sex and romance department, you're impatient, direct, sometimes abrasive, and are rarely shy about being the aggressor. Your passionate, impulsive nature makes you leap before you consider what you're doing and with whom and gets you into trouble frequently when you're younger. The wrong partners teach you pretty quickly that every choice has a consequence and that all choices require a little forethought.

As you mature, your powerful sex drive may still steer you into relationships that are better left alone, but experience helps mitigate some of the damage. What you're really looking for is a partner who appreciates your abilities, puts you at the center of attention, and applauds your every triumph. The person should also be committed to you, love you unconditionally, and have sex whenever you want to. That, at any rate, is the superficial ideal. On a deeper level, you would like a committed relationship in which you and your partner are equals who enjoy the same thrills, passions, and interests and have the freedom to explore your respective creative abilities.

Professionally, you shine in any of the creative fields and should explore several before you decide. Some to consider are acting, entertainment, fashion, communication, music, and politics. Whatever you choose, your ego is healthy enough to stand up to whatever it takes to get to where you want to go. And your pioneering spirit will put you exactly where you need to be to trailblaze.

Best Matches: Venus in Aries or Leo, Venus in Sagittarius, Sun in a fire or air sign.

Examples: French composer and pianist Claude Debussy, Aldous Huxley, Monica Lewinsky, Martha Stewart, Prince William

MARS IN TAURUS♂ ♉

You have a certain style that distinguishes you from other people. It isn't just your flamboyant flair—although that's plenty in and of itself—or your quick wit or the warmth you exude. This style is something unique to you—your trademark, your signature, the way other people identify you.

This combination of fire and earth in two fixed signs makes you stubborn in your opinions and beliefs and indicates that you build your career and just about everything else in your life with care, hard work, and persistence. Other people think you know exactly where you're going and how you're going to get there and, most of the time, you do.

In those rare moments when your belief in yourself falters, you may redirect your attention, casting around for some other path that seizes your interest or your passions. If you find such a path, you may even follow it and pour your considerable energy into it. But it's far more likely that you will discover what you really want to do early in life and then branch out once you've established yourself. In other words, you aren't a quitter. You don't leap into something else because you have failed. The word "failure" doesn't exist for you.

You're a whiz when it comes to managing and investing money. Good thing, too, because you love spending it. You're as generous with other people as you are with yourself. As long as you earn more than you spend, you're in great shape. But as soon as the plus and minus columns shift, you have trouble cutting back and may slide into debt.

You're a deeply sensual person, sexually passionate, and you don't have any hang-ups about sex purely for the sake of sex. You're direct about your intentions and expect other people to be equally direct. When they're not, it surprises you. When you fall for someone, however, you tend to fall hard and if it's the right someone, you commit without a second thought. You're usually monogamous in a committed relationship and are appalled and deeply hurt if the other person strays. But you don't hold grudges; you tend to forgive, forget, and move on.

Thanks to your Leo Sun, anything theatrical holds an appeal for you. But you can excel in virtually anything you attempt professionally, as long as it holds your interest and is something at which you shine. The more self-sufficient the profession is, the more freedom you have and the happier you are.

Best Matches: Venus in Taurus or Leo, Sun in Taurus, Venus in an earth sign or fire sign, Mars in an earth sign.

Examples: Lucille Ball, Fidel Castro, Madonna, Robert De Niro, Alexandre Dumas, Sydney Omar, Garrison Keillor

MARS IN GEMINI ♂ ♊

The energies of this fire/air combination work well together. The brilliance of your Leo Sun is channeled through the areas that Gemini rules: communication, the intellect, conscious thought, travel, and learning. It's likely that you'll have more than one profession and although this doesn't usually happen simultaneously, it can. You're a multitasker, and this along with your quick wit, versatility, and curiosity are your greatest assets.

The primary interest of your Leo Sun is *you;* the main interest of your Mars in Gemini is *other people*. With this combination, you never have to concern yourself about how you'll get to know people, about being guided to the right people or to the right information at the right time. Your Mars in Gemini will take care of it. Think of this placement as a kind of signal that radiates outward in every direction from the center of your life, attracting opportunities, networks, a web of people who share and support your interests.

You enjoy intellectual discourse, the sort of discussions where everyone is trying to get his or her point of view across and all the points of view, of course, are different. During these kinds of discussions, you may attempt to draw attention to yourself by assuming center stage and espousing your views. This is exactly in line with your Leo Sun and you'll be completely successful when you do this. However, the point of these kinds of discussions lies with your Mars in Gemini, not your Leo Sun; the point is to listen and absorb information. This is the one area where you'll experience conflict with this combination.

Your sexuality vacillates. One moment, you're totally into the person you're with, involved and caught up in the Sexual Zen of Now, and the next moment, your mind is zooming in a million directions, the phone is ringing, a fax is coming through, you're thinking about the places you need to go and the people you need to see, and those beautiful Zen moments are sliding away. It's nothing personal, no reflection on your partner. It's just how it is.

Even when you're in a fully committed relationship that is satisfying on nearly every level, you can experience vacillation in your sexuality. And that's okay. Nowhere is it written that sexuality must be confined to the body. If you have a partner who honors your mind and your creative abilities, that's really where the sex begins.

Best Matches: Venus in Gemini or another air sign, Venus in Leo, Mars in an air sign, Sun in a fire or air sign.

Examples: This one has quite a lineup. Loni Anderson, Neil Armstrong, Coco Chanel, Zelda Fitzgerald, Sean Penn, Matthew Broderick

MARS IN CANCER ♂♋

You're a flashy homebody. Your pizzazz, your style, your sense of color and fashion are all reflected in your home and personal environment. You like bold, bright colors that are arranged according to *your* likes and tastes, and may use Feng Shui—the Chinese art of placement—in your home or work space. If you don't use Feng Shui, you should look into it. You have an instinctive understanding of energy and Feng Shui is all about facilitating the flow of energy in a given space, whether it's your home, office, or just a room.

Fashion trends probably appeal to you, too, and you undoubtedly have a closet jammed with many boldly colored clothes. You may go through phases where you favor a particular color or range of colors; then your mood shifts and suddenly those clothes won't do anymore and you need a whole new wardrobe in a different spectrum of colors.

Physically, your hair is unusual in some way and you may play around with its color—brunette one month, blonde or redhead the next. It's all part of that Leo need to find the best look and that Mars in Cancer need to feel comfortable and at home in your own skin.

You enjoy being the center of attention, but not necessarily in a sweeping, general sense. You want to be someone else's center of attention—one special person, if possible—and you will go to great lengths to accommodate the quirks and habits of that special person. If that special person turns out to be not worthy of your attention and love, it's difficult for you to extricate yourself emotionally from the relationship. Mars in Cancer can cling to a relationship (or anything else) that has exhausted itself.

You have had (or will have) your share of uncommitted relationships where the main attraction is just sex. But even sex can get boring without, at the very least, common interests, and those interests only go so far. Deep down, you're looking for someone who enjoys what you enjoy, who regards home as a castle, and who wants to have a family, roots, and perhaps a deep connection to a particular community.

Professionally, you do well in anything where you have a great deal of freedom. You have the motivation, discipline, and singular vision to succeed at any home-based business, as long as it's something that makes you look good. Whatever you choose, you'll nurture it and strive to attain some sort of security within that field.

Best Matches: Venus in Cancer or Leo, Venus in an air sign, Mars in a water sign, Sun in a fire or air sign.

Examples: Physicist and UFO expert Stanton Friedman, Yves St. Laurent, Frederick Ogden Nash, Gracie Allen

MARS IN LEO ♂ ♌

As a double fire, double fixed combination, you're one huge powerhouse of energy. People aren't just attracted to you; they seek to plug themselves into your seemingly inexhaustible supply of energy and optimism in the hopes that some of it will rub off on them.

When you're in your glory, you're like royalty holding court with the subjects of the land. You expect your subjects (admirers)

to cheer your efforts, to show their appreciation outwardly (applause, adulation), and to generally make it known that you're the greatest thing since sliced bread. Your arrogance annoys other people or, in worst case scenarios, drives them away.

However, in your ordinary life you're passionate, optimistic, hard-working, and you make the most of your considerable raw potential. You're a genuinely creative individual, with great dramatic flair and a flamboyant style. When these qualities find a creative niche or outlet, nothing can stop you from succeeding—except your own need to be appreciated and occasional bouts with self-doubt. Some professions at which you would excel are acting, art, writing, athletics, and music. You do well in business, but not in a subservient position. CEO would be just fine. You also would do well owning your own business. Generally, your belief in yourself and in your capabilities is strong and steady. You have warmth and charisma, and are generous from the heart.

You aren't shy at all when it comes to sex. Your directness can be refreshing for a partner who values it, but may put off a partner who prefers subtlety. You don't have any problem with sex in uncommitted, non-monogamous relationships, and during certain periods in your life, you may actually prefer those kinds of relationships. But you don't take rejection well. While most of us can be hurt when our hearts or egos are on the line, for you this is *really* true. You experience some self-pity and slink off somewhere to lick your wounds, but you always rebound and rarely hold grudges.

Once your heart gets tangled up in a relationship and the feelings are reciprocated, you are faithful and loyal to your mate and expect the same in return. You also expect to be the center of your mate's attention and to be fully supported in all that you do. You won't play games. When you have something to say, you say it. When you're angry, you express it.

The weakest part of your body is your heart, so regular aerobic exercise would be beneficial to you. You might want to give meditation a try, too, just to keep yourself grounded and in balance.

Best Match: Venus in Leo or another fire sign, Mars in a fire or air sign, the Sun in Leo or another fire sign.

Examples: Artist Aubrey Beardsley, Wilt Chamberlain, Alex Haley, Herbert Hoover, Peter Jennings, Kenny Rogers, Martin Sheen, Esther Williams

MARS IN VIRGO♂︎♍︎

Think of Jackie Onassis, who had this combination. Her leonine hair. The precision of her style. Her discreetness about her personal life. When she was thrust into the limelight, she rose to the occasion, but she guarded her privacy and that of her children.

This combination doesn't feel particularly good. It's like an itch you can't reach. You're convinced it's going to drive you crazy. The secret to living with this combination and using its potential to the fullest is mastering the itch. Mind over matter. The power of your will.

You have a gift for details, for connecting the dots. Communication is one of your greatest strengths and whether it's the written word or the spoken word, your facility with language can fill other people with passion, romance, zeal, mystery, and beauty. When you believe in something completely—whether it's a concept, a system, an idea, another person, a project, or a job—nothing can stop you. No obstacle is too large, no challenge is too challenging.

You're not an information junkie, as combinations with Gemini can be, but information is important to you. You like being informed and when you need to know something, you gather all the information you can before making a decision. You also have strong intuition, though, and quite often the information you gather only confirms what you already knew intuitively.

You may be interested in health and medicine. Whether it's mainstream medicine or alternative health depends on your particular experiences, but in either case you're conscious of what you eat, how you exercise, and how you look and feel. You would like a partner who complements your interests and your style. If you're a nonsmoker who is into regular exercise and good nutrition, then you're not going to be attracted to a couch potato surrounded by a cloud of smoke. Or, if you *are* attracted, the relationship won't last.

You're sexually discreet. If you opt for one-night stands with people who are married, you don't blab it all over town. Even if the person isn't married, you keep your own counsel. You're usually cautious in sexual matters, but when the chemistry is right, caution is the first thing to bite the dust. In a committed relationship, you're faithful and loving, and you relish honest communication. You do have exacting standards, though, and when the other person doesn't measure up, you try to extricate yourself with as much grace as possible.

You've got a temper, but you're not the type to explode in public. Besides, once you let off steam, that's it. The whole thing blows over.

Best Matches: Venus in Virgo or another earth sign, Venus in Leo, Mars in an earth sign, Sun in a fire sign or earth sign.

Examples: This is a varied lineup: Emily Brontë, musical shaman Jerry Garcia, Rosalynn Carter, Julia Child, Magic Johnson, Jackie Onassis, Jose Silva, author and reincarnation researcher Helen Wambach, Wesley Snipes

MARS IN LIBRA ♂ ♎

If you're really honest with yourself (and everyone else), you'll readily admit that you love beautiful things. You love how they look, how they feel, and how they make you look to others. You also like what is beautifully mysterious, an image or a piece of art or a person who triggers an internal question.

Even though this fire/air combination gets along incredibly well, there's one area that can prove challenging. Your Leo Sun glories in the limelight, likes to be seen and discussed over dinner by the common folks. But your Mars in Libra is far more interested in the commoners, in why they think as they do and what makes them tick, anyway.

Oh, who cares what makes them tick, the Sun says irritably.

I do, Mars replies.

And Mars says it with such force and conviction that the Sun shuts up and Mars gets its way.

As a result, relationships are one of the primary forces in your life. It isn't that you're off looking for love all the time (although you may be), just that you enjoy companionship and don't like to spend much time alone. You aren't shy about initiating a relationship, but in any relationship, committed or otherwise, you run the risk of bending over backward to make things work. You're too willing to compromise. You won't do this indefinitely, though, and if and when you see that the relationship isn't growing or changing, you won't hesitate to end it. But you probably won't end it until you've got something else going, and even then you may not make a clean break. You really don't like hurting anyone and you dislike confrontational situations, so you may carry on two relationships simultaneously until you muster the courage to extricate yourself from the relationship that no longer works. This often causes the very thing you're trying to avoid. Best to be up-front right from the start.

Once you find the right person and are in a committed and mutually loving relationship, your sexuality flourishes—as long as the two of you are in harmony most of the time and your partner has the same aesthetic sensibilities that you do.

Best Matches: Venus in Libra or Leo, Venus in a fire or air sign, Mars in an air sign, Sun in Libra.

Examples: Whitney Houston, Bill Clinton, Sally Struthers, Alfred Hitchcock, Tipper Gore, Jerry Falwell, Roman Polanski

MARS IN SCORPIO ♂ ♏

Fire and water. It doesn't take a nuclear physicist to figure out how these two elements interact. But despite the elements, this combination works pretty well because Mars co-rules Scorpio, so the planet feels relatively comfortable here.

You're independent, intense, and as a double fixed combination, have definite opinions about everything. It takes a very convincing argument to change your mind once it's made up and even then you may stick to what you know rather than risk banking on something new or unknown. Professionally, you do well with your own business or company, but also would excel in trust law, psychology, insurance, recycling, medicine, surgery, politics, banking, or any kind of engineering. You also have artistic or theatrical talent that deserves to be nurtured and developed.

You're passionate and sensual and don't have any qualms about being involved in a relationship based purely on sex. There is, though, one exception to all of the above. If you were brought up in a home that was excessively religious, where sex was viewed as bad or distasteful, then you may have some heavy emotional baggage that gets in the way of your sexual enjoyment.

For you to commit to a relationship, several criteria have to exist. The other person has to win your trust, proving that he or she is worthy of your attention, time, and energy; the person has to be crazy about you and demonstrate this in flamboyant and excessive ways; and the person has to share some of your interests and values. While this last part is true of most combinations, it's especially true in a combination that involves Scorpio.

One of the more interesting and frustrating dichotomies for people who have this combination involves intimacy. Your Leo Sun is compelled to spill everything, every little thought, insecurity, doubt, certainty, and wound—in short, nothing less than your entire personal history. But Mars in Scorpio is secretive. Despite your love for your partner and the level of your honesty, there are some things you simply won't divulge. These secrets belong to you and you alone. Even so, when you find someone with whom you share respect and love, you're a faithful, loving partner.

You usually have excellent insight into other people's motives, but less insight into your own. You are somewhat selfish when it comes to your own dreams and aspirations and yet, can be astonishingly generous with your time, energy, and money. You also have a soft spot for children. If you don't have children of your own, then you're close to nephews, nieces, or other children who are like your own flesh and blood.

Best Matches: Venus in Scorpio or another water sign, Venus in Leo or another fire sign, Mars in a fire or water sign, Sun in a fire sign.

Examples: Ray Bradbury, Dag Hammarskjöld, Orville Wright, Princess Anne

MARS IN SAGITTARIUS ♂ ♐

With this double fire combination, your energy is nothing short of remarkable. You go until you drop. You have great personal warmth, a generous heart, and such an abundance of optimism that other people are drawn to you in droves.

You need and demand a lot of freedom and do best in professions that allow it. Forget the time clock or a boss breathing down your neck. Forget the usual nine-to-five routine. You're much too restless for clocks, schedules, and bosses. Besides, your talents lie elsewhere—drama, the arts, writing, psychology, the travel industry, publishing, even the practice of law—if you can be disciplined enough to get through three years of law school and study for the bar. Whatever your choice, make sure that it's also your passion.

Sexually, you're uninhibited, direct, and often blunt. When you're interested in someone, you don't play games. You aren't the least bit coy. When other people are intimidated by your direct approach and back off, you're genuinely perplexed. It never occurs to you that some people like the game of seduction to be a bit more subtle. You aren't very discriminating about your partners, either, which is due as much to your spontaneity as it is to your impatience. When you want something—or someone—you want it *now*.

Your personal freedom is so important to you that you probably end a number of potentially healthy relationships out of fear that once you commit, you might as well be in prison. If you do finally settle down, you still demand an inordinate amount of freedom and aren't the type to call home every night while you're on the road. This is fine as long as your partner is the same type or thoroughly accepts you as you are.

Less evolved people with this combination can be blowhards who philosophize endlessly about *their* beliefs, *their* spirituality, *their* take on how everything works. They talk until the audience has gotten up and left. Some even keep right on talking to an empty room because they love the sound of their own voices.

You may have a mystical streak that is actually deeply spiritual in nature. In exploring this facet of yourself, you'll find that by listening to the voice of your intuition, you make fewer mistakes and are able to progress more rapidly toward whatever it is you're trying to achieve.

Best Matches: Venus in Sagittarius or another fire sign, Venus in an air sign, Mars in a fire sign or air sign, Sun in Sagittarius.

Examples: Samuel Taylor Coleridge, Dustin Hoffman, Carl Jung, H.P. Lovecraft, Shelley Winters

MARS IN CAPRICORN ♂ ♑

The influence of Capricorn in this combination is major and it's called *ambition*. You have such a deep need to achieve something for which you'll be recognized that you'll go to great lengths to make it happen. It may not come about quickly, but backed by the passion of your Leo Sun and the pragmatism of Mars in Capricorn, it definitely *will* happen.

Now let's look at the rest of the equation. You're a consummate planner, and you plan and strategize even when your Leo Sun is demanding *fun, drama, and attention.* At times, the weight of the real world may keep you so grounded that you forget how to be playful and creative. And if you forget that for too long, then your life descends into a joyless rut of repetition, gross materialism, and naked ambition.

You excel in any profession where you can see tangible results for your hard work. The arts appeal to your Leo Sun, business appeals to your Mars in Capricorn. These combined energies could produce the CEO of a movie studio or your own production company, a writer whose measured, steady output earns acclaim, an athlete . . . well, you get the idea. You don't recognize the word *limitations* and *failure* happens to other people, not to you. You have an indomitable belief in yourself and your abilities, and that alone will take you very far.

You're somewhat reserved when it comes to your sexuality. Even though your Leo Sun craves attention and does whatever is necessary to get it, when it comes right down to the bottom line, you aren't the type to indulge in one-night stands. In less evolved people with this combination, though, there could be a tendency to use sex to advance their own ambitions, power, and prestige.

In an ordinary relationship that has no agenda, your sex drive comes out of hiding and you and your partner discover just how powerful it actually is. Within the parameters of commitment and mutual love and respect, you flourish. Now that your personal life is taken care of, you can turn your energy toward achieving your ambitions. But you must take care not to neglect the relationship. If you arrive at the top alone, you may realize that the sacrifice was too great and life at the top is too lonely. But if you can get to the top of wherever you're going with your partner beside you, then you've pretty much got it all.

Cultivate gratitude and a little humility along the way so that when you look back over your life, you can see how you have made a significant difference.

Best Matches: Venus in Capricorn or another earth sign, Venus in Leo or another fire sign, Mars in an earth sign, Sun in a fire sign.

Examples: Peter Bogdanovich, George Hamilton, Annie Oakley, Valerie Harper, actress Frances Nguyen

MARS IN AQUARIUS ♂ ♒

Fire and air love each other nearly as much as fire and fire. This combination gives you intellectual drive and a flamboyant personal style that is somehow channeled into your intellect and ability to communicate.

You thoroughly enjoy people and value their individuality and their respective talents and abilities. If you're a teacher, you have a gift for bringing out these abilities in others. If you're an actor or a writer, you're able to get down inside a character's head and show the rest of us how he or she thinks.

This combination, however, means that your Sun and Mars are opposed to each other. Oppositions feel the way a rubber band looks when you stretch it out as far as it can go without popping. It's an internal strain, a tautness that never really goes away, but which you can learn to work with. For instance: You've just shared an idea or project you have with the people in your writing group. They tear it apart. They dissect it. They make it clear that they think the idea is stupid and that it won't work.

You're so fixed in your beliefs about your idea or project that you immediately go on the offensive and argue its merits. The argument becomes quite personal. You end up alienating the members of your group, and, ultimately, can't salvage the idea. The better route would be to assess whether the criticisms are valid. *Use the criticism to your advantage.*

When this kind of tension enters the sexual arena, you're drawn to the wrong people and your relationships risk disintegration into one loud and very long shouting match. Sex becomes a contest of wills, a struggle of ideals, a clash of values and vision.

While the sign of your partner's Venus is always important in terms of compatibility and general chemistry, with a Sun/Mars opposition it becomes a vital determining factor in whether the relationship will work. Be sure to check out the compatibility suggestions below.

In the right relationship, you and your partner respect each other's need for freedom, individuality, and creative endeavors. Your passion for each other begins in a shared vision of what is possible and may extend outward into a larger social context to effect change.

Best Matches: Venus in Aquarius, Leo, or in another fire or air sign, Moon in Leo or Aquarius, Mars in an air or fire sign, Sun in Aquarius, or another air sign, or in a fire sign.

Examples: Mae West, actor William Powell

MARS IN PISCES ♂ ⨯

You're a sensitive, moody person with an imagination as huge as the Pacific Ocean. And that imagination cries out for creative expression. Anything in the arts appeals to you and with good reason. It's the one field where your imagination and talent can be developed and nurtured. Whether it's art, music, dance, writing, or some other creative endeavor, you have a lot to contribute. But the arts aren't your only possible venue. Any field where your compassion comes into play would suit you.

One woman with this combination cast around for years, jumping from one job to another, until she sat down one night and listed her strengths and weaknesses and took a hard look at what she wanted to accomplish in her life. Today, she's a storyteller who specializes in hospice work with children. She combined her imagination and her compassion to create a niche for herself and, in doing so, she performs a service. The work also satisfies her Leo Sun, because it puts her on center stage and she's working with children.

You can be extravagant. Throughout your life you may go through periods when it's difficult to make ends meet. In some people with this combination, the urge to spend, spend, spend stems from some inner need to fill an emotional void. Once the void is identified and understood, the pattern is broken.

You're a true romantic, sentimental and deeply emotional. You enjoy being courted with gifts and surprises, anything that illustrates just how much your partner cares. You also are passionate and sensual. If you get involved in a relationship based solely on sex, it will work only until your emotions get tangled up in it, which they eventually will. It's tough for you to detach emotionally from anything you do. In the right relationship, you are a faithful and loving partner. The best kind of relationship is one in which you and your partner are equals in a creative profession and share the same spiritual beliefs.

As with any combination that involves Pisces, there's always a risk that compassion is mistaken for love and you end up in a martyr/victim relationship. With a Leo Sun, though, this is less likely to happen; Leo just won't stand for too much that detracts the focus of attention from herself. Still, you should be aware of this possible dynamic.

Generally, you aren't possessive, although your jealousy can be stirred up when your significant other doesn't pay enough attention to you.

Best Matches: Venus in Pisces or Leo, Mars in a water sign, Sun in a fire sign.

Examples: Dorothy Hamill, Phyllis Schlafly, Leon Uris

SENSE-MEMORY EXERCISE FOR SUN IN LEO

Mars represents our physical senses. Each of us has at least one sense that is stronger than the others. Perhaps you have a finely honed sense of taste or touch. Maybe your hearing or sight is acute. Your strongest sense, whatever it is, provides you with immediate and reliable information about yourself or others, your environment, and your personal world.

In the space below, describe an instance where one of your physical senses played a vital role. This experience can be positive or negative or anything in between. Be detailed and specific.

_____

_____

_____

_____

_____

The incident or situation you've just described pertains to your second question. If the connection isn't immediately apparent, look for the metaphor.

A man with his Sun in Leo described his first sight of Edinburgh Castle during a trip to Europe twenty years earlier. He was overpowered by its sweeping majesty, and felt as if he finally had come home. He took over a hundred photos so that he could capture the light against the castle at different times of the day. The photos were the start of a lifelong hobby of travel photography.

His second question in the inventory at the beginning of part two was: *When will I meet a special woman?*

He interpreted his description to mean that he would meet her while traveling (perhaps to Edinburgh or Scotland?), that she might be in a creative profession or a photographer, and that there would be a sense of recognition when he met her.

8

Sun in Virgo ☉ ♍

THE ANALYST
Mutable Earth

"I am discerning."

Strengths: Mental quickness and agility, detail-oriented, efficient, dutiful, fulfill their obligations to others, excellent communicators, usually well-organized

Weaknesses: Critical of self and others, can be obsessive about details, a worrier

Sexual Blueprint: It all begins with a mental spark.

You're a discriminating individual with a penchant for details that is unsurpassed in the zodiac. While you may not always be able to see the big picture at first, you're able to home right in on dots that connect the bigger picture. When you're truly interested in something, you plunge into the subject and research it until you have gathered every minute detail that you need.

Like Gemini, your sign is ruled by Mercury, the planet of communication. In some way, shape or form, communication probably plays a major role in your professional life. You may be attracted to writing or public speaking, editing, music, acting, or the entertainment business in general. You also would make an excellent manager. You have a strong need to be of service to others in some capacity. Perhaps you volunteer for a nonprofit organization or charity that supports causes you believe in. Or maybe you donate part of what you make to a particular charity. For some Virgos, "service" is simply helping friends and family members through difficult times.

You can be extremely self-critical, part of the Virgo quest for an idealized notion of perfection. *I'm not good enough. . . .* Or smart enough or rich enough or educated enough. There are endless variations on this self-criticism theme. This searing critical streak can also be turned on other people whom, for one reason or another, you find lacking in some way.

You're often inscrutable in terms of sex and romance. You may seem emotionally remote at times, then open, receptive, talkative. A changeling. People have a tough time figuring you out. You don't entertain romantic illusions as a rule. You see what there is, as it is, and then try to improve on it. This is the Virgo way.

SUN IN VIRGO AND . . .

MARS IN ARIES♂♈

You probably feel a good deal of tension with this earth/fire combination, a kind of continual tug-of-war between caution and impulsiveness, discretion and blunt honesty.

While your Virgo Sun usually works in a quiet, measured way

toward some clearly defined goal, your Aries Mars rushes forward, sampling a little of this, a little of that. The challenge is to channel all the energy of Mars into a creative endeavor or profession that genuinely interests you, and then to pursue it diligently, with attention to the details, with precision and exactness.

You're known as an innovator, an idea person, and quite often in your professional life you're the one chosen to launch something new. You may have problems completing things that you start, but this tendency is far less pronounced when the Aries Mars is combined with an earth sign like Virgo, who feels obligated to finish what he or she starts. But if you notice that you have a tendency to abandon projects, take steps to rectify it willingly.

You enjoy change, but you enjoy it best when you initiate it. When change is thrust upon you—we're talking about major shifts like a job change or an unexpected move—it's important to ask yourself what the deeper message is. What's the universe trying to tell you? Have you become entrenched somehow in what you're doing? Maybe you've been itching for a change but fear has held you back. Once you start brainstorming your own life in this way, the answers you find may surprise you.

Your sexuality vacillates between impulsiveness and caution, impatience and patience, passion and a certain coolness. It depends on who is in charge—your Virgo Sun or the Mars in Aries. The best mix is somewhere between the two extremes. Allow your considerable intuition to guide you when you're attracted to someone new, and don't hold back with the person who has won your trust and proven worthy of your attention and affection. The precarious balance between these two energies requires a constant adjustment and fine-tuning.

While your Aries Mars won't have second thoughts about sex without commitment, your Virgo Sun might. This could translate as an impulsiveness in choosing sexual partners—and subsequent regret that you acted so rashly. Then again, it may be just what your cautious Virgo Sun needs to shake up the status quo. In either case, your passion is ignited by a partner whose courage and enthusiasm for life match yours.

Best Matches: Venus in Aries or in Virgo, Venus or Mars in a fire sun, Sun in an earth sign.

Examples: Singer Cass Elliot, short story writer O. Henry

MARS IN TAURUS♂♉

As a double earth combination, your gift is being able to make even the most esoteric ideas practical. You have a lightning-quick intellect that easily distills complex information and you're able to communicate this information in a way so that people understand it. Your communication ability—whether written, verbal or expressed through an artistic medium—is one of your greatest strengths.

You're inordinately patient and everything you do reflects this patience. You may not be the speediest worker in the zodiac, but you nearly always complete what you start. There's something in you that just can't quit—whether a job, profession, or a relationship. When you commit, it's usually for the long haul.

You excel in any profession that deals with communication, teaching, entertainment, athletics, banking, journalism, or any kind of self-employment. The most important thing to consider, though, is that you love what you do and feel that your work contributes somehow to the larger family of man.

You may have a deep interest in life after death, reincarnation, mediumship, quantum physics, synchronicities—anything that helps you understand the inner workings of the cosmos. Call it mysticism or eccentricity, this interest propels you to explore many diverse belief systems, where you seek the common thread. Travel provides a way to learn about the beliefs of other cultures and people and may be something that you do extensively at certain periods in your life.

You're attracted to people who share your interests in these matters. In your most intimate relationships, these ideas and belief systems are likely to play a major role. While your Mars in Taurus doesn't have any qualms about relationships that are based primarily on sex, your Virgo Sun needs a mental connection first. A sexually uncommitted relationship will work only as long as the intellectual spark exists.

In a committed relationship, all the sensuality of your Mars in Taurus flourishes and you find comfort in having a solid foundation from which the rest of your life and creativity can unfold. Despite the flexibility of your Virgo Sun, you can be strikingly stubborn about issues that matter to you. Sometimes this manifests as a certain pickiness or criticism toward others or, worse, toward yourself. But these bouts of self-criticism are probably relatively rare because Taurus always seems to have an innate sense of her own worth.

Best Matches: Venus in Taurus, Venus in Virgo or Capricorn, Mars in an earth or water sign, Sun in an earth sign.

Examples: Jesse James, J.B. Priestley, Alison Lurie, Michael Jackson, James Van Praagh

MARS IN GEMINI ♂ ♊

You're one of those people with a seemingly inexhaustible supply of physical and mental energy. Some people refer to you as having a lot of "nervous energy," but nerves really have little to do with it. It's your mind that is constantly busy, churning and scrutinizing, communicating, formulating, racing about. You probably don't need much sleep and, even if you do, sleep is what bites the dust first when the pressure is on. You benefit from catnaps or from short periods of meditation or relaxation where you re-charge your batteries and then, like a Duracell battery, keep mov-ing on.

Professionally, you excel at writing or any other form of com-munication. Whatever career you choose, your output is prolific. You're able to do more than one thing at a time and may have several careers over the course of your lifetime. If you have one main career, you're likely to have several sidelines that also bring in money.

With this combination, the lens through which you perceive the world and your experiences is primarily mental. Something has to make sense to you intellectually for you to fully understand it. There are many times, though, when your intuition is running at full tilt and if you listen to what it's saying, you can bypass your intellect altogether. This isn't as contradictory as it sounds. Mutable signs—and this is a double mutable combination—are known for their flexibility and adaptability. When your intuition provides you with information that you need quickly, you accept it and run with it.

Sexually, you're sometimes tough to pin down. People perceive you as one thing and then are surprised to discover you're much different than what they thought. Part of the confusion stems from Gemini's duality. Represented by twins, there are often two distinct sides of your personality—the light and the dark, the in-tellectual and the intuitive, the social butterfly and the loner. For you, sexuality always begins with a mental spark, an intellectual camaraderie in which you and your partner share similar philoso-phies and beliefs. If that spark doesn't exist, then regardless of how attractive someone is, you're not interested.

If the mental spark exists, though, then the relationship is worth pursuing. Deep down, in your heart of hearts, you're a romantic. But instead of moonlit beaches, you prefer an evening at a bookstore that has a sidewalk cafe or a jaunt with your partner to someplace you've never been before. Each of us has our own definition of romance, and yours always begins with that mental camaraderie.

Best Matches: Venus in Gemini or another air sign, Venus in Virgo, Sun in Virgo, Mars in an air sign.

Examples: Jean-Claude Killy, author Neale Donald Walsch, Senator Bob Kerrey

MARS IN CANCER ♂ ♋

You approach nearly everything in your life in an intuitive, detailed way. If, for instance, you're told that something is true or factual, you probably nod your head, then accept or reject the truths or the facts through your intuition. When you're younger you may not even be conscious that you do this. But you invariably reach a point where you become aware of this internal process and if you're smart, you'll explore it with all the excitement and enthusiasm that you bring to the intellectual side of your life.

Your intuitive approach to life may lead you into some mighty strange places, at least by conventional standards. But you have a deep and abiding need to understand the world in which you live and how you fit into it, and are constantly testing the parameters of your free will. You may explore various spiritual philosophies, taking a little from one, a bit more from another, constantly piecing together a belief system that feels intuitively right for you.

If possible, get into any profession that provides the freedom you need to explore and express your own creative and spiritual goals. You're a consummate communicator and excel at making the abstract concrete. The creative arts, medicine, science and research, or even owning your own business are all great choices.

Sexually, you can be elusive, mysterious, enigmatic. It isn't intentional; you're not playing games. It simply takes a very special type of person to attract you. You need not only a mental spark, but an intuitive connection with the person. You're particularly adept at "reading" the other person through his or her behavior, interests, and conversations, as well as through what the other person *doesn't* say or do. Your intuitive antennae are always twitching—receiving, transmitting, and reading signals about other people.

When you do find the right partner, it's unlikely that a purely sexual relationship will satisfy you. You're looking for something much deeper in a partner. It doesn't have to be a committed relationship that ends in marriage, but it does have to be a relationship in which you—and your partner—can grow and evolve emotionally, spiritually, and creatively. You want a partner whose curiosity, creativity, and life quest match your own.

When you do commit to someone, you aren't the type to stray. You have better and more constructive things to do with your time. Besides, what's the point of committing if you aren't absolutely sure about your partner?

Best Matches: Venus in Cancer or in Virgo, Sun in Cancer, Mars in a water sign.

Examples: Anne Archer, Ingrid Bergman, Taylor Caldwell, Stephen King, Maria Montessori, H.G. Wells, Edgar Mitchell, Richard Gere

MARS IN LEO ♂ ♌

Whatever you do is done with flair, precision, and a bold self-confidence. You seem to know exactly where you're going and how you're going to get there. Even when you don't know, others think that you do because you project such optimism and certainty.

You make things happen in your life with your drive, creativity, determination, and enthusiasm. Your charisma is like a magnet that attracts people and opportunities. Your creativity is important to you, and everything you can do to nurture and develop it will benefit you on many levels. You probably have talent in writing and acting, and may come up with some new and creative way to combine the two. Teaching, business, cosmetics, astrology, theater, the arts, writing . . . the world is wide open for you professionally. All you have to do is choose, commit, and pursue. But along the way, it's important to be aware of several possible pitfalls:

Arrogance. Mars in Leo isn't known for being humble, but if you come across as being an arrogant know-it-all, you'll alienate the very people who can be the most helpful. Your Sun in Virgo will help greatly in this regard. Virgo rarely has an ego.

Insistence on your own way. Even though your Virgo Sun is flexible and adaptable, your Mars in Leo isn't. It's wisest to listen to other people's ideas and admit the possibility that you may not always have the best or only answer.

Being the center of attention. Few things are more boring than a person who strives to be constantly in the limelight.

With all that said, these qualities probably don't apply to you very often unless you have a lot of Leo elsewhere in your chart. But if you see these patterns of behavior emerging in yourself, take steps to correct them.

You're comfortable with your sexuality and are undoubtedly honest about what you're looking for in a partner or from a partner. Your frankness can be disconcerting to others, especially people who aren't as clear as you are about what they want. Given the exacting nature of your Virgo Sun, you may have a list of qualities you're looking for in a sexual partner or in a long-term relationship. The qualities are probably quite specific, which is fine as long as they aren't so precise that you close yourself off to possibilities.

You're a passionate person with powerful emotions. You can use these emotions to create the life you want.

Best Matches: Venus in Leo or another fire sign, Venus in Virgo, Mars in a fire sign, Sun in a fire or earth sign.

Examples: Leonard Cohen, Timothy Bottoms, Amy Irving, Sophia Loren, River Phoenix

MARS IN VIRGO♂♍

As a double Virgo, all the attributes of the sign are emphasized. You have a precise, detail-oriented, and analytical mind, and perceptions as sharp as glass. You're efficient and practical in just about everything you do and are a hard worker. When you don't understand something, you keep asking questions and digging for information until you're able to pull many disparate pieces together to form a cohesive, comprehensible whole.

You're mentally restless and impatient. Your mind moves at a lightning-quick speed and when you're really caught up in the excitement of the moment, you talk fast and furiously. Your wry wit and wonderful sense of humor attracts many different types of people, so you rarely lack for friends or potential lovers. The challenge for you is to maintain this wit and humor when things get you down.

You can be incredibly harsh on yourself, picking apart your every flaw and imperfection and holding them up to some idealized version of what you *should* be. This doesn't serve any purpose. It undermines your self-confidence and sends you into periodic blue funks where everything you do or say doesn't seem to measure up. When you find yourself doing this frequently, try a technique recommended in *The One Minute Millionaire*. Wear a rubber band around your wrist. Every time you have a negative thought about yourself or someone else, or you catch yourself speaking negatively, snap the rubber band. It won't take long for your inner saboteur to equate negativity with a physical sting, thus discouraging that saboteur from rearing its head.

Physically, you're striking in some way—unusual eyes, gorgeous hair, or perhaps a voice that sounds like music. Thanks to all your nervous, restless energy, you benefit from some sort of regular physical exercise. Whatever you choose, make sure it's something that you enjoy. Otherwise you probably won't pursue it.

It's doubtful that you make a habit of one-night stands or get involved in relationships that are built strictly on sex. You have a great sense of propriety in that regard. Besides, there has to be a mental spark between you and another person for you to be interested at all. The other person has to be able to communicate as strongly and clearly as you do. Sometimes even the spark isn't enough. You need an intuitive recognition that the other person is cut from the same cloth that you are. When you do feel this kinship, your passion surges, your heart opens up, and your creativity blossoms. In other words, why settle for less than what you truly want?

It may be that in your most intimate relationships, you first get to know the person as a friend and then gradually discover the scope and breadth of your mutual interests.

Best Matches: Venus in Virgo or another earth sign, Venus in a water sign, Mars in an earth sign, Sun in Virgo or another earth sign.

Examples: Dorothy Parker, Peter Sellers, Raquel Welch, B.B.

King, Hank Williams, Upton Sinclair, William Saroyan, Louis
XVI, Lyndon Johnson

MARS IN LIBRA ♂ ♎

You have a creative bent that really cries out for nurturing. It may
be in the area of communication, the arts, music, acting, or in a
certain type of business. You have great finesse in dealing with
people and have a refinement about you that attracts not only
artistic people but also individuals who share your values and
worldview.

You have a real talent for communication and may be attracted to writing, public speaking, counseling, or some other
facet of communication that allows you to share your knowledge
with others. You're able to see the many sides of a given issue, an
ability that makes you a terrific mediator and which may attract
you to the practice of certain types of law.

You seek to establish balance and harmony in your life and are
miserable when things are chaotic. Even though you're able to
recognize areas of imbalance in other people's lives, it's difficult
for you to do the same thing in your own life and in your personal
relationships. Meditation or a spiritual discipline like yoga or tai
chi can help in this regard. Your Virgo Sun will help, too, offering
up details about what is out of balance.

Any combination with Libra usually indicates a romance
along the lines of a Meg Ryan movie. Girl meets boy, boy sweeps
girl off her feet, boy and girl separate, boy and girl get back together again and live happily ever after. It's vastly more complicated than that for you, but you get the idea. You enjoy the
whirlwind of romance, the idea of being in love, and the comfort
and companionship of a partner.

Your Virgo Sun may be a bit fussy about potential partners and may even have a rather specific list of the person's qualities. But for Mars in Libra, it boils down to a couple of things: Is there chemistry? Does the other person share your aesthetic values? Do you feel good when you're with the person? Where your Virgo Sun needs the mental spark, that Libra Mars needs something a bit more elusive—the other person's appreciation and acceptance of who and what you are.

Intimacy is rarely a problem for you. You like sharing your thoughts and feelings with another person and regard sex as one of the purest forms of communication. After all, the body doesn't lie. This combination of earth and air is usually loyal and monogamous in a committed relationship. However, you could have a tendency toward dishonesty if you get into a situation where your feelings don't run as deeply as your partner's. You hate hurting anyone, so you may string your partner along, hoping for an opportune moment to break the news, while you simultaneously begin a new relationship with someone else. It's best to listen to the cautionary voice of your Virgo Sun in this situation and be as honest as possible right away.

Best Matches: Venus in Libra or in Virgo, Mars in an air sign, Sun in Libra.

Examples: Jorge Luis Borges, Colonel Percy Fawcett, Samuel Goldwyn, Tommy Lee Jones, Arnold Palmer, Christa McAuliffe

MARS IN SCORPIO ♂ ♏

The energy of this earth/water combination is expressed through intense emotions and great attention to detail. You're not a dabbler. When you get into something—a job, a project, a relationship, a quest of any sort—you dig for the bottom-line answers. You don't accept other people's truths as your own. In fact, you don't accept anything blindly. Always, you must satisfy your own intuitions first. Everything you hear and read is tested against some inner gauge. If it resonates, you explore it further. If it doesn't resonate, it ceases to be of any interest at all to you.

This process is usually unconscious. However, at some point in your life, you'll begin to question how it works and the questioning makes the process conscious.

You're inclined toward secrecy—not necessarily because you have things to hide (although you might), but simply because trusting others is difficult for you. Your inner sanctuary is exactly that—a sanctuary, a private place large enough for just you. If you're going to allow someone else into the sanctuary, he or she first must earn your trust by proving to be a loyal friend, lover, or spouse.

People with this combination often have intense, compelling eyes, thick hair, and a kind of smoldering sexuality. You may not be an exercise buff, but try to find some type of exercise that you would enjoy doing regularly.

Your enormous passions can get you into trouble in relationships. When you're younger, you may seek out sexual partners with nothing in mind except sex. As you mature, you probably become more discriminating and have more clarity about what you really want. You meet someone and immediately your psychic antennae twitch. You study the person's eyes, the way he or she speaks, and you listen for the things that aren't said. You read between the lines with great insight and when you pay attention to what that insight is telling you, your choice in partners falls more closely in alignment with your desires and needs.

In a committed relationship, monogamy is your preference. You may be something of a control freak at times and power games and power issues are your weapons. You have to guard against that pattern in your most intimate relationships. In the end, it all comes down to just one issue: trust. If you trust the person you're with, then the relationship works. If the other person violates your trust, you cut them out of your life with a brutal swiftness.

Best Matches: Venus in Scorpio or in another water sign, Mars in a water or earth sign, Venus in Virgo.

Examples: Robert Blake, Jeremy Irons, Charlie Sheen, Eldridge Cleaver, Terry Bradshaw, author and psychic Ingo Swann, Oliver Wendell Holmes

MARS IN SAGITTARIUS ♂ ♐

Earth and fire generally aren't very compatible. But Virgo and Sagittarius are both mutable signs, which reinforces your flexibility and adaptability. Your adaptability is intrinsic to your survival instincts. You're the type of person who could be dropped on a deserted island with nothing more than a backpack filled with some essentials and you would figure out how to survive.

Your talent for precision and analysis is best exposed in some form of communication, in politics, spirituality, higher education, the law, or the arts. You're always looking for the bigger picture by piecing together information, personal experiences, and your intuitive wisdom about how the world works. You're happiest when you're working for yourself. You chafe against any restrictions that are placed on you, whether by a job, a relationship, or a political structure.

Depending on your mood, age, and other life circumstances, you approach experiences in one of two ways: from a strictly left-brain, rational slant or from an intuitive, more holistic perspective. The two are contradictory, but you're able to accommodate such contradictions and work out your own method for melding the two.

You usually are bluntly honest about what you feel and what

you're looking for in a relationship. When people are put off by your bluntness, you figure they aren't worth your time. You enjoy sex and the context of the relationship doesn't make much difference to you.

You value your personal freedom so much that you have trouble committing to anyone. Deep down, you probably have specific criteria that you're looking for in a partner. Even when you find someone who meets your criteria, you may not commit. It all depends on timing. You're optimistic by nature, though, and are always hopeful about any relationship in which you get involved.

Your discrimination may not be the best when your heart gets involved, though. Your impulsiveness and passion often get the best of you. So it's sometimes wisest to think before you leap and to listen to the niggling voice of your Virgo Sun. You know that voice, that little whisper that says, *He's got really poor taste in socks*. Granted, a poor taste in socks doesn't mean the person is unsuitable, but it's the little details that often are the most telling.

You can recognize an injustice a mile away and if it's something about which you feel passionate, you will go to bat for the person or the cause without any hesitation.

Best Matches: Venus in Sagittarius or another fire sign, Mars in a fire sign, Venus in Virgo, Sun in Virgo or Sagittarius.

Examples: Ken Kesey, Arthur Koestler, Agatha Christie, Jimmy Connors, Greta Garbo

MARS IN CAPRICORN ♂ ♑

The energy of this double earth combination strives for practicality and efficiency. Whether it's esoteric concepts, or your projects, emotions, ambitions, or spiritual beliefs, it always comes back to *How can I make this useful?*

This combination is ambitious from an early age. You have talent in communication, business, the arts, or working with the elderly. You need to be in charge of whatever you do and although you work harder and longer hours than most of your peers, your bossiness and dogmatic approach may alienate you from coworkers. You build your career with care, patience, and a constant awareness of the ultimate goal. You're an excellent strategist and when you spot an opportunity that furthers your agenda, you seize it and incorporate it into your strategy. You have a talent for gathering people around you whose goals and dreams support your own and instinctively know how to draw out the best in them.

You can be somewhat detached and unemotional when it comes to sex and relationships. It's a defense mechanism, an unwillingness to allow anyone inside the walls you have constructed so carefully around your heart. It's also a result of your need for order and efficiency in your own life. In other words, you may equate relationships with emotional chaos. This attitude means that you don't need a committed relationship to enjoy sex. You're able to have a strictly sexual relationship without your emotions getting involved.

When commitment enters the picture, however, you discover a depth of passion, warmth, generosity, and love for your partner that surprises you. You realize that relationships don't have to spell emotional chaos and that your partner may be your most loyal and dedicated ally, fully supportive of your ambitions, strategies, and dreams.

Earth signs are grounded, but a surprising number of double earth sign people are highly intuitive. The challenge is to listen to your intuition, to recognize its validity and place in your life, and to heed its guidance. There will always be a part of you that balks at intuitive help, that insists on a left-brain scrutiny of intuitive information. And that's fine when you have the time and the energy to go through the process. But when you don't have the time, when you have to make a quick decision about something, go with what your gut says.

Best Matches: Venus in Capricorn, Virgo, or Taurus, Mars in an earth sign, Sun in Capricorn or Virgo.

Examples: Leo Tolstoy, actress Elizabeth Ashley, Lily Tomlin, Johann Goethe

MARS IN AQUARIUS ♂ ≈

Your independence and individuality are pronounced and you have a deep respect for these qualities in other people. Your vision and foresight lead you into some strange and little-traveled regions of the mind and into areas that other people consider eccentric or extreme. But you could care less what other people think of you. Your thrust in life is primarily mental. You use your vastly original mind and your considerable willpower to manifest new opportunities, friends, and just about anything else you want.

You usually aren't conservative or traditional in any sense of the word. You like experimenting with anything that is cutting-edge, avant-garde. You're attracted to quantum physics, astrology, alternative health, electronics, anything that might allow you to bust old paradigms and find new and exciting ways of doing things.

Since both Virgo and Aquarius are thinking signs, this combination isn't very active physically. But you benefit from physical activity and it doesn't matter what it is as long as it gets your blood moving and you enjoy it. That last part—*enjoyment*—is key. The more you enjoy it, the more often you'll do it, and the healthier you will be. Regular physical exercise also grounds you, bringing you into the moment and into an acute awareness of your body.

Sexually, anything goes for your Mars in Aquarius. But your Virgo Sun is far more cautious. How you bridge this internal dichotomy depends on other elements in your chart, but there are several possibilities. You might swing back and forth between caution and abandon. Or you might make a conscious decision early in your life to be one way or the other. Or you may just go with the Aquarian urge to experience whatever you can without losing your independence, but temper that with an astute awareness of what it would take to make you commit to someone.

Some possible specifications? Your partner would have to give you a wide berth to do what you want, when you want and where you want. You wouldn't have any problem giving these same freedoms to your partner. Your partner would have to understand that your friends and the people with whom you associate are important to you, and wouldn't expect you to give them up. He or she would have to accept that you have causes, beliefs, and very strong opinions. Of course, there won't be any sort of relationship at all without an intellectual camaraderie between you and your partner, so most of your specifications won't be an issue!

Best Matches: Venus in Aquarius or another air sign, Mars in an air sign, Mars or Sun in Virgo.

Examples: Buddy Hackett, Lauren Bacall

MARS IN PISCES ♂ ♓

Imagination. Courage. Great intuition. Sounds like a dream, but at times this combination can be difficult to navigate. Even though the two elements—earth and water—get along just fine, Virgo and Pisces are opposed to each other in the zodiac. This makes you argumentative—not only with other people, but with yourself, too. These arguments with yourself go something like this:

Virgo Sun: *Get all the details. We need to know everything.*

Pisces Mars: *Hey, chill out. I have a feeling that things are just fine.*

Virgo Sun: *Your feelings and hunches have been known to be dead wrong.*

Pisces Mars: *Not in this case. Now shut up and let me relax.*

The best way to use the energy of this combination is through your creativity. With an imagination as large as the Pacific Ocean and the ability to analyze and dissect every little bit of information that crosses your path, there is little that you can't accomplish given discipline, desire, and focused will power. You excel in just about any type of creative profession, but also would do well in communication, any type of research, alternative medicine and health, psychiatry, or the fashion industry.

Your sexuality is difficult to define. You can go through long periods of celibacy even while you're dreaming about the perfect, ideal mate—the person with whom you can share everything, your soul mate. You define what you want through these fantasies, but unless you back the dreams with action in your daily life, they remain only dreams. You need to get out and meet people, open up your possibilities and options. If you always back your visualizations with concrete action, you can manifest just about anything you desire. Even a soul mate.

The biggest challenge you face is that you want a partner who is, well, *everything*: lover, friend, spiritual companion, creative equal. If and when you find that person, you'll be faced with yet another challenge—accepting the fact that your partner is human. He or she will have flaws, will make mistakes, will be on the same quest for perfection that you are. But until that quest is fulfilled, you are simply two imperfect human beings who love each other. Isn't that enough?

You have a practically infinite well of love and generosity to bring to the right person, the right relationship. So despite the challenges, get busy visualizing, imagining, and doing.

Best Matches: Venus in Pisces or another water sign, Mars in a water sign, Venus or the Sun in Virgo.

Example: David Copperfield

SENSE-MEMORY EXERCISE FOR SUN IN VIRGO

Mars represents our physical senses. Most of us have at least one sense that is stronger than the others. Maybe you've got great hearing or exquisite taste buds. Maybe your sight is as sharp as a hawk's. Your strongest sense, whatever it is, provides you with immediate and reliable information about yourself or others, your environment, and your personal world.

In the space below, describe an instance where one of your physical senses played a vital role. This experience can be positive or negative or anything in between. Be detailed and specific.

_____

_____

_____

_____

_____

The incident or situation you've just described pertains to the second question you created at the beginning of part two. If the connection isn't immediately apparent, look for the metaphor.

A teenage girl with her Sun in Virgo told a story about a dog, a golden retriever named Jessie. The dog had been given away by its original family because one of the kids developed asthma and all the pets had to go. Jessie ended up in a drug-sniffing program, where she was trained to find drugs in school lockers. She washed out of the program and was taken home by the cop who ran the program. His family already had two dogs and was looking for a good home for Jessie.

The teenage girl convinced her family to adopt Jessie, but because they had cats, her parents decided to try Jessie for a couple of days on a trial basis to see how the dog and the cats got along. The teenager described the most minute details of Jessie's arrival at her house—how she immediately found a spot next to the girl's father (the hard sell who really had to be convinced), and how she greeted each of the cats as if she had known them for years. Her power of observation was acute.

"Her immediate loyalty and love for our family was obvious from that very first hour. She fit right in. It was like she recognized us as her rightful family."

Her question was about who her first boyfriend would be. She immediately realized from her story about Jessie that her boyfriend would be someone who "fit right in" with her family, "almost like he belonged there."

9

Sun in Libra ☉♎

THE ROMANTIC
Cardinal Air

"I'm a romantic, a mediator, an artist."

Strengths: Great people skills, able to see both sides of any issue, good mediation talents, artistic and/or musical abilities, aesthetic sensibilities, appreciates harmony and balance in life, pacifist, natural diplomat

Weaknesses: Difficulty making decisions, can lose self in sensual pleasures

Sexual Blueprint: Romance is everything.

Pity the fool who figures you for a pushover. Beneath that pleasant, sociable exterior lies the insight of a psychic. You're such an astute observer of people that you usually can spot a phony before he even opens his mouth and although you'll be pleasant, you'll find some courteous and perfectly legitimate excuse to move on. You're a natural diplomat who strives to see the best in people even when the best isn't what's shining.

You're the true romantic of the zodiac, the person who really does love those moonlit beaches and candlelit dinners in some secluded spot where intimate conversation can be exchanged. You can be as passionate as Scorpio, as chatty and charming as Gemini, and as rash and impulsive as Aries. But in each instance, your energy is focused on relationships, people, the arts, mediation, counseling, and the quest for balance and harmony.

You're a flirt who is able to talk to anyone about almost anything. When involved in a relationship, you enjoy bringing your partner small luxuries—concert tickets, CDs by some exciting new musician, tickets to the opera, books by an author you love. You like being courted in the same way. Sexually, you can be coy yet honest, cool but passionate, reckless yet measured. In other words, you are a mass of contradictions when it comes to sex. How this plays out for *you* depends on the strength and clarity of your free will.

In the end, though, you're looking for a partner who courts you even after twenty years of marriage and who still sees the essential good in life, love, and everything else that matters.

SUN IN LIBRA AND . . .

MARS IN ARIES ♂♈

Okay, here's the scoop. Aries and Libra are opposed to each other in the zodiac, an aspect called an opposition that means an almost unbearable inner tension. This tension has no resolution; at best, you can simply learn to live with it.

Mars in Aries is a loner; the Libra Sun is a people person. Mars in Aries craves freedom and independence; the Libra Sun wants to be part of a couple. Mars in Aries is rash, impulsive; the Libra Sun is more dilatory and contemplative. The list of dichotomies is long, but the resolution is simple: you have to work with this energy. It takes effort, commitment, and understanding.

You eagerly explore the unknown and the cutting-edge in the arts, relationships, and causes, and within the scope of your own life and experiences. When you're passionate about what you're doing, you're a tireless worker. Your abundance of physical energy keeps you on the move from dawn to midnight. You keep up this pace until you either drop or get sick. Achieving balance is the key to using this combination to its fullest potential. And balance, as you undoubtedly know by now, is one of your more difficult challenges.

You have great initiative and drive, and when your goals are clearly defined in your mind, you can accomplish practically anything. The only catch is that if you lose interest in what you're doing, you may walk away from it and leave other people to finish what you started. This tendency may be mitigated by your Libra Sun, which is sensitive to other people's feelings and finds it distasteful not to follow through on commitments.

You're sexually precocious, passionate, and impatient—a bundle of adjectives that can spell trouble in your sexual relationships. Your Mars in Aries can function just fine in a relationship based strictly on sex, but at some point your Libra Sun will demand something more and this is where the challenge comes in. Aries Mars craves independence, the Libra Sun craves companionship. Somewhere between these two extremes lies the answer. The route you take to find that intermediate ideal can be either difficult or easy. It all depends on the degree of awareness that you bring to the challenge.

In a committed relationship, you usually are torn between the need to have things *your* way and an equally demanding need to accommodate your partner's needs. This tug-of-war is another challenge that you'll have to work with to find a satisfactory middle ground. But take heart. In your scheme of things, once you're in love, love conquers all!

Best Matches: Venus in Aries or a fire sign brings sexual passion. Venus in Libra or an air sign, Mars in an air sign, or the Sun in an air sign or a fire sign works just fine.

Examples: Jesse Jackson, Anne Rice, e.e. cummings, Linda McCartney, Paul Simon

MARS IN TAURUS ♂ ♉

At first glance, this combination seems difficult. What, after all, do air and earth have in common? But Libra and Taurus share Venus as a ruler, which means they are looking for the same things in life; only their approaches differ.

Your creative abilities are strong. You may have talent in art, music, communication, or athletics. A natural diplomat, you have powerful people skills and are able to mediate disputes with judicious fairness. Your diplomacy may be a talent you use professionally, but it's also a skill that you use in your daily life. You can be inordinately stubborn about your point of view, beliefs, and values. Even when you're accommodating someone else's needs, a part of you is thinking about how the other person should be more sensitive to *your* needs.

This combination usually has a commanding sexuality that is evident on several levels. Physically, you are probably attractive, with one or several distinctive features. You have a pleasant speaking voice that puts other people at ease. You aren't a screamer; in fact, shouting, anger, and disharmony disturb you. Your neck may be somewhat thick, and it, your throat, and your lower back are the weakest parts of your body. Your sex drive is strong and you don't need a committed relationship to enjoy it. All you need is physical attraction.

However, if the relationship doesn't evolve or grow, you may feel the urge to move on. But you probably won't until there's someone else in the picture, which means there could be some duplicity on your part. Your best bet in this situation is to be honest about your feelings and *then* either stick it out to see if anything changes or make a clean break. This same scenario applies to your committed relationships, too. Avoid dishonesty.

In a committed relationship, your sexuality and passion flourish and come alive in ways that may surprise you. You discover that within the parameters of commitment, you have companionship and love, a good sex life, and the stability that your Taurus Mars enjoys. You suddenly have energy to pursue creative interests with your partner, and if the relationship is truly solid, you may decide you would both be happier working for yourselves. If you go into business together, you will both work long and hard to make a go of it.

Best Matches: Venus in Taurus means an abundance of sensuality. Venus in Libra brings a similarity in aesthetics and artistic sensibilities. Mars in an earth sign, or the Sun in an air or earth sign works well, too.

Examples: Chuck Berry, Julia London, Wallace Stevens

MARS IN GEMINI ♂ ♊

People think of you as a networker and an information broker. Through your vast web of acquaintances and friends, you connect people to each other with the same ease and sheer joy with which you cull information. Part of what draws people to you is that you're a good listener and are genuinely interested in other people—who they are, why they are as they are, what motivates them, the texture of their lives.

As an inveterate collector of trivia, facts, and stories, you're always on the lookout for common threads in seeming disparate bits of information and for the common threads that connect people, ideas, belief systems, techniques, and spiritual views. Your memory for this kind of information is remarkable and one of your great strengths. It's part of what makes you a great storyteller, an ability that you use in your daily life and that you could develop professionally. F. Scott Fitzgerald had this combination, and whether he was writing about a character's mental breakdown or the lives of the rich and famous, he excelled at describing this kind of minutia.

You're a sociable person, always on the go, meeting friends at museums, bookstores, coffeehouses, or theaters. If you're female, then you're looking for a partner who is as sociable and gregarious as you are and who isn't hesitant to speak what he feels and thinks. Male or female, your criteria for a relationship are relatively simple: your mind must be won over first; the other person has to share your artistic sensibilities and enjoy other people; and the person has to be able to communicate as easily as you do.

These items remain true regardless of the nature of the relationship. In fact, your sexual expression isn't much different in a committed relationship than it is in an uncommitted relationship. Either way, as long as the mental link exists, you yield to the moment. You have a great capacity for intimacy, and once you're in a committed relationship, you are a loving partner.

Best Matches: Venus in Gemini, Libra, or Aquarius means great communication in the relationship. Venus in a fire sign heightens the sexual tension. Mars in an air or fire sign or the Sun in an air sign work well.

Examples: Catherine Deneuve, F. Scott Fitzgerald, Oliver North, Tanya Tucker, Julio Iglesias

MARS IN CANCER ♂ ♋

As a double cardinal sign combination, your energy is highly focused and directed. But the planets in these two signs form a 90-degree angle to each other, an aspect known as a square that creates friction and resistance. This suggests that you may experience conflict about *where* your energy should be directed. Your Libra Sun is "other" oriented; your Cancer Mars is "inner" directed. The chasm may seem huge at times, but it isn't insurmountable.

Your home and family are important to you and it's likely that your artistic sensibilities are reflected in your home and personal space. You may have striking artwork on the walls, a Steinway piano in the living room, or furnishings that are aesthetically unusual in some way. Or your home may be orderly and neat, with unique touches that speak of harmony and peace. You enjoy music of many kinds, but have a fondness for the classical stuff; it soothes you.

One of the best expressions of the Libra/Cancer energy is through a home-based business that utilizes the strengths and passions of both signs. This might be in the arts or music, counseling, therapy, hospice or nursing work, alternative medicine, or the care of children or animals. Regardless of what you do to earn a living, it's vital that you zero in on the one thing that you love more than anything else and try to work this into your professional life.

Your sexuality fluctuates depending on your mood. Sometimes, sex is the least most important thing in your life. Other times, it rises to the top of your list. In both instances, sex isn't the real issue. It's just a byproduct of what you're really looking for—not just companionship, but a partner whose needs and interests match yours on an emotional, intuitive, intellectual, and spiritual level. The whole nine yards, in other words.

Yet there's a part of you that doesn't want that at all, that fantasizes about living in some Greenwich Village loft, working meticulously at your art or your music or writing the great American novel. Then there's a part of you that fantasizes about doing this same thing with a partner, the two of you subsisting on cheese, bread, and wine while perfecting your art together.

If and when you find the perfect partner, you commit fully. That person then becomes not only your lover, but your closest friend and an extension of your own soul.

Best Matches: Venus in Cancer or in Libra brings about almost perfect understanding of each other's needs. Venus in a water sign or air sign, Mars in Cancer or Pisces (Mars in Scorpio is much too intense for you), or a Sun in an air sign would also work.

Examples: Richard Harris, Cheryl Tiegs, Harold Pinter, P.G. Wodehouse, Dr. Joyce Brothers, Adlai Stevenson

MARS IN LEO ♂ ♌

These two energies work great together. They form a 60-degree angle known as a sextile, which facilitates an exchange of energy between the two planets. You have warmth, a generous heart, and high energy. You believe in your ability to achieve whatever it is you want in life and you aren't afraid to pursue it.

Your professional strengths are varied. You're good with people, able to draw them out and engage them in conversations in which they reveal themselves. You have a strong sense of the dramatic and your own emotions are likely to be powerful and readily expressed. Creative self-expression is a primary force in your nature and, one way or another, it will find an outlet. Best to channel it into a creative profession if you can, otherwise the need turns inward and attracts the kinds of experiences that only drain your energy.

You never lack for friends and acquaintances and your dynamic personality attracts all types. You usually have an intuitive feel for the ones who may cause you trouble and manage to send them on their way. The exception to this is when one of the less than desirable types happens to have the gift of gab and flattery and puts you in the spotlight. In other words, you listen to your ego rather than your intuition and probably pay a rather steep price for it.

You're physically attractive, with hair that is extraordinarily lovely or otherwise unusual in some way. Libra rules the lower back and many Libra Suns seem to have back complaints of one kind or another. Leo rules the heart, so regular aerobic exercise is important in the maintenance of your general health. Your heart is important in a metaphoric sense, too. The wider it opens emotionally, the healthier you are.

The best kind of relationship for you is one in which you and your partner are working together creatively. The worst is the kind that ends up on Lifetime TV as an original movie. Somewhere between the two extremes lies ordinary life. Even if you find the ideal partner, the two of you still have to get through the day-to-day stuff together, and this may not be so easy at times. You can be opinionated and stubborn about certain things and don't like to be pushed into making a decision before you're ready.

Sexually, you don't have to pause to make a decision. The chemistry is either there or it isn't. You feel it. If the chemistry is there and the commitment isn't, that's okay, too, at least as long as you're emotionally satisfied. Once that emotional satisfaction withers up, you're gone.

Best Matches: Venus in Leo or another fire sign, Venus in Libra or another air sign, Mars in a fire sign, the Sun in a fire or air sign.

Examples: Dick Gregory, physicist Niels Bohr, Helen Hayes, Jim Henson, Sigourney Weaver, Thomas Wolfe

MARS IN VIRGO ♂♍

This air/earth combination may feel a bit strange at times. You need to connect with other people, but you notice their flaws all too quickly and are sometimes put off by what you perceive. By pushing the other person away like this, you immediately limit your options.

With this combination, there's a tendency to be either self-critical or critical of others. If your criticisms concern other people, you may not voice it; your Libra Sun, after all, dislikes being mean or crude and, even more, can't stand disharmony. What's likely to happen in this situation is that things build and your list of flaws grows until something else acts as a trigger for an explosive tirade in which nothing is held back.

The other possible manifestation of this combination is that you funnel your critical mindset and penchant for details into a creative pursuit or into your professional life. It's a healthier and more productive way to handle the energy, and once it becomes habitual there're virtually no limits to what you can achieve.

Your sexuality sometimes puzzles you as much as it does your partners. You enjoy sex, particularly in a relationship where there's a mental and artistic chemistry, and can be tremendously passionate and intimate with your partner. But sometimes you just aren't interested. It's as if your libido has left town and your sexual energy is poured into other facets of your life. If you scrutinize the situations in which this happens, however, you may find that some other, deeper issue is at work. Perhaps you're dissatisfied with the relationship, but don't want to admit it to yourself or to your partner. Perhaps you're under severe stress at work. If you look deeply enough and are honest with yourself, you'll be able to pinpoint the *real* reason for your disinterest.

Your body is often the best gauge of what's going on inside of you. If you have allergies, then ask yourself who or what in your immediate environment you are allergic to. If you go through a period where you are accident-prone, look for the message within the context of the accident. If you're prone to heartburn, look for the real reason your "heart" is "burning."

Mars in Virgo can be somewhat fastidious, rather like a cat that can't stand to get its paws wet. Even though the inclination is softened somewhat by your Libra Sun, you may be fussy about what you eat, the texture of your clothes, the way your bed is made, or the way your partner dresses or combs his or her hair. There's a pattern here and when you become aware of it in one area of your life, you begin to spot it in other areas, including your relationships.

In any relationship, such details can be quite telling. They may force you to focus on what you really feel, and why. In fact, such details may be one way in which your intuition speaks to you. Listen to it carefully.

Best Matches: Venus in Virgo spells a fastidious relationship; Venus in Libra or another air sign means excellent communication and mutual artistic interests; Venus in a fire sign brings passion. Sun in an air or earth sign are also good.

Examples: John Dean, Karen Allen, activist and ex-priest Philip Berrigan, John Dewey

MARS IN LIBRA ♂ ♎

In the world of the quintessential romantic (you), love and beauty are, well, just about the most important things that exist.

Okay, so maybe that statement is a slight exaggeration—but only slight. As a double Libra, your notions of love and romance, and beauty and art are exceptionally powerful motifs in your life. You're a relationship-oriented person. That means that when things in the relationship area are going well, everything else in your life hums right along. The reverse is also true. No one is more miserable than a double Libra when a relationship begins to unravel, or collapses altogether.

You're the very paragon of cooperation and accommodation. But you may carry this trait too far, bending like a straw to meet your partner's needs and desires. You get something in return, of course, but the returns may not be entirely to your satisfaction— i.e., Where's the romance? Where's the violinist who plays while you and your partner dine at the edge of the sea? Where are the flowers, the surprise concert tickets, the moonlit walk through some exotic village?

There's considerable passion and a capacity for deep and lasting intimacy with this combination. But certain requirements have to be met first. Your partner must have aesthetic sensibilities that are similar to yours. He or she must appreciate music, art, books, and the beauty inherent in daily life. He or she must enjoy people, even if the nature of the enjoyment differs from yours. He or she must appreciate *you* and show that appreciation. Sorry, but an occasional hug won't cut it. You need genuine demonstrations, stuff that comes from the heart, and you need a lot of it. In return, you'll do whatever needs to be done to make the relationship work.

You approach most things in your life with a balanced, judicious perception. You immediately recognize unfairness when you see or experience it and seek to remedy it, if it's within your power to do so. This tenet is certainly true in your most intimate relationships, but its expression may be stymied by your unwillingness to create so many waves that a situation turns ugly and confrontational. Yes, that's what you despise most of all: confrontation. It just doesn't fit in with your idea of how life should be.

When you find your niche—in a relationship, a profession, a creative endeavor—you are singular and dedicated in your passion. As a rule, you dislike crudeness in any form, and yet there are always exceptions. Comedian Lenny Bruce, for example, had this combination, and made a career out of the very things this combination should abhor. In every double Libra combination there is some small part that rebels against what your archetype is supposed to be. Go figure. Blame free will.

Best Matches: Venus in Libra or another air sign heightens communication. Venus in a fire sign heightens the sexual chemistry. Mars or the Sun in a fire or air sign works also.

Examples: Lenny Bruce, Art Buchwald, Johnny Carson, R.D. Laing, John Lennon, novelist Michael Palmer

MARS IN SCORPIO ♂ ♏

There is more to you than meets the eye. Beneath that amiable exterior lies an astonishing intensity, powerful desires, and the soul of a spiritual warrior.

Thanks to the air/water elements in this combination, things can feel mighty uncomfortable until you learn from experience how to use this energy to achieve your fullest potential. The ease or difficulty of working with this combination depends on what you're doing. If you're conducting research, counseling others, or are involved in a creative profession, the energy enables you to delve deeply and relentlessly until you find whatever you need or are looking for. You're able to call upon your vast reservoir of intuition.

The area where this energy may prove most problematic is in relationships. While your Libra Sun is affable and generally open and up-front with other people, your Scorpio Mars is far more circumspect, solitary, and secretive. Your Libra Sun enjoys being involved in a relationship, but your Scorpio Mars has serious reservations. Your Libra Sun trusts people until they prove to be untrustworthy, but your Scorpio Mars trusts only when trust is won. These contradictions between the urges of your Sun sign and the dictates of your Mars sign are best resolved through a conscious awareness of how you act in relationships and by clearly defining what you're looking for.

One of the best uses of this combination's energy lies in the insight it provides into other people. This can prove to be invaluable in your most intimate relationships, allowing you to understand your partner's deepest thoughts and fears more readily.

You usually are comfortable with your sexuality and probably don't have any hard and fast rules about whether a relationship should be committed or not for you to enjoy sex. You have a powerful sex drive, but what you're really after isn't sexual satisfaction per se. For you, sex is the most immediate and direct route to communion with another person and it's that connection that you're after, that baring of souls.

You may be somewhat controlling in your most intimate relationships. This can have some unpleasant repercussions when the person you're trying to control rebels. If you repeatedly find yourself in situations where power is an issue, it would behoove you to discover why control is so important to you.

Best Matches: Venus in Scorpio or another water sign increases passion, sexuality; Venus in Libra or another air sign brings mutual communication; Mars in a water sign means heightened intuitive connections and deeper emotions between you and your partner. The Sun in Libra or another air sign also work well.

Examples: Mickey Mantle, Olivia Newton-John, Eleanor Roosevelt, Deepak Chopra

MARS IN SAGITTARIUS ♂ ♐

With this combination of air and fire, you're in search of deeper spiritual truths and in one form or another that quest dominates your life. Until you're able to identify the quest, it may feel like an internal itch, an almost unbearable restlessness that you can't explain or describe to anyone else.

The quest can take any number of forms, but usually involves an exploration of your worldview and deepest beliefs about life, death—the whole nine yards. As you explore this area, you may need to express what you discover, somehow, to share it with others through a creative medium. This sharing is part of your larger journey and its nature is determined to some extent by your commitment to your ideals.

Your people skills are extraordinary. If you speak publicly, you're able to move your audience with your wisdom. If you write, you're able to communicate your ideas clearly and in a way that touches your readers. If you act, you become the character you portray. At every turn, your creative expression is the fulcrum that helps you balance and understand your quest.

Your relationships—close friends, as well as your partners and your children, if you have any—somehow become pivotal to your quest. They expand your vision or take you in startling new directions you might not have discovered on your own.

You don't have any rules about sex without commitment and, at certain times in your life, may prefer that kind of relationship. No strings, no expectations, plenty of freedom. You won't compromise your ideals and beliefs just to make a relationship work. You'll get plenty of flak from your Libra Sun on that score. Libra is famous for its ability to accommodate everyone else's needs. But your ideals and beliefs are intrinsic to who you are and you're looking for a partner who appreciates that precisely because he or she also has ideals and beliefs worth fighting for. In your heart, you have always loved the rebels best.

In a relationship that meets your specifications, your passion is as vast and unknowable as the ocean. You're more than willing to shoulder your share of responsibilities, to accommodate but not to sell out, and to be free without hurting anyone else. Beyond that, you make no promises and give no guarantees. You will love fully and faithfully, but never blindly. You will always say your piece, even if you say it with a bluntness that sets your partner reeling.

The unintentional duplicity that is sometimes evident with this Sun sign won't have much of a chance against the need of your Sagittarius Mars to be bluntly frank.

Best Matches: Venus in Sagittarius or another fire sign brings passion, adventure, romance; Venus in Libra or another air sign indicates a free-flowing communication; Mars in a fire or air sign, Sun in Libra or Sagittarius or another air or fire sign are also excellent combinations.

Examples: T.S. Eliot, Christopher Reeve, John Sayles

MARS IN CAPRICORN♂♑

In astrological terms, the planets in this combination form a 90-degree angle to each other, an aspect known as a square. Squares create tension and friction that are impossible to ignore. You either deal with them or they continue to surface again and again. However, this combination consists of double cardinal signs, which generate dynamic, forceful energy that galvanizes you to action.

You have ambition and drive and once you set your sights on a goal, you pursue it with dedication and hard work. You plan and strategize well, and rarely lose sight of what you're doing and why. However, you can become obsessed with your work and your ambitions that any semblance of balance in your life vanishes. When you're locked into this workaholic mode, you forget how to relax or have a good time and ignore your personal relationships. This is sure to drive your Libra Sun crazy. Your Sun needs to socialize, to explore the arena of human relationships. If you get too wrapped up in work, your Sun will rebel and then you really will feel the tension and friction of this combination.

You're looking for a partner who shares your values and worldview. Until you find that person, you enjoy a variety of relationships and don't necessarily need commitment to have one that is strictly sexual. Mars in Capricorn is somewhat conservative, though, so an uncommitted sexual relationship won't last long if it doesn't evolve into something else.

Your organizational skills sometimes carry over into your relationships and may be construed as controlling. This, in turn, can lead to power struggles where your partner chafes at the structures you impose and you then try to accommodate your partner's needs by ignoring your own. Overcompensation, in other words, may be something you have to deal with in any intimate relationship.

In your ideal relationship, your capacity for intimacy and your sexuality deepen and flourish. This frees up energy that you then pour into creative endeavors or into achieving your ambitions.

Best Matches: Venus in Capricorn or another earth sign is the best, making for a grounded relationship. Venus in Libra highlights romance; Mars in an earth sign, Sun in Libra or Capricorn would also work.

Examples: Nancy Kerrigan, Timothy Leary, Franz Liszt, Aleister Crowley

MARS IN AQUARIUS ♂ ≈

In this double air-sign combination, the planets form a 120-degree angle to each other, an aspect known as a trine that makes for an easy exchange of energy. Your strengths are primarily intellectual and visionary. You have great insight into what makes people tick and it's rare when you can be fooled into thinking a person is something he or she isn't. For that matter, you usually are able to spot phony agendas as easily as you spot phony people.

You value and respect individuality and nurture it in your children, if you have any, and in your friends and partners. Despite your Libra Sun's need for relationships, you can be fiercely independent. You can also be opinionated, stubborn, and fixed in your beliefs. Due to your emphasis on the mind, a dichotomy may exist between what you profess to believe and how you actually live day to day. If and when someone points this out to you, you become defensive and find a dozen excuses for the discrepancy. Bottom line? You don't always walk the talk.

In affairs of the heart, your mind must be won first. But the winning involves some marked differences from combinations that involve Gemini. First and foremost, you must retain all your independence for pursuing your interests, friendships, and causes. You must be able to do what you want, when you want it (within reason, of course), and your partner absolutely has to understand that the relationship isn't the only thing that exists in your life.

Even when the ground rules are established, you aren't about to rush into a committed relationship. You can enjoy sex without commitment just fine and aren't the type to worry about if or when the scales will tip into something else. You attract more than your share of eccentric and artistic people and if your partner is one of them, then none of these issues will be issues for either of you.

Your sexuality may not conform to anyone else's standards, but you're comfortable with it nonetheless. In the right relationship, your capacity for intimacy is excellent precisely because you're such a good communicator. You're not a particularly secretive person and don't usually hold back details of your personal history, or your thoughts, beliefs, and feelings. You aren't a volatile person who blows up over every little thing. However, when your buttons are pushed—and those buttons generally concern freedom issues—your temper erupts swiftly.

Your visionary abilities allow you to see cutting-edge trends before they arrive and can be used in any profession. But whatever you do should allow you the greatest amount of personal and creative freedom as well as freedom to support your many causes, whatever they might be.

Best Match: Venus in Aquarius, Libra, or Gemini emphasizes communication; Mars in an air sign or fire sign heightens the sexual side of the relationship; Sun in an air sign also would work.

Examples: Lee Iacocca, Jimmy Carter, Truman Capote, Lee Harvey Oswald

MARS IN PISCES ♂ ⟩(

This combination can also be quite visionary, but in a different way than Libra/Aquarius. Your approach to just about everything is exceptionally intuitive and emotional. If something feels right, you go with it. If it doesn't feel right, you may go with it anyway—and then regret it. Once this happens often enough, you learn to listen to your intuitive voice and to follow its advice.

Your emotions, intuition, and imagination are the most powerful forces in your life. To some extent, they depend upon and nurture each other. When you feel something strongly enough, for example, then your imagination and intuition seem to open up automatically. Sometimes your imagination speaks first, other times your intuition is first in line. The order doesn't matter; it's the content of the visions, dreams, feelings, and images that is important.

You do well in any work or profession where you have artistic freedom or in which your compassion can shine—nursing, medicine, social work, counseling, psychology, or work in hospitals, prisons, or hospices. This same compassion, however, can get you into trouble in relationships when you take a wounded soul under your wing. Compassion is an admirable trait, but if your emotions get mixed up with your mission, you could find yourself in the twilight zone of the martyr/savior syndrome.

To break out of this syndrome requires an adjustment in your thinking and a conscious awareness of the deeper belief that attracts the experience. It also requires that you channel your compassion into other venues, perhaps into a creative passion that you haven't yet developed fully. It all depends, really, on what you want to make of your life, what kind of legacy you would like to leave behind.

Frequently, the higher inspiration of this combination gets

clouded when you're involved in an intimate relationship. You're looking for nothing less than your soul mate, but in the real world a soul mate may seem impossible to find. So you make do with other relationships, some of them less than satisfactory, or you simply do without and throw yourself into your work or your spiritual and psychic development. The challenge with this combination is to maintain your path, whatever it is, and not to indulge in escapism. If you can rise to that challenge, then the rest will unfold in its own time.

Best Matches: Venus in Pisces or another water sign, Venus in Libra or another air sign, Mars in a water sign, Sun in an air or water sign. Best to stay away from Venus or Mars in Scorpio. The energy is simply too intense.

Examples: Carrie Fisher, Chris Carter (creator of *The X-Files*)

SENSE-MEMORY EXERCISE FOR SUN IN LIBRA

Mars represents our physical senses. Most of us have at least one sense that is stronger than the others. Your sense of smell or taste may be powerful. Maybe your hearing is as acute as a dog's. Your strongest sense, whatever it is, provides you with immediate and reliable information about yourself or others, your environment, and your personal world.

In the space below, describe an instance where one of your physical senses played a vital role. This experience can be positive or negative or anything in between. Be detailed and specific.

_____

_____

_____

_____

_____

The incident or situation you've just described pertains to the second question you created in the inventory at the beginning of part two. If the connection isn't immediately apparent, look for the metaphor.

A young woman with her Sun in Libra wrote a poem that described her experience with a ghost in the house where she lived as a child. Whether the ghost was "real" or not was immaterial; to her, it had been real enough so that the terrifying ordeal had stuck in her memory for more than thirty years. Her description concerned her sense of hearing—the noises the ghost made, the frantic beating of her heart as the noises got closer and closer to her bed.

Her second question was: *Should I marry my boyfriend?*

She realized, from what she'd written, that certain aspects of her relationship with her boyfriend terrified her and that she wasn't "hearing" (listening to) that message.

10

Sun in Scorpio ☉ ♏

THE POWERFUL
Fixed Water

"I'm a paradox even to myself."

Strengths: Exceptionally intuitive, great courage, innate curiosity, industrious, passionate, rich inner life, inherent sensuality, profound spiritual beliefs

Weaknesses: Never forgets a slight, everything is black or white, power freak, controlling, exceedingly stubborn

Sexual Blueprint: Sex is a conduit to the genuine communion.

Secretive. Powerful emotions. Passionate. Sexual. Regeneration. Destruction. Rebirth. Resurrection. Piercing insight. These are some of the usual keywords for Scorpio that you'll find in astrology books. All of them are true, but aren't the full story.

Your true power lies in your emotions, which are so intense

and focused that they permeate everything you do, every choice that you make, every thought that you think, every dream that you have. Your emotions are the lens through which you view yourself and your world and at times they are so powerful that they nearly overwhelm you.

Scorpio is one of the most misunderstood signs, often associated exclusively with intense sexuality. While this is certainly part of who you are, sex just for sex doesn't interest you. You're after the deeper stuff, the whys and whats that help mold an individual and sex is a means to that kind of knowledge. Even when you're involved in a relationship that is purely sexual, there're always more dimensions to the relationship for you.

Your secrecy is due to lack of trust and a reluctance to let just anyone into the private sanctuary of your being. Any partner who wants commitment from you must win your trust and it's not easily won. Beneath your smoldering sexuality and your penetrating insight lies a toughness that other people sense but may not be able to define. You're an enigma even to the people who know you best. Much of the time you're a mystery to yourself as well, puzzled by the forces that seem to move your life.

SUN IN SCORPIO AND . . .

MARS IN ARIES ♂ ♈

This combination is a tough one. It's not just the fact that water and fire don't mix, but that Mars in Aries can be a relentless bully that always vies for top-dog position and your Scorpio Sun doesn't take kindly to bullies. As a result, you experience a fierce internal tug-of-war over certain issues and situations.

In your professional life, for example, you probably feel conflicted between your desire to plunge ahead and a need to make decisions in a more measured, contemplative way. You rush into projects or relationships rashly and impatiently only to regret it later when you realize you've made a big mistake. In sexual situations, you act on impulse rather than allowing yourself a little time to mull things over. Your central personal conflict boils down to a struggle between your impatience to pursue any experience for the thrill and your need for the bottom-line truth of any experience. The first approach is superficial, the second approach is anything but.

Regardless of the situation, there are several ways to integrate these two energies so that you can take full advantage of this powerful combination. Your abundant physical energy needs several outlets. One outlet should be daily physical exercise. This will mitigate your restlessness and make it easier to focus on the rest of your life.

A creative outlet is just as vital to your health and happiness and the spectrum of possibilities is vast. You can excel in the arts, in business, medicine, research—anything that allows you to explore your ideas and to get to the core of whatever you're pursuing. You're an innovator, so it won't be surprising if you carve some new niche for yourself that allows you to use any number of your talents and provides the freedom you need in your professional life.

In relationships, you're really difficult to pin down. People who meet you for the first time are struck by your smoldering sexuality and how personable you are. The two qualities, when bundled together, can create the impression that you are unconventional sexually, that just about anything goes. This may be true with certain people in certain situations, but isn't a general rule. And maybe that's the whole point, really. What works today with person A may not work tomorrow or next month with person B. It all depends on how you feel *in the moment*.

There's plenty of passion with this combination, and once trust is established, you're capable of great intimacy as well.

Best Matches: Venus in Aries would seem to be the ideal match, at least as far as your Mars sign is concerned. But, given your powerful Scorpio Sun, you might consider a Venus in Scorpio, especially if you're looking for intense sexual experiences. Mars in a fire sign would work better than Mars in either Cancer or Pisces, which Aries would overpower. A Sun in a water sign would work well, too.

Examples: Helen Reddy, Art Garfunkel

MARS IN TAURUS♂ ♉

You have a quiet intensity that feeds your creative abilities in a way that is mysterious to other people and perhaps to you as well. As a double fixed sign, you're incredibly stubborn and when it comes to your creative expression, your way is the only way. This may not be true all of the time, but it takes a very convincing argument for you to change your mind once it's made up.

Once you set your sights on a goal, it takes nothing short of a nuclear blast to keep you from attaining that goal. You probably came into the world knowing what you wanted to do, and if that passion is strong and relentless enough, you'll achieve whatever you set out to do. It's likely that you have talent in music, art, or acting. You're also good at handling and investing money. You enjoy investigating topics that are truly mysterious and always look for the deeper truth, the deeper reality.

Physically, you're strong and you may have some sort of regular exercise regimen that increases or maintains your inherent strength. Sometimes with this combination there's an awareness of the physical body as a spiritual vessel, so that you follow a discipline that enhances both your physical self and your spiritual beliefs.

Your nature is deeply passionate, though not always trusting. You usually know immediately whether you like or dislike someone you just met and this first opinion rarely changes. Your powerful will and intuition work tirelessly on your behalf, making you aware of the deeper nuances in any relationship. Your sexuality is a primary force in your life and you don't need commitment to enjoy sex. The parameters of a relationship matter less to you than the content, the texture, the inner workings of your partner.

When you do commit, you're a loyal and loving partner and expect the same in return. Since Scorpio and Taurus are opposed to each other, though, you tend to approach everything, including relationships, with contentiousness. *I'm going to win.* Or: *It has to be done the way I want it done.* This attitude is the primary challenge in any of your intimate relationships. If you can nurture flexibility in yourself and try to go with the flow, the challenge can be met and conquered.

Best Matches: Venus in Taurus or another earth sign, Venus in Scorpio, Mars in an earth sign, Sun in Taurus.

Examples: Jamie Lee Curtis, Indian mystic Sai Baba, Leon Trotsky, Will Rogers

MARS IN GEMINI ♂ ♊

This water and air combination forces you to be flexible when you would rather do things in ways that are tried and true. You explore your diverse interests in depth, always seeking the common thread, the underlying theme that connects one idea with another, even when the ideas seem to have no link whatsoever.

Your friends and acquaintances are as diverse as your interests. They come from many walks of life and from a variety of professions. You're genuinely interested in other people—their stories, personal histories, motivations—and in some way, this interest is translated into your creative vision. You're a consummate communicator, able to express yourself clearly through a diversity of mediums. But when it comes to your private life, you clam up.

Your sexuality is a puzzle, even to you. Sometimes sex is uppermost in your mind, your main priority, the focus of your existence. Other times you're more interested in exchanging ideas and philosophies; your thrust is more mental. This is the essential paradox of a Scorpio/Gemini combination. Your Scorpio Sun is secretive by nature, but your Gemini Mars isn't; your Scorpio Sun gives you a smoldering sexuality, but your Gemini Mars makes you appear to be footloose and carefree.

Resolving the paradox requires that you stand apart somewhat from yourself and observe how you approach sexual relationships—how you act, what you do, and what you think and feel at the time. Granted, this isn't the easiest process, but it provides great insight into your own sexual and emotional needs. The process will appeal to your Gemini Mars, which enjoys gathering information of any kind and it will appeal to your Sun because it feeds Scorpio's need to understand herself.

You're a natural flirt, and that won't end just because the nature of your relationships change. Even when in a committed relationship, you enjoy flirting and lively conversation with people you find attractive. This doesn't mean that you're interested sexually in everyone with whom you flirt. Once you commit, you tend to be loyal as long as your partner is loyal, and your capacity for intimacy and true depth of understanding expands and deepens over the years.

Best Matches: Great chemistry with someone who has a Venus in Gemini or Scorpio, or in another air sign. A Venus in Pisces would be overwhelmed by your Scorpio Sun, but a Venus in Cancer might work if you share the same values about home and children. A Mars in Libra or Aquarius would never be boring, and with a Sun in Gemini, you might spend so much time talking that you never get down to sex!

Examples: Joni Mitchell, Lauren Hutton, Mamie Eisenhower

MARS IN CANCER ♂ ♋

You're an intensely emotional person whose views of just about everything are very subjective. This combination is nearly as secretive as that of double Scorpio. It's not so much that you have anything specific to hide (although you may) but simply that you prefer to keep your private life private.

You place a lot of emphasis on your home, your roots, and your ancestry. Your family is extremely important to you and if you have children of your own, you may be overprotective and somewhat controlling. In fact, control issues may crop up periodically in your life—regarding either the control you exert over others or the control others attempt to exert over you.

Even though many people with this combination work nine-to-five jobs, those aren't the best venues to fulfill your great potential unless you have a lot of creative freedom. The ideal is a profession in which you can use your intuition and your creativity to work at a deep, imaginative level. A home-based business would work well for you, as would any sort of entrepreneurial venture, where you find a niche in the market and seek to fill it.

As a double water sign, your sexuality is all about emotion. Although the Scorpio in you probably doesn't have any problem getting involved in relationships that are strictly sexual, your Cancer Mars may balk and urge you to withdraw if the relationship doesn't evolve into something else. There will be times in your life, though, when sex is all that you want from a relationship because it's simpler and less involving, so you build a little wall around your heart.

Walls, of course, are meant to be scaled or pierced or torn down and eventually someone will come along who will serve that purpose. Then you become an emotional torpedo, zeroing in on the bottom line, the deeper truth about your partner and the relationship. This powerful combination won't tolerate lies and deception, and at the first hint of either, you break the ties and move on.

But in a mutually committed relationship where you and your partner are true equals, you have the potential for great happiness.

Best Matches: Someone with a Venus in Cancer is ideal. A Venus in Scorpio may result in a relationship that is so intense that you crave moments when you can surface for air. A Venus in Pisces might be overwhelmed by all that Scorpio energy, but a Mars in Pisces would fit right in with your Cancer Mars. A Cancer Sun would work, too.

Examples: Albert Camus, Pablo Picasso, Henry Winkler, Burt Lancaster

MARS IN LEO♂♌

As a double fixed sign, you're stubborn, rarely changing your opinions once they're formed, and you fight for your beliefs and ideologies. With this combination, Mars and your Sun form a geometric angle called a square, which produces friction or resistance between the two energies.

The friction here is between your penchant for secrecy and your need for an audience. Hillary Clinton exemplifies this combination. During the Monica Lewinsky scandal, she kept her personal feelings private, then subsequently sought the limelight through her successful run for senator. Scorpio never forgets a slight and Leo, despite the bravado, can be deeply wounded.

You're ambitious, usually know what you want, and view every obstacle merely as another challenge to overcome. You refuse to allow the word "surrender" into your vocabulary. Although the square is challenging, it gives you tremendous inner resources to achieve just about anything you want. It also makes your intimate relationships difficult.

Sometimes control issues are at the center of the difficulty. You refuse to be controlled by anyone, yet you may feel a need to control your partner, who in turn rebels by doing something to violate your trust. Once that trust is violated, the relationship is never quite the same. Other times, the difficulties in relationships surface because despite your need for privacy, you love the limelight, applause, recognition, and drama. If your partner has more of the limelight than you do, you may resent it. Or if your partner is the shy, retiring sort, he or she may resent *your* limelight. There's no easy way around these issues except to be aware of them and try to work with them positively as they come up.

You can be deeply protective of your partner and children, but also expect them to be as independent and resilient as you are. You're direct about your sexuality and sexual needs even when your Scorpio Sun is screaming at you to keep your mouth shut and let your partner figure it all out. You want to be recognized for your abilities, but even more than that, you want to be loved and understood.

Best Matches: Someone with Venus in Leo is best. Sparks fly, the chemistry boils. Venus in Scorpio is intense, extremely sexual and sensual. Mars in Scorpio is also intense, but could lead to power struggles. Sun in Leo is good, too, except that then you're both vying for the limelight.

Examples: Hillary Clinton, Kevin Kline, George Eliot, Clifford Irving, Demi Moore

MARS IN VIRGO♂︎♍︎

Water and earth: the energies of these two should flow together seamlessly. You're a precise, analytical person and also highly intuitive. When you're humming along the path in life that is right for you, your left and right brain have equal say. You get into trouble, though, when one overpowers the other. Then things tip into an imbalance that can manifest itself according to the house placements of your Sun and Mars (see Chapter 2).

Let's say that your Virgo Mars is in the fifth house and your Scorpio Sun is in the seventh house. If you're going through a period where you're being overly analytical about everything, then you probably are analyzing and dissecting your creativity, children, and pleasurable sexual experiences (fifth house) as well as your intimate and business partnerships (seventh house).

You do well in any profession that deals with health, medicine, research, community or social services, science, or the arts. Your Scorpio energy gives you the ability to probe deeply into whatever you do, and the Virgo energy makes you a perfectionist for whom details are vital. When you apply this combination of energies to a profession about which you are passionate, there's no limit to what you can achieve—*if* you can avoid self-criticism. Virgo Mars can be a paragon of pickiness—either toward other people or herself.

Sexually, you may be somewhat finicky. You aren't taken in by someone with a slick line, the right clothes, or a gorgeous face and body. You probably are most interested in the person's health habits, spiritual beliefs, motives, and ambitions. One-night stands probably aren't for you. You prefer a relationship that evolves over time, with mutual interests and passions unfolding in a natural way.

Virgo Mars is more emotionally detached than your Scorpio Sun, which makes you more balanced than, say, a double Scorpio combination. Sometimes, though, particularly when you're in a left-brain analytical mode, your detachment in a relationship can run to extremes. During these periods in your life, your interests turn more toward the mind and the intellect than toward emotional and spiritual issues. If you're in a committed relationship, it's important to reassure your partner that your period of detachment does not reflect a lessening of your love. Otherwise, miscommunication and power struggles may ensue.

Best Matches: Venus in Virgo tends to be a relationship with intellectual chemistry. Venus in Taurus can be sensual, Venus in Capricorn ambitious. Venus in Scorpio promises intensity while Venus in Mars is intensely sexual, with possible power issues. A Sun in Scorpio puts you both on the same life wavelength.

Examples: Whoopi Goldberg, Carl Sagan, Indira Gandhi, Georgia O'Keeffe, Bonnie Raitt

MARS IN LIBRA ♂ ♎

Other people perceive you as gracious, balanced, judicious, and fair-minded. You are all of those things, but beneath that gracious exterior lies a tougher, more intense individual rarely seen by other people. This water/air combination is never a matter of "what you see is what you get."

You enjoy the arts in any form and may have artistic or musical talent yourself. You don't settle for easy answers, easy knowledge, easy anything, so if you make your living in the arts, then your approach is thorough and probing. You constantly dig deeper into yourself, seeking the material that you need to create something that outshines your competitors.

You are sexually precocious, experimental, and curious. You

don't need commitment to explore your sexuality and at certain times in your life, you'll prefer *not* being committed. Your challenge is that when you want to end a relationship, you may not be up-front about it because you don't like hurting anyone's feelings. So you get involved with someone else, who doesn't know about your first partner, until you muster the courage to tell the first partner what's going on. Then, of course, the second partner may find out what's happening and the deception catches up with you. This kind of circuitous deception can get confusing quickly, so even if you have to hurt someone, honesty really is your best policy.

You enjoy being romanced. You enjoy the flush and buoyancy of the initial stages of a relationship, the sense that you've been swept into an unexplored country, the lightness of being. Moonlit beaches, soft music, gifts of roses: you picture yourself as Meg Ryan in *Sleepless in Seattle*. This kind of romance hooks you fast.

It is said that for a Libra, relationships are everything. Scorpio doesn't share that need, so there may be conflict between your need for companionship and your need for solitude and privacy. But if your partner is the right partner, then even Scorpio can adjust and learn to love being in love.

Best Matches: You have good chemistry with someone whose Venus is in Libra or another air sign. A Venus or Mars in Scorpio will be exceptionally intense, and power struggles may ensure. A Sun in Scorpio or another water sign would be good, too.

Examples: Bill Gates, Richard Burton, Kate Capshaw, Michael Crichton, Lyle Lovett, and Pat Buchanan

MARS IN SCORPIO ♂♏

Your life is filled with emotionally intense experiences and dramatic ups and downs. You live within a pressure cooker of sweeping, powerful emotions and these emotions attract experiences, situations, and people that reflect your inner state.

You do best in a profession where you can use your emotions and intuition in a creative way and without too much interference from other people. Any of the arts would suit you, but so would scientific or medical research, investigative work, finances and business, the law, the healing arts, massage therapy, astrology, and metaphysics. In fact, you can achieve anything as long as you're passionate about it and bring the full power of your will to manifest what you need, when you need it.

As a double Scorpio—two planets in that fixed water sign—you're stubborn and exceptionally intuitive, and your emotions rush through you like some powerful river. Nothing in you is ambivalent. Things are black or white, right or wrong, good or bad. There are no gray areas. You can be so inflexible and opinionated that you aren't the easiest person with whom to work or to live. These traits can make your professional life challenging, to say the least. That's one of the reasons you should attempt to work for yourself.

This combination is both sexual and deeply spiritual, and for you that's no contradiction. There's always a spiritual component to your sexual experiences. You don't intellectualize about sex or your sexuality as some of the air-sign combinations do. For you, it all unfolds on an instinctive level, with lovemaking as its own language. You don't vocalize much of what you feel in a relationship and with the right partner, there won't be any need to talk about what you or the other person feels. You both already will know.

You have a tremendous capacity for passion and when you really let loose, it's the sort of passion that has few limits. Anything goes. You lose track of time and space and sex becomes a kind of transcendental experience. Not too bad a way to spend a week-end!

If you have children, you are somewhat overprotective and controlling. As with any Scorpio combination, control issues will surface until you have conquered the need to control and learned to be more flexible and to go with the flow. Even when you learn this, though, always pay attention to your intuition. It won't ever steer you wrong.

Best Matches: Venus in Scorpio is the absolute best, the perfect partner. But Venus in Cancer or Taurus would be just great, too, since both are compatible with Scorpio. Mars in a water sign would work and so would a Sun in Scorpio or in Cancer.

Examples: Leonardo DiCaprio, Sally Field, J.A. Jance, Jonas Salk, Dylan Thomas, Martin Scorsese, Mackenzie Philips of The Mamas & the Papas, Laura Bush, Grace Kelly, Shere Hite

MARS IN SAGITTARIUS ♂ ♐

You've got spit and fire and an independent streak that is nearly as intense as your restlessness. You need a lot of personal freedom to come and go as you please and do *not* do well with a boss breathing down your neck and issuing orders.

You're always on the lookout for the larger picture of whatever you're involved in, whether it's a creative project or a relation-ship, and need to know how that bigger picture fits into your life. Or vice versa. This need can become a personal quest, one of the things in your life that propels you into a multitude of diverse ex-periences. You may not even be consciously aware that you're on a quest, but at some level, you do know and you honor that quest.

You aren't the type to live your life according to other people's ideas about what is correct or acceptable. In this sense, you very definitely go your own way and if your way differs too much from the norm, you'll get downright sneaky about doing what you want to do when you want to do it. One way or another, you will live your life your own way. A good example of this is Prince Charles. He married the right girl and made her a princess and the mother of the next heir to the throne and he did all this because royal protocol demanded that he should. But by all accounts, he continued his relationship with Camilla Parker Bowles.

While the Sagittarius part of the equation is chatty and personable and more than willing to talk about personal beliefs and spirituality and just about anything else under the sun, the Scorpio part of the equation clams up when confronted with anything personal. You don't recognize anything paradoxical about your behavior because, for you, there's no paradox. It's business as usual. It's just how things are.

In a relationship, however, this can be a major challenge. An intimate relationship, by its very nature, requires honest communication—and that may be one of the reasons that you avoid committed relationships. Sex is great, sex is fun, sex is a need that must be met. But in your scheme of things, sex doesn't require commitment.

When you do commit, your partner—and this is the ideal—will be nothing short of extraordinary. He or she will share your love for foreign travel, will have similar spiritual beliefs and a similar worldview, and will be filled with as much enthusiasm for life as you are. Sex with this person will be like something from a Hemingway novel—the earth will shake, fireworks will explode behind your eyes, and you'll know you have met your match.

Best Matches: Look for a Venus in Sagittarius or another fire sign for passion and adventure. Venus or Sun in Scorpio deepens sexuality. A Sun in Sagittarius spells mutual independence.

Examples: Goldie Hawn, Billy Graham, Prince Charles, Voltaire, George Gallup, Lee Strasberg

MARS IN CAPRICORN♂♑

Ambition is your middle name. This isn't meant in a derogatory sense, as in "naked ambition." Your ambition is the sort that is achieved through careful strategy and planning, always with an eye on the ultimate goal. You don't achieve at the expense of others.

With this combination, your Sun and Mars form a harmonious angle to each other called a sextile. This angle or aspect indicates that the energy between the two planets flows smoothly, almost effortlessly, and with a water and an earth combination, how could it be otherwise? Water feeds the earth and the earth absorbs water to produce vegetation, which in turn produces food and oxygen. Water prevents earth from turning to dust. Translated, this means that in everything you do, you seek practical results and applications. It's not enough for you to have an idea; you act to make the ideas practical, useful, and efficient.

You do well in any profession where you can use your intuition (Scorpio) and your ambition (Capricorn) to further man's knowledge of himself and his world. You're as good in business matters as you are in the arts. You have a talent for making money and yes, money buys freedom to pursue your goals in your own way. But making money is rarely the endpoint of what you want to achieve. It's a means to an end.

You can be stodgy and conventional at times. You insist on doing things the conventional way or on honoring the traditions of society, the community, and your family. But at other times, your Scorpio Sun energy takes over and you don't give a damn about traditions or conventions; you're more interested in deeper issues.

You're comfortable with your sexuality, and it, like most things in your life, has a practical purpose. It's a means through which you come to know yourself better and, in the right circumstances and with the right person, allows you to explore a side of yourself that can be as wild and experimental as you can imagine. Sex also brings you a kind of elemental comfort in that you feel less alone, less isolated. You can share things with a sexual partner that you can't (or won't) share with a close friend, a sibling, or with your mother!

In the right relationship, whether it's committed, purely sexual, or some weird permutation of either of these, you meet the part of yourself that is part goddess (or god). And then everything else clicks together and, oops, suddenly you are exactly where you are supposed to be, with your life unfolding around you.

Best Matches: Venus in Capricorn or another earth sign. That's the best. It brings practicality and grounding to the relationship. Then Venus in Scorpio or a water sign, Mars in an earth sign, and the Sun in either a water or earth sign.

Examples: Just look at this diverse lineup: Teddy Roosevelt, musician/singer Tom Paxton, Arctic explorer Richard Byrd, Julia Roberts

MARS IN AQUARIUS ♂ ♒

Yes, you're probably a visionary in some area of your life and you're able to see cutting-edge trends long before the rest of us do. As a double fixed sign, you also are very stubborn, slow to change your mind once it's made up, and even slower to change your beliefs and opinions. You'll always listen to a convincing argument about why you're wrong or mistaken, but even then you won't necessarily change your mind. This inflexibility can be useful at times, but when it goes to extremes, it can affect you physically.

You're a creative individual who brings foresight into everything you do. If you make your living in any facet of the arts, you do so with relentless determination and an independent spirit, and always remain true to your own vision. You also would do well in business or as an entrepreneur. You're attracted to any profession that allows you to use your mind and your intuition, and which doesn't restrict your freedom in any way.

You honor individuality and yet are aware of the human collective—that we are all connected at some level and that what affects one, affects all. When you're judgmental about other people, you probably don't voice it unless you're angry, and even then you may keep your opinion to yourself. One of the prevalent themes in your life is to formulate some sort of worldview that is uniquely yours. This evolves as much through your experiences as it does through your intuitive grasp of spiritual laws.

Your Sun and Mars form a challenging angle to each other known as a square. Squares create friction. Where your sexuality is concerned, that friction shows up in your vacillation between passion (Scorpio) and complete emotional detachment (Aquarius). A partner, particularly one who doesn't know you well, can find this disconcerting and confusing. But this fluctuation from one extreme to the other may be part of what your partners find so intriguing about you.

Before you commit to any single relationship, you need to be sure that your partner understands your need for personal freedom to pursue your ideals, your friendships, and your association with groups that share your ideals. Once you find a partner who grasps what you're really about, your capacity for intimacy deepens. In the right relationship, your sexuality comes alive in new ways and may surprise even you!

Best Matches: Venus in Aquarius means good communication and a forward-thinking relationship; in Scorpio sexuality is heightened. Venus in an air sign, Mars in an air or water sign, and the Sun in a water or air sign also would work well.

Examples: Kurt Vonnegut, Grace Slick, Charles Bronson, Winona Ryder, Christian Barnard, Adam Ant

MARS IN PISCES♂︎♓︎

You often are so intuitive that it's spooky—not just for others, but for you, too. You often perceive things that other people don't, the hidden nuances, the unspoken words, the language of the soul. Call it what you want—intuitive, psychic, clairvoyant; it doesn't matter, they all fit. As a double water sign, your intuition and emotions are your most powerful allies.

You function at such deep levels that quite often the mundane details of daily life escape you. Your imagination is simply too vast to grasp and deal with all the petty details. While your neighbors are out mowing the lawn and washing their cars, you're dreaming of man's prehistory or searching the skies for UFOs or researching some fantastic conspiracy that you read about on the Internet. Through your imagination, you can reach so far within yourself that you tap into the ocean of the collective unconscious.

Physically, you probably have large, expressive eyes and a soft, rounded face. You may have a tendency to gain weight easily. Your hair is probably unusual in some way. Your feet are sensitive, beautifully formed, and you benefit from foot reflexology.

You do well in any artistic field where your imagination and intuition are free to roam and create. You also would do great in any profession in the medical or hospice field, counseling, research, or investigative work. You may have more than one profession over the course of your life, but whatever you do, above all, make sure that you love it.

Your sexuality is all about emotions, intuition, and spirituality. Sounds weird, but that's just how it is for you. You probably aren't interested in casual sex; you want the whole romantic, soul-mate package and really, nothing less than that will do. Finding that partner could be a challenge for many signs, but you're so psychically aware that you'll recognize the person as soon as you meet him or her. It will feel like you've finally come home. There's sure to be a past-life connection.

Even soul mates, though, have challenges to meet and issues to resolve. So even if you find the perfect partner, it doesn't mean you can sit back, kick up your feet, and be assured of bliss and happiness forever. But it does mean that within the parameters of commitment, your sexuality blossoms, your capacity for intimacy deepens, and you can probably overcome Scorpio's secrecy.

Best Matches: Venus in Pisces, Scorpio, or Cancer would mean intuitive connections, and deep emotional bonds. Mars in an earth sign and the Sun in Pisces would work well, too.

Examples: Bo Derek, Caroline Wyeth

SENSE-MEMORY EXERCISE FOR SUN IN SCORPIO

Mars represents our physical senses. Most of us have at least one sense that is stronger than the others or provides information more quickly about our physical environment. Perhaps your sense of touch is extraordinary. Maybe your sight is exceptionally powerful. Your strongest sense, whatever it is, provides you with immediate and reliable information about yourself or others, your environment, and your personal world.

In the space below, describe an instance where one of your

physical senses played a vital role. This experience can be positive or negative or anything in between. Be detailed and specific.

_____

_____

_____

_____

_____

The incident or situation you've just described pertains to the second question you created in the inventory at the beginning of part two. If the connection isn't immediately apparent, look for the metaphor.

An elderly man, a widower with his Sun in Scorpio, described an experience he'd had years earlier in which his sense of taste played a major role. He was in India during the Second World War and described his first taste of Indian curry. Hot. Spicy. Incredible.

His second question concerned whether he should encourage a relationship with a widowed friend of his dead wife. The woman had been stopping by the house frequently, bringing him casseroles and desserts, and since they were already old friends there was an easy camaraderie between them. From his description of the curry, he decided the time to act was now.

II

Sun in Sagittarius ☉ ♐

THE OPTIMIST
Mutable Fire

"Everything will work out for the best—because I say so!"

Strengths: Innate optimism, the sort for whom the glass is always half full rather than half empty, truth seeker, independent, humorous, vivacious, charming, athletic, an explorer and traveler, sees the larger picture

Weaknesses: Can be overzealous about spiritual beliefs, boastful, impatient, cuttingly blunt, irresponsible, acts like a rebellious adolescent when he doesn't get his way

Sexual Blueprint: Love me if you want, but never tie me down.

An interesting thing happened on your way into the life you're living now: you were born Sagittarius! That means that your soul's mission is to look for the bigger picture, the larger truth—the cosmic biggies. It also means that you have charm, charisma, presence, a curiosity that rivals that of Gemini, an interest in foreign cultures and people, and a fascination with spiritual thought. But let's go back to that first attribute.

The soul. It may seem to be a paradox that a book about sexual astrology includes stuff about spirituality and the soul. But that's a big part of what Sagittarius is about. In one way or another, your spiritual or religious beliefs are a major theme in your life. So are books and publishing, the law, foreign cultures and people, foreign travel, independence, and anything to do with the higher mind. This all sounds rather lofty, but in less aware Sagittarians, it can get pretty boring, especially when the Sadge gets on his soapbox and starts preaching.

However, Sagittarians who are more aware rarely preach and there are few people more fun to be around, more into life and everything it has to offer, and more dedicated to their ideals. Many of the best psychics I've met are Sagittarians. They're able to use their talent to see *your* bigger picture.

Paradox, it seems, is a big part of your journey.

SUN IN SAGITTARIUS AND . . .

MARS IN ARIES ♂ ♈

If you were born in frontier times, you would be driven out of town because you refused to toe the line, to live the politically correct life according to the consensus morality of the times. You would be a witch or a warlock, an animal communicator, an herbalist, a healer, a rebel through and through.

Fortunately for you, we're a bit further along on the evolutionary scale (but not by much), and nowadays there are other venues of expression for someone like you. Whatever you do professionally, rest assured that it will be radically different from everyone else in your college graduating class (except other Mars in Aries people) and that in some way, shape, or form, your pioneering spirit will be evident.

As a double fire sign, you're passionate, independent, reckless, and fearless. You go parachuting for the thrill of it. You rock climb because it's *fun*. And you don't know the meaning of the word *vertigo*. There will always be other people, the judgmental sort, who think you're—well, okay, let's say it—nuts, bonkers, totally out to lunch—but hey, so what. Variety is the spice of life and all that, and experience is what you're here for. Besides, you don't give a damn what other people think.

This attitude is sure to drive your mother crazy and won't endear you to bosses, supervisors, or authority figures in general. That's okay, too. You can talk your way out of a wet paper bag if you have to. Your independence forms the core of your survival instincts.

In the sexual arena, all of these personality attributes come into play. You don't need any kind of parameters to enjoy sex, and enjoy it you do—fully, delightfully, lustfully—and it's so great in the moments that it's happening that you don't bother thinking about mañana. You're in the here and now and if it feels good, why not do it? So when you wake up in the morning with a hangover or the feeling that something monumental has happened (but can't recall exactly what it was), well, you'll deal with it. You'll remember. And in the meantime, there are five million other things to throw yourself into.

In a committed relationship (which probably won't happen when you're in your teens or twenties and maybe not even in your thirties), your ideal partner will have a firm grasp on who you are and what you're about. You'll insist on your own independence, but be jealous of time he or she spends away from you. You'll be volatile, but will cry out in frustration when your partner is that way. But then there's the sex. And somehow, that makes all the difference.

Best Matches: This one is a no-brainer. A Venus in Aries, Sagittarius, or Leo will create such chemistry and sparks that the two of you may not even get out of bed in the morning. A Venus or Mars in any of the air signs will keep things intellectually stimulating. A Sun in a fire sign is dynamite, too.

Examples: Beau Bridges, Emily Dickinson (who poured all this passion into her creative work), Leslie Stahl, James Thurber, Kevin Costner (think *Dances With Wolves*) Rod Serling

MARS IN TAURUS♂♉

You have astonishing reserves of physical energy and strength. You probably are athletic or enjoy sports. You should have some sort of regular physical exercise program that keeps you aerobically fit and flexible. Running combined with yoga or tai chi would be beneficial.

You can be infuriatingly stubborn at times, using methods that have worked in the past even if those methods don't work as well now. But thanks to your more flexible Sagittarius Sun, you usually can be convinced to try something new. With this fire/earth combination, anything you do professionally has to show tangible, practical results. Your Sagittarius Sun brings in the ideas and your Taurus Mars implements them in a grounded, pragmatic way. You would do equally well in the arts or in business, banking, finance, or owning your own business.

You're an acquisitive person who may collect art or certain types of music, and you enjoy beautiful, harmonious surroundings. You probably also enjoy travel, especially the kind that happens spontaneously, where you take off for parts unknown with little more than a backpack and some cash. You take pleasure in foreign countries and cultures, enjoy the foods and learning about the people and their mythologies and worldviews. The nomad in you would enjoy a job or profession that involves travel.

Even though this is a fire/earth combination, Sagittarius and Taurus share certain traits when it comes to sex. You probably are fairly comfortable with your sexuality most of the time. You tend to be frank about sex, your own needs, and what you're looking for. People who are accustomed to more circumspection and coyness in sexual matters probably find your honesty unsettling. But other people's opinions rarely hold much influence over you and when others are put off by your directness, you go elsewhere.

Sex is important to you, though. Your nature is deeply sensual and your sense of touch well developed. You enjoy partners who honor your freedom and independence, but who find the same kind of pleasure that you do in sex. You have little use for conventional relationships, so sex without a commitment is rarely an issue for you. When you do commit, you do so for the long haul, as long as the sexual relationship is mutually satisfying.

Your intimacy quotient may be erratic at times, particularly if you're feeling stressed by work. But during those periods, sex is the way you communicate and your need for it may be higher than usual. Even though Sagittarius is chatty, Taurus is often more circumspect; this disparity may require adjustment and fine-tuning until you learn to merge the energies.

Best Matches: With someone who has Venus in Taurus, the relationship is deeply sensual. Venus in one of the other earth signs would work well, too. Venus in Sagittarius or another fire sign creates sparks and excitement. Mars in an air sign brings excellent communication. A Sun in Leo can be sexually explosive.

Examples: Louisa May Alcott, Richard Crenna, Stalin

MARS IN GEMINI ♂ ♊

With this combination, your Sun and Mars form an aspect called an opposition, where the two planets are 180 degrees apart. They form a kind of fulcrum, balancing each other and yet never reaching agreement. Where Sagittarius seeks the big picture, the larger truth, Gemini collects the pieces of information that comprise that truth. Sagittarius does things in a large, sweeping way, Gemini is more interested in the quickest way. Both are impatient, but for different reasons. Sagittarius is future-oriented, Gemini is more of a here-and-now type. Both are people people, but their approaches differ. What one lacks, the other has.

The trick to navigating a natal opposition lies in learning to balance the demands of each planet involved. This can be particularly challenging in your profession and work and in regard to sex and your sexuality.

Professionally, for example, your Sagittarius Sun needs an enormous amount of freedom to pursue your job in the way that you believe it should be done. But if you're working for someone else who is controlling or has a vision that doesn't fit your vision, then you can count on there being friction. Your Gemini Mars, air to the Sagittarian fire, approaches everything intellectually. If the intellect is engaged and happy, if there are people around with whom to socialize, then life is good.

You do well in any profession that deals with communication, the arts, animals or animal rights, sports, medicine, travel, the law, higher education, the public, politics, astrology, metaphysics, or religion. You're good at spotting upcoming trends and have a knack for being in the right place at the right time. Your creative drive is strong and when you allow your intuition to guide you in this area, you rarely make a wrong move.

Your sexuality often puzzles you as much as it does your partners or potential partners. One moment you're the life of the party, chatting away a mile a minute, flirting with everyone who crosses your path. The next moment you're in a blue funk and all you want to do is go home. Blame the Gemini duality for that. Your sexuality depends on which of the Gemini twins is in charge on a given day: the twin who is full of life and curiosity or the bookish twin who just wants to be left alone.

Freedom is an issue for you in any relationship, even one that is uncommitted and based purely on sex. You need a lot of freedom, and not because you're headed off to spend time with another lover. You have causes, missions, and passions that must be tended. If your partner, committed or uncommitted, shares this part of your life, great. If not, well, that's okay, too. Chances are you share other commonalities and if you don't, the relationship won't last and you'll be on to other things, other relationships.

Life with you is rarely boring. When you find a partner who appreciates your diversity and innate optimism, then life is not just very good; it's the closest thing to paradise on earth.

Best Matches: Venus or Mars in Gemini or another air sign heightens communication and intellectual interests. Venus in Sagittarius or another fire sign spells passion, adventure, and independence. Sun in an air sign or fire sign works well, too.

Examples: Beethoven, Jim Morrison, Henri Toulouse-Lautrec

MARS IN CANCER ♂ ♋

Imagine Indiana Jones mixed up with stay-at-home witch Sandra Bullock in *Practical Magic*, and you have an inkling of what this combination is really about. Action and dynamic living are up against intuition, magic, and the cosmic carpet ride into the great beyond. And it's all inside *you*. To describe the combination as challenging doesn't say the half of it. Fire and water will never see eye to eye on anything. However, there are ways to use this energy to your advantage.

If you can approach everything you do from an intuitive level, life will flow more easily. You know you've got plenty of intuition, but usually you're so restless and impatient to get wherever you're going that you don't take the time to listen to your inner voice. The next time you walk in to a party, allow your intuition to precede you. Let it move and flow around the room, testing the atmosphere, getting a sense of the people. Then go where it goes. Don't fight it, just do it.

This process will save you time and grief in the long run and not just with sexual relationships and romances. Use it at work, in your personal life. You tend to be exceedingly blunt and sometimes it's best to just shut up and keep your thoughts to yourself. Your intuition will let you know when to speak and when to remain silent.

Sexually, things can get real strange for you. Your Sagittarius Sun insists on being free, nomadic, unfettered, and often irresponsible, but your Cancer Mars is a homebody who wants his or her own space, own house, pets, *things*, perhaps even a family. Your Sun enjoys sex within any context, but your Mars is more conventional, preferring sex with commitment. Somehow you need to find a satisfying bridge between these two extremes. Intuition, again, may be the answer.

If your intuition tells you to hop into bed with that attractive stranger with the soulful eyes, then by all means do so. But if it screams at you to back off, then you should listen—or you're sure to regret it later. You want someone with whom you can share your deepest feelings and thoughts. All too often, your Sagittarius Sun chooses the wrong types and your Mars just goes along with it. You have a strong nurturing instinct; this instinct is best served by developing your own creativity, intuition, home life, and vision, rather than by mothering a partner.

Perhaps, in the end, you really are looking for a partner who will nurture *you*, your relationship, your intimacy, and whatever you build together.

Best Matches: Venus in Cancer would be great, with immediate soul recognition. Venus in Scorpio or Pisces would be good, too. Venus in Sagittarius or another fire sign would work, although there might be issues about who is right. Mars in a water sign or the Sun in a fire sign would be just fine also.

Examples: Science-fiction writer Philip K. Dick (*Minority Report*, *Blade Runner*), Mary Martin, John F. Kennedy Jr.

MARS IN LEO ♂ ♌

As a double fire-sign combination, your life is about dynamic action, passion, drama, and creative drive. You have leadership ability, a fearless nature, and a determined will. You also have a rather large ego that demands constant stroking, applause, and recognition.

If you consider your job to be *just a job*, your ego can hurt you professionally. You always have the feeling that you're slated for greater things—certainly something greater than a regular nine-to-five job. This feeling creates inner resentment toward bosses and coworkers who aren't as ambitious as you are, but who may be higher in the company's scheme of things. Rather than nurturing your resentment, you're better off developing your creative talents in your free time or trying to find work in the creative field that interests you.

Professional possibilities for this combination run the gamut: the arts, business, publishing, travel, teaching, acting or public speaking, public relations, academia—anything that puts you squarely on center stage. You're great with people, who are attracted to your warm and generous spirit and the fire and passion with which you tackle just about everything in your life. You have a real soft spot in your heart for children, animals, and people who are (down on their luck), so at some point in your life you may work or volunteer in a profession related to these areas.

Your sexuality is passionate, erratic, unpredictable. Your Leo Mars has such a need to be recognized that you can be won by flattery and sometimes the people who win you don't have your best interests at heart. Fortunately, your Sagittarius Sun can spot a phony quickly, although your Leo Mars may not want to listen. And if the sex is good, it may take you a while to wake up to reality.

In any kind of relationship, you demand a lot of personal freedom, yet you can be possessive and jealous if your partner doesn't pay you the kind of attention you think you deserve. But in a relationship where you and your partner are in sync emotionally, spiritually, and physically, all your warmth, generosity, passion, and love blossom. In the right relationship, you're monogamous, sensual, and sexual, and you love having a partner and companion.

Best Matches: Venus in Leo, Sagittarius, or Aries causes sparks to fly. Mars in a fire sign is passionate, but you may experience periodic clashes of wills. Mars in an air sign would mitigate the clashes. The Sun in either a fire sign or an air sign would work, too.

Examples: William Blake, Bob Guccione, Ross MacDonald, Edna O'Brien, Augusto Pinochet, Frank Sinatra

MARS IN VIRGO♂

These two planets are 90 degrees apart, an aspect called a square. Squares tell a great deal about the challenges a soul chose before coming into life and with this combination, the basic challenge is the friction between your ego and overall personality, your life force, and your physical and sexual energy. But let's get specific.

Your raw potential is considerable and your talents, many and varied. You're a perfectionist who culls the smaller details, the nuances, and then connects them to create the larger picture. The larger picture at any given time may be something as huge as your life or a personal relationship or something as small as a particular creative project. Sometimes this process works in reverse: you already have the larger picture and you seek the details you need to bring that larger picture into reality.

Professionally, your options are practically infinite. Communication, the arts, acting, travel-related industries, academia, publishing, teaching, metaphysics, and public relations are all areas you would enjoy. Whatever you do, it should be something that provides you with a lot of personal freedom (Sagittarians hate to punch a clock) and opportunities to use both your left and right brain.

You're conscious of your health (or should be) and may be interested in nutrition and alternative treatments for common ailments. When you're stressed or feeling blue, the emotion may manifest itself as an upset stomach or an ache in your hips or perhaps strained muscles in your thighs. If you're not athletic, you should consider a regular exercise routine that helps you burn off the restless mental energy of Virgo and the nervous energy of your Sagittarius sun.

Sexually, you can be extremely picky about your partner even when your Sagittarius Sun is screaming, *Go for it and worry about the details later.* A special kind of chemistry has to exist before you get involved sexually with someone. It's difficult to define what that chemistry is, but you recognize it when you feel it. There are exceptions to this general rule, of course. Nothing is ever set in stone with a Sagittarian. Also, this combination is a double mutable, which means that you may change your mind from moment to moment.

Communication and common interests are vital to that special chemistry. There's a part of you that is deeply mystical and spiritual, and you need to be able to share this with any partner that you have. That doesn't mean this quality has to exist in every relationship you have, but it must be part of any intimate partnership for the relationship to endure.

Best Matches: Venus in Virgo or Sagittarius, Venus in an earth sign, Mars in an earth sign, Sun in a fire or earth sign.

Examples: Joan Didion, Paul Schaeffer, Ellen Burstyn, Kenny Loggins

MARS IN LIBRA♂︎♎︎

Fire and air. Just about perfect. Your physical and sexual energy feed right into your overall personality. These two planets are 60 degrees apart, forming an aspect called a sextile. Sextiles are considered to be points of ease that facilitate an exchange of energy between two planets. In everyday terms, it means you have seemingly endless reserves of energy and that your creative ideas usually find expression. You're forceful and determined about achieving your goals, especially your creative goals.

Relationships are also important to you; your energy finds its best expression with and through other people. You would do well in the law, public relations, any of the arts, counseling, mediation, academia, and publishing. If you have your natal chart, the house placement of Mars will describe the area of life where your physical and sexual energy is most likely to find its fullest expression.

If, for instance, it falls in the fifth house, then your creativity, sex life, and your children will be the focus of the energy. If it's in your third house, communication, siblings, travel and relatives will be the focus. In the tenth house, your focus would be on your career and profession. Simply look up the meanings of the houses in Chapter 2 to find the specific focus on your Mars energy.

You have many ideals and are able to communicate them through your creativity. You also try to live them in your daily life, through a balanced, judicious approach to everything you do. Balance and harmony, the very qualities that you seek to instill in your life, often elude you until you learn to balance yourself first. Try meditation, yoga, or a similar discipline to achieve balance.

Now, down to the nitty-gritty. A relationship that meets your emotional, spiritual, and physical criteria is vital to your happiness in life. As a romantic, you feel most alive when you're involved *and* in love and if great sex is a part of that package, so much the better. When you're younger, sex may be your biggest priority, but as you get into your late twenties (usually between the ages of 26 to 30), companionship and relationships become more important. Sometimes the Libra Mars placement indicates that marriage happens later in life and, given your freedom-loving Sagittarius Sun, this is a distinct possibility.

Once you find the relationship that fits your ideal, your life seems to unfold according to some larger design that you're aware of, but can't always see in its entirety. Sometimes sexual intimacy allows you to glimpse this larger picture and you may feel, then, that there's a hint of destiny about the way your future is unfolding.

Best Matches: Venus in Libra or another air sign or Mars in an air sign brings many friends and heightens communication; Venus in Sagittarius or another fire sign means passionate emotions and a dynamic relationship; Sun in a fire or air sign work well, too.

Examples: David Carradine, Thomas Carlyle, Nancy Mitford, Jonathan Swift, Keifer Sutherland, Charles de Gaulle, Jeff Bridges

MARS IN SCORPIO ♂♏

The good news about this combination is that it provides you with an intense curiosity that compels you to delve deeply into whatever you do. The challenge is that fire and water don't see eye to eye on much of anything. However, if you can use your piercing intuition and insight to serve the Sagittarian need for the larger picture, then you'll be well on your way to mastering the energy of this combination.

Your intuition is one of your strongest assets and it allows you to amass information without connecting all the little dots, something that no doubt appeals to your restless Sagittarius Sun. You're able to assess strangers almost instantly. When you enter an unfamiliar situation your psychic antennae work endlessly, testing the waters, gathering information. This process happens at the speed of light and allows you to make quick decisions about anything.

Professionally, you have a pretty clear idea about your strengths and how you would like to apply them. Public relations, medicine, travel, surgery, publishing, communication, metaphysics, recycling, trust law: any of these professions would suit you. However, the more independent you are in your work and profession, the happier you are. With your intuition and foresight, you should be able to spot upcoming trends and create a marketing niche for yourself.

Scorpio is always associated with sex, and this association is accurate, as far as it goes. But it isn't the full picture. Scorpio Mars doesn't have sex just to have sex. There are always deeper motives, unconscious urges and needs at work. Despite the independence and cavalier attitude of your Sagittarius Sun, you want to be understood by your partner. Deeply understood. A soul understanding. Some of your most intimate relationships, in fact, will be with past-life connections, people you recognize instantly.

You're passionate by nature and enjoy sex, but aren't necessarily a romantic as, say, any combination with Libra is. Your Sagittarius Sun is direct about sexual matters (and everything else), but your Scorpio Mars is far more circumspect and secretive. Your sexual needs are most likely expressed through a kind of smoldering sensuality that settles in your eyes and in the movements of your body.

In the right relationship, at the right time in your life, your capacity for intimacy burgeons and you suddenly realize this entire sex-and-romance business isn't nearly as difficult as it once seemed.

Best Matches: Venus in Scorpio or Sagittarius are the people with whom you experience sexual fireworks and the deepest understanding. Mars in a water sign works well, too, as long as the person's Sun is in a fire sign.

Examples: Eugene Ionesco, Chuck Mangione, William F. Buckley, Bruce Lee, George Santayana, Dionne Warwick

MARS IN SAGITTARIUS ♂ ♐

You enter a room and conversation stops. Eyes turn your way. You don't even have to do anything for this to happen. It's called *presence*, a mysterious quality that celebrities attempt to cultivate, but the bottom line is that you either have it or you don't. And you have it in abundance.

In this double fire combination, the Sun and Mars are conjunct, a powerful aspect in which two planets occupy the same sign. Conjunctions accentuate and heighten the qualities of the sign. Turn back and read the description of the Sagittarius Sun. Now double all those qualities, good and bad, and you have some idea of what this entails.

Your personal quest for the bigger picture and the larger truth is sure to involve a lot of traveling. The travel can be physical or mental, emotional or spiritual, or some combination, but one way or another, your search takes you into strange, uncharted places, mysterious countries of the mind or the globe. You may not always be conscious of what you're looking for, but you can't ignore the compelling urge to search, well, for *something*.

With this combination, there is usually some kind of contact with foreign countries and people or a creative expression that involves Sagittarian themes. Sometimes you become the vehicle through which larger forces work. Elian Gonzalez is that kind of double Sagittarian. He fled Cuba with his mother in a boat filled with refugees, the boat sank, and he was the sole survivor, allegedly aided by a pod of dolphins that kept him afloat. When his father left Cuba to come to Miami to retrieve his son, Elian's plight polarized Miami's Latino community and caused Janet Reno, then attorney general, to order police to storm his cousin's house and seize the boy.

You're incredibly comfortable in your own skin and absolutely at home with your sexuality. Your sexual standards will never conform to those of society, but that doesn't bother you at all. You're frank and completely honest about your sexual needs and patterns and if other people are disturbed by that, you dismiss them without a second thought. You're looking for someone who is as fearless as you are, who thirsts for the same kind of knowledge and isn't put off by surprises or sudden changes in plans. You are, after all, a double mutable sign as well as double fire, and that means you're flexible enough to go with the flow, whatever that may be. And that ability is your greatest strength.

Best Matches: Here's another no-brainer. Venus in Sagittarius or another fire sign. That not only spells chemistry, it's earth-shaking, explosive, addictive. Venus or Mars in an air sign isn't too shabby, either, in that communication would be exceptionally smooth. Sun in a fire sign or air sign.

Examples: Joe DiMaggio, Teri Garr, Richard Leakey, G. Gordon Liddy, Mark Twain, Patty Duke, Elian Gonzalez.

MARS IN CAPRICORN ♂ ♑

Fire. Earth. You don't expect them to be particularly agreeable. Yet when channeled in the right way, this combination produces some amazing people. Uri Geller. Steven Spielberg. Christina Aguilera. And that's just for starters.

The secret seems to lie in the Capricorn Mars ability to build and it doesn't matter whether you're building a novel, a screenplay, an empire or a career. The other part of the equation lies in the ability of the Sagittarius Sun to see the larger scope of whatever you're doing. So when you build, you do so within the context of a larger goal or picture. Granted, this isn't a conscious process all of the time. It's not as if you're sitting around, shuffling pieces to see where they fit and trying to figure out whether to make *ET* first or *Schindler's List*. You're too busy living and doing and creating. These two planets work together in a *process*.

Your Sagittarius Sun makes you a dynamo of activity. But with your Capricorn Mars, it's not senseless activity, rushing here and there just to keep moving. Capricorn grounds everything you do and makes the results practical. You can achieve just about anything you set your sights on in any field you choose. You have the inner strength and fortitude to go the long haul, and you know how to plan and strategize. Your determination to achieve attracts people who support what you do and attracts situations and opportunities that allow you to test and refine your techniques.

All of this energy is great for your professional life, but there can be hell to pay in your personal life. Your freedom-loving Sagittarius Sun keeps you playing the field, so you probably won't settle down at a young age. Or, if you do settle, the partnership may not endure the vast inner changes that you experience. Your partnerships at any age are unlikely to be traditional, although this tendency is softened somewhat because Capricorn Mars needs tradition and parameters. As you get older, the energies of these two planets may propel you into new spiritual dimensions and it is important that your partner, if you have one, be a part of the journey.

A lot of passion is inherent to Sagittarius and even to Capricorn Mars, but your sexual passion is often mixed up with your creative passion until the two become indistinguishable. You may have a creative sex life or a sexy creative life or some amalgam of the two.

Best Matches: Venus in Capricorn or Sagittarius, Venus in a fire sign or earth sign, Mars in an earth sign, Sun in a fire sign or earth sign.

Examples: Steven Spielberg, Uri Geller, Samuel L. Jackson, Walt Disney, Christina Aguilera, Woody Allen, Ed Harris, Rex Stout, Christina Onassis

MARS IN AQUARIUS ♂ ≈

These two signs get along amazingly well. They form an angle to each other known as a sextile, an aspect that indicates ease and an easy exchange of energy. Both signs have foresight and vision, and both are true freedom lovers. Sagittarius is more flexible than Aquarius, more willing to adapt to change, but Aquarius is more willing to take on responsibility, especially when that responsibility concerns humanitarian causes.

You're a talented individual with some firm opinions about yourself, how the world works, and your place in it. You're an individualist who has little use for established paradigms and conventions. Regardless of what you do professionally, you're happiest when you have an inordinate amount of freedom to pursue your passions and to come and go as you please. You can spot upcoming trends easily and usually can figure out some way to incorporate these trends in your work.

Your friends and group associations are important to you and many of them support the same causes and ideals that you do. The beautiful quality to this combination is that you refuse to see anything as an obstacle. Where another person may see an insurmountable wall and back down, you see a transparent veil and simply push it aside and walk through to wherever you're bound. You believe that anything can be overcome with equal parts mind, willpower, and action.

Sexually, you're nearly as unconventional as the double Sagittarius combination. You call your own shots, create your own parameters, define your own boundaries and bottom lines. Early on in life you probably have some idea of what you want to do with the time you're allotted on the planet and since you can't know that exact number of years, you intend to make use of every second.

When you get involved in a relationship, you usually do so without any preconceived notions of where it's going. You're fully in the now. Yes, you have plans, but those plans don't necessarily include a partner. If and when a partner enters the picture, you're direct about your needs and expectations, sexual and otherwise, and if your partner has problems with any of it, well, adios and good luck, and you're on to the next adventure. You're not afraid to spend your life alone, if that's how things pan out. You can survive anywhere.

In a committed relationship, you give freely and deeply of yourself and enjoy the intimacy of companionship. When you give your heart, you're also giving your soul. But few relationships in your life will add up to your entire life; that is, you don't live just to love and be in love and have great sex. You live creatively, to fulfill your potential.

Best Matches: Venus in Aquarius or Sagittarius energizes the relationship and brings free-flowing communication; Venus or Mars in a fire or air sign or the Sun in fire or air also work well.

Examples: Dave Brubeck, Phil Donahue, Ridley Scott, Stone Phillips, Charles Schultz, Ben Stiller

MARS IN PISCES ♂ ♓

Fire and water. You don't have to be a physicist to figure out what happens when these two elements get together. All too often, your impulse toward action may seem to be squelched by your impulse to just kick back and daydream. This isn't implying laziness—you'll never be lazy with a Sagittarius Sun—but it does indicate a vast and sometimes incomprehensible imagination. That said, this is a double mutable combination, so your ability to adapt to any situation or circumstance is one of your primary assets and the foundation of your survival instincts.

Any combination that involves Pisces suggests profound intuition, insight, spirituality, and imagination. It also suggests some physical traits—large, compelling eyes, feet that are beautifully formed or unusual in some way, and either a tendency to gain weight or an innate grace in body movements.

You're easily hurt, and sometimes take things personally that aren't intended that way, but your Sagittarius Sun refuses to acknowledge it. You're sensitive to your environment and are something of a psychic sponge, absorbing the moods and feelings of the people around you. This "psychic absorption" is just one of the reasons you should associate with positive, upbeat people. The other reason is that the more optimism you have in your life—liberally supplied by your Sagittarius Sun—the healthier and happier you are.

In whatever you do professionally, your imagination allows you to tap into the collective mind for inspiration and ideas that your energetic Sagittarius Sun then carries out into the larger world. Whether the profession is in sports, finances, entertainment and the arts, politics, or music, you have a wonderful grasp of the higher forces and the larger picture.

The clash between Sagittarius and Pisces is most noticeable in your sexuality and in your love life. Sagittarius craves freedom and no commitments, but Pisces wants a soul union. Sadge can be enormously irresponsible and Pisces, very moody. When you put these two qualities together, the result is someone who is tough to live with and even tougher to get to know. Pisces can be celibate for long periods of time, but Sagittarius has a powerful sex drive. Finding the middle ground is your biggest challenge.

One possibility lies in a partner whose creative interests, talents, and spiritual beliefs are similar to yours. In a sexual or committed relationship founded on creative and spiritual similarities, the problematic issues become less important. You grow into each other's lives and everything else unfolds quite naturally from that.

As with most combinations that involve Pisces, always be aware that you can fall into the martyr/savior syndrome in matters of the heart. Go into any relationship with the full awareness that you can't change the other person. Either love them as they are—or look elsewhere.

Best Matches: Venus in Pisces, Cancer, Scorpio brings great intuitive awareness of each other's needs. Venus in Sagittarius or Mars in a fire sign means passion and a dynamic relationship. The Sun in a water or fire sign also works.

Examples: Chris Evert-Lloyd, John Paul Getty, Liv Ullmann, Francisco Franco, Tom Hayden, John Milton, Tina Turner

SENSE-MEMORY EXERCISE FOR SUN IN SAGITTARIUS

Mars represents our physical senses. Most of us have at least one sense that is stronger than the others or provides information more quickly about our physical environment. Perhaps your sense of touch is extraordinary. Maybe your sight is exceptionally powerful. Your strongest sense, whatever it is, provides you with immediate and reliable information about yourself or others, your environment, and your personal world.

In the space below, describe an instance where one of your physical senses played a vital role. This experience can be positive or negative or anything in between. Be detailed and specific.

The incident or situation you've just described pertains to the second question you asked in the inventory at the beginning of part two. If the connection isn't immediately apparent, look for the metaphor.

A middle-aged woman with her Sun in Sagittarius had such a deep fear of flying that for years she had taken a train from Florida to New York to visit her family. Then there was a family emergency that necessitated her taking a plane to New York. She described the plane trip—all the sights, sounds, tastes—everything that constituted her fear and its impact on her senses. Her second question was whether she should marry or just live with the man she was seeing.

From the description she'd written, she realized that it didn't matter whether she lived with or married the man. It was commitment that she feared (sounds like a typical Sadge!), and her fear stood between them. She decided that she had to overcome her fear (like the fear of flying) for the relationship to evolve any further.

12

Sun in Capricorn ☉♑

THE ACHIEVER
Cardinal Earth

"I'm not as tough as I seem."

Strengths: Singular focus, pragmatic, efficient, achievement-oriented, goal-oriented, ambitious, brings the abstract down to earth

Weaknesses: Set in ways, can be emotionally cold and detached, too serious at times, ambition can take over, hungry for power, materialistic, worries a lot, seeks status

Sexual Blueprint: I play for keeps.

Other people often find you mysterious. They regard you as something of an enigma. Truth is, much of the time you're an enigma to yourself. You puzzle over your drive, your stamina, and your relentless need to achieve.

For some of you, the achiever shows up early in life. You're the kid on the block who organizes the neighborhood lemonade stand, strategizes about how to boost sales, organizes and delegates the activities—and then goes on to make a tidy little profit. As you get older, the lemonade stand becomes a college degree, a doctorate, a career as a writer, singer, or actor, building a business, becoming a CEO, the head of the FBI (Hoover), or becoming a legend (Humphrey Bogart). You get the idea. Whatever you are building in your life, you do it patiently, with careful planning. You rarely veer from the path you've set except in response to a sudden, unexpected event or situation. Then you're forced to take detours, but even your detours have purpose.

You aren't the type to get involved in casual affairs. You're much too traditional in that regard and besides, you don't like wasting time. You have a clear sense of what you're looking for in a partner and if you don't see those qualities quickly, that's it for you. When you go wrong in your choice of partners, it's usually because you've been seduced by someone's status or wealth.

SUN IN CAPRICORN AND . . .

MARS IN ARIES ♂♈

There's no love lost between fire and earth. Capricorn and Aries form a 90-degree angle to each other, an aspect called a square that creates tension and brings particular qualities or issues into stark focus. However, Aries and Capricorn are both cardinal signs, so they use energy in a singular, focused way. Aries gives you the get-up-and-go and the passion to pursue what you want in life. But it also laughs at your traditional values and sends you straight into trouble where sex and romance are concerned.

It's not that your judgment in this area is flawed, only that you are often so impatient about cutting to the chase that you end up with sexual partners who are unsuited to your temperament. They may be rash and reckless, inconsiderate and bossy—and really, bottom line, who needs it? You'll find that when you allow your Sun sign to lead you in terms of sex and romance—i.e., when you control your impulses—things actually turn out much better.

In your work or profession, this combination can manifest itself in several ways. You may start things that you don't finish because you lose interest. You may burn the candle at both ends, sacrificing sleep, exercise, and proper nutrition until you collapse. Or, if you're smart, you make sure that you want to take on a project before you actually do it and then you fulfill your obligations even if you reach the point where the project no longer interests you. This same process should prevail in your relationships, but it may take considerably more practice to get to that point.

In a committed relationship—and that's the Capricorn Sun ideal—your sexuality explodes to life. You can't get enough of your partner's body, mind, or spirit. Then, just as abruptly and inexplicably, you detach and turn your focus back to your ambitions, your career, your materialism. Where's the middle ground? What's the bridge between one extreme and the other? As one person with this combination expressed it, *Both sides are me and I'm learning to merge them.*

Your creativity is one way to merge the two energies successfully, and if you share that area with a partner, so much the better. Sometimes, the extremes in any combination are there to force us to pay attention, to resolve some issue that we've agreed to tackle this time around. That may be what the Capricorn Sun and Aries Mars are really about.

Best Matches: Venus in Aries creates sexual fireworks, but may also bring certain issues to the surface, namely independence— who has it, who doesn't, and who wants it. A better match would be Venus in an earth sign like sensual Taurus or a Mars or Sun in Taurus.

Examples: Stephen Hawking, Carl Sandburg, Rod Serling

MARS IN TAURUS♂♉

These two earth signs complement each other nicely. They form an angle known as a trine, an aspect that enhances self-expression. The Taurus Mars lightens the personality of the usually far-too-serious Capricorn and confers a sensuality that Capricorn usually doesn't have.

You really are relentless in the pursuit of whatever you hope to achieve, and even though you don't work quickly, you are always thorough and you plan details with great care and precision. Your self-expression tends toward pragmatism in all things—from your profession and career to your creativity to your love life, and even to the way you raise your children. You're self-reliant, independent, and willing to go the extra mile to make sure the job is done well.

This combination isn't known for its passion. However, Taurus Mars is inherently sensual, so there's an element of sensuality in all that you do. If you're an outdoors type, which many earth combinations are, then you don't just go hiking. You hike with your senses wide open, aware of the texture of the air, the blueness of the sky, the solidity of the ground under your feet, the wildlife that breathes around you. You bring this same attentive quality to your relationships.

You're looking for a partner who is as sensual, grounded, and practical as you are. Despite your double earth combination and its emphasis on practicality, there's a bit of the mystic in you who explores cosmic questions. It would be great if your partner had some of that, too. Since you're reserved around other people unless you know them well, potential partners sometimes mistake you for an ice queen. They can be either intrigued or put off by your reserve. Those who are intrigued figure they'll crack the ice; those who are put off aren't worth your time.

The interesting thing is that it doesn't take all that much to crack the ice. Behind that reserved facade beats the heart of a sensualist with an endless reservoir of love, affection, and loyalty for the right person. Your Capricorn Sun isn't interested in casual affairs, but your Taurus Mars definitely goes in that direction, particularly when you're younger. At various points in your life, your Capricorn Sun will dominate your sexuality and at other times your Taurus Mars will be in charge. Of course, if you work with these energies consciously, *you* will be in charge.

Best Matches: Another no-brainer: look for someone whose Venus is in Capricorn or Taurus. However, there are some other excellent combinations as well: Venus or Mars in passionate Scorpio or sensitive Cancer, or a Sun in Taurus.

Examples: Muhammad Ali, J. Edgar Hoover, Robert Bly, Tiger Woods, Isaac Newton

MARS IN GEMINI ♂ ♊

Air and earth don't have any special issues with each other in the astrological scheme of things, but they aren't the coziest of couples, either. However, Gemini is the consummate communicator and provides you with everything you need to lighten up your approach to life, to be witty and fun-loving.

You're physically restless and certainly need some sort of exercise outlet to burn off that energy. Otherwise, you may stay awake nights, counting sheep, fretting, and wondering if you should pop one of those sleeping pills you keep in the medicine cabinet.

It's probably a good idea if you have a hobby or even several hobbies that distract you from your intense ambition and need to succeed. Maybe you enjoy writing or doing art or photography in your spare time. Perhaps you're into animals or collect antiques or rare books. Whatever your love, nurture it and develop it; eventually, you may forget about your aspirations for that CEO spot and open your own rare books store or animal training business. You would do very well with your own business, particularly if it's oriented toward contact with the public.

Your have excellent and varied creative talents and can attain whatever you reach for, in whatever profession you choose. Thanks to the versatility of Gemini, you may have more than one profession over the course of your life or could have several simultaneous professions. Your Capricorn Sun will have to be dragged kicking and screaming off a predetermined path to do this, but once you do it, you find that you like the diversity.

Sexually, you aren't as traditional as a double Capricorn. Casual affairs aren't forbidden in your scheme of things. They actually may be your preference at times when you don't want to make an emotional investment in a relationship, but enjoy intimacy with a particular partner. You're attracted to people who have lively, curious minds and who communicate well and quickly. You like to be seduced and courted in typically Gemini ways—through ideas, books, communication and writing. The more creative the seduction is, the more you like it. One Capricorn woman with a Gemini Mars received e-mail love poems from her partner while they were dating and before sex had entered the picture. These poems showed a sensitive side of him that she hadn't seen before and convinced her he was someone with whom she wanted to get emotionally involved.

Best Matches: Venus in Gemini, Libra, or Aquarius would

create mental sparks and excellent communication. Mars in any of the air signs would mean great intellectual rapport. Venus in Sagittarius or Leo would create sexual chemistry.

Examples: Martin Luther King, A.A. Milne, Terry Moore

MARS IN CANCER ♂ ♋

Sun in Capricorn and Mars in Cancer form an opposition to each other, an aspect of 180 degrees that creates a delicate fulcrum of tension between your self-expression and your physical and sexual energy. The house placements of both the Sun and Mars are important in this equation, so make sure you check your natal chart and read the house placement descriptions in Chapter 2.

However, despite the opposition, this combination works to your advantage in several ways. Cancer, a water sign, softens your Capricorn ambitions, makes you less, well, relentless, and also confers a deep intuition. Since water and earth nurture and sustain each other, the energies of the two planets have great potential for working in sync.

You do best in a home-based business. It may be a creative enterprise or provide a service or be strictly business related. Whatever it is, it provides the context in which you use your organizational skills in tandem with your intuitive abilities. Left-brain/right-brain. Whatever profession you're in, you're there because it satisfies some deep inner blueprint for happiness and not just because it pays you well. How does the saying go? Do what you love and prosperity follows? The adage fits this combination.

It's doubtful that casual affairs interest you. You're looking for a partner who feels home and family are important, who is perceptive and supportive of what you do, and whose sexuality is similar to your own. You're less materialistic than other combinations with Capricorn, less impressed by status and success and the trappings of American life. You like comfort, yes, but you don't sell out. You don't prostitute yourself for money or status.

You approach sex and relationships intuitively. If it feels right, then in your mind, it *is* right. As a double cardinal combination, you probably are frank about what you're looking for sexually and in a relationship. You won't tolerate dishonesty or duplicity and if you encounter it in a committed relationship, you break things off without regret and simply move on. You're a loyal and loving partner, and expect the same in return.

Best Matches: Venus in Cancer works beautifully, giving you an intuitive and emotional connection with a partner. Venus or Mars in Taurus is more sensual. With a Venus in Capricorn, you and your partner would see eye to eye on most of your professional concerns. A Sun in Cancer or Capricorn would work well, too.

Examples: Diane Keaton, Naomi Judd, David Lynch, Nostradamus

MARS IN LEO♂♌

Earth and fire. There's no love lost between these two and the combination requires a constant fine-tuning before you can utilize the energies to your benefit. But the Leo Mars adds warmth, generosity, and passion to your personality and pushes you out into public.

You have a need to be recognized for your talents and achievements. But your Capricorn Sun negates some of Leo's constant need for applause and center stage, and allows you to use your ease before the public in a way that benefits you professionally and personally. With your drive, ambition and talent for self-expression, the sky literally is the limit for you professionally. Leo is the sign of actors and actresses, so if you have any dramatic talent at all, it's worth nurturing. But you would do well in any communication profession.

Your sexuality is something you grow into as you age. You're comfortable enough with it, but there's always a little kid inside of you who wants more affection, more words of praise, more appreciation, more, more, more. And it's this part of you that is easy to seduce with shows of affection that may not have anything to do with how the other person really feels about you. When you're being seduced in this way, your Capricorn Sun is screaming that you're being scammed, that you had better wake up and get real. Whether you listen or not depends on the depth of your need for applause.

In a relationship where your partner truly cares for *you* rather than the persona you project, your passion is a primal force and your capacity for intimacy rarely wanes. Even when your focus is on your career or ambitions, you maintain a steadfast loyalty to what you and your partner have built together.

You prefer monogamous relationships—besides, who has time to juggle several simultaneous relationships?—and despite the conservative nature of your Capricorn Sun, love being swept off your feet. You enjoy the whirlwind of romance, the essential mystery. You can be jealous and possessive, particularly if you feel you aren't getting the attention and love you so justly deserve, and those qualities will destroy a relationship faster than almost anything else. Trust may be something that you have to learn.

Your natural flamboyance can work with you or against you, depending on other factors in your natal chart. Make sure that you check the house placements for both your Sun and your Mars. These placements describe the areas of your life in which these two energies are most likely to manifest themselves.

You have a powerful will and sooner or later learn that when you bring the full force of your will to your career or relationship or to whatever you're doing, your inner beliefs shift and your experiences reflect that.

Best Matches: Venus in Leo or another fire sign is passionate. Venus in Capricorn or an earth sign translates as practical. Mars or the Sun in a fire sign, especially if it's Aries, can create conflicts of will.

Examples: Robert Duvall, Odetta, Yves St. Laurent, Ogden Nash, Robert Mitchum

MARS IN VIRGO♂♍

These two fit together like the proverbial foot and shoe. Double earth. Highly practical, efficient, and goal-oriented. Also, there's a part of you intrigued by mysterious and mystical experiences and people. It seems paradoxical for a double earth sign, but there you have it.

You're something of a perfectionist, especially when it comes to your work. You need to have all the small details just so. This tendency can manifest itself as a finely tuned discrimination or can just be flat-out picky. And there *is* a difference. When your perfectionism is exhibited as pickiness, someone else is usually on the receiving end. Be critical of others often enough and you alienate the very people who might otherwise support your endeavors.

You're mentally quick, with an enviable ability to recall details, and have a keen, dry wit. You're a relentless worker who rarely flinches when given additional responsibilities and isn't afraid to go the extra mile required to get any job done. You don't take shortcuts and may not even know the meaning of the word. Laziness isn't part of your lexicon. Professionally, you do well in the arts and entertainment, in the communication field, in service-oriented work, or in working with the elderly. Medicine or scientific research are also good choices. Whatever you do, your hallmark is practicality. You're always asking how you can translate something into a form that other people can use.

You're looking for a partner who complements your talents, plans as well as you do, is goal-oriented, and isn't the least bit timid about standing up to your sometimes formidable personality. Casual affairs aren't your thing. You don't mind uncommitted relationships, but prefer that sex evolves from the relationship rather than the other way around. Your partner should take care of him- or herself physically. We're not talking about an Olympic athlete here or even a jock. Your partner should simply be aware of his or her health and maintain it through nutrition, exercise, and all the other things the experts say lead to a long, healthy life.

In the absence of this kind of partner, you date but keep your options open. Celibacy doesn't bother you, especially when your sexual and physical energy is being poured into your career. Seduction for you begins with the intellect, through communication and joint creative endeavors. In a committed relationship, you value communication above almost everything else and sex becomes one way of communicating.

Best Matches: Venus in an earth sign, any earth sign. But for sensuality, pick Venus or Mars in Taurus. Venus or Mars in a water sign would be a good fit, and so would a Sun in an earth or water sign.

Examples: Tim Matheson, John Carpenter, Ted Danson, Shari Lewis, Sissy Spacek

MARS IN LIBRA ♂ ♎

This double cardinal combination is a powerhouse of energy. You're focused, often singular in your vision, and you're oriented toward people and relationships. Your Sun and Mars form a 90-degree angle to each other called a square, an aspect that creates friction and resistance. Quite often, the square acts as a springboard for achievement, pushing you ever forward.

Your artistic inclinations showed up early in your life. You may have been the kid in your neighborhood who played the flute or sketched incredible drawings of animals or people. You enjoy art, museums, concerts, films. You may have an artistic or musical talent that you've nurtured and have turned into a professional asset. You're a social creature, fascinated by relationships—being involved in them, studying them, working with them. You have excellent insight into other people and easily spot the imbalances in their lives.

When you attempt to turn this insight on your own life, the task is more difficult. A square with Mars can result in contention, so you may experience periods where your self-expression conflicts with your sexuality in some way. You really do seek harmony and balance in your own life and when things are on track, you know exactly how to achieve it. The trick is to recall this sense of balance when chaos encroaches on you.

In relationships, your focus is on maintaining a fine balance between your needs and those of your partner. All too often, Mars in Libra bends like a straw to accommodate everyone else's needs. This tendency is diminished by your Sun in Capricorn, which doesn't bend easily for anyone, but the propensity exists, so be aware of it. You're sexuality has high and low cycles that depend to a large extent on what else is going on in your life. If you're feeling comfortable with your life, your sexual desires are usually heightened and sex is just one of the ways in which you and your partner communicate. If you're in a low cycle, then sex probably isn't very high on your list of priorities.

There's an element of duplicity with the Libra Mars that results from a reluctance to hurt anyone's feelings. In this scenario, you start up another relationship before you end the one you're in. The best way to remedy this tendency is to imagine yourself in the other person's shoes. If you were the person being dumped, wouldn't you prefer to know it right up front?

Best Matches: Venus in Libra or another air sign, Mars in an air sign. Venus in Capricorn or another earth sign, the Sun in an earth sign.

Examples: Elvis Presley, Mary Tyler Moore, Andrew Johnson, Johannes Kepler

MARS IN SCORPIO ♂ ♏

An intriguing combination. Here, the Sun and Mars are 60 degrees apart, forming an aspect called a sextile that facilitates a smooth exchange of energy. You have ambition, drive, stamina, and profound insight into the workings of the world, people, and yourself. You're curious about what makes people tick and use your creativity to explore that curiosity. And then, using the strengths of your Capricorn Sun, you build something around what you have discovered. Or you build it as you're discovering.

Take J.R.R. Tolkien. Story has it that the hobbits were born when he began telling one of his children bedtime tales. But always, there was something much deeper going on. Through the trilogy of *Lord of the Rings*, Tolkien explored large themes—good versus evil, magic, love, the transition from one world order to another, and the dynamics of the hero's quest. True to the nature of this Sun-Mars combination, Tolkien dug deep within himself and his own experiences for the material in the trilogy.

Regardless of what your work or profession is, you don't do anything halfway. When you set out to achieve a particular goal or ambition, you do so with intense focus and insight and refuse to settle for easy answers. Your insight and intuition often border on prescience. Take a look at the house placement of Mars in your natal chart. This will tell you in what area of your life your prescience is strongest. If your Mars is in the fifth house, for example, then your prescience (and your sexual and physical energy) are focused in the area of creativity, children, and pleasurable sexual experiences. Mel Gibson, who has this combination, with Mars in Scorpio in the fifth house, is father to seven children, was voted sexiest man alive, and won an Oscar as best director for *Braveheart*. His Capricorn Sun is in the sixth house of daily health and work, indicating that the creative drive of his Mars is expressed in his daily life.

You aren't the type for casual affairs. You're looking for genuine commitment, a genuine partner, and when you find such a person, you're unerringly faithful and loving. You can be jealous and possessive, though, and if left unchecked, this trait can be your undoing. Try to channel those feelings into your creative life.

Best Matches: Venus in Scorpio spells sexual explosions. Venus or Mars in Capricorn will work, too, and so will Venus, Mars, or the Sun in a water or earth sign.

Examples: J.R.R. Tolkien, Mel Gibson, Albert Schweitzer, Jon Voight, Henry Miller, Barry Goldwater

MARS IN SAGITTARIUS ♂ ♐

This combination can be difficult because the natural exuberance of Mars in Sagittarius is often squelched by the more serious-minded Capricorn Sun. Or, in a less likely scenario, Capricorn shirks its responsibilities and, following the Sagittarian energy, shucks all responsibility and takes off for parts unknown.

The best way to meld these two energies is to merge your ambition with some type of cause or mission or to pour it into your creativity. One way or another, Sagittarian themes will play a big part: travel, foreign countries and foreign-born individuals, publishing, spirituality, metaphysics, the higher mind, education, academia.

A major benefit of this combination is that with any goal you set, you're able to glimpse the larger picture of what you're trying to achieve. A certain prescience that often accompanies Sagittarius Mars may crop up at various points in your life. It may manifest itself as an intuitive sense about some future event or situation, a face that floats before your eyes as you're falling asleep, or a gut feeling that is hard to ignore. Sometimes you glimpse probabilities, which is a useful creative talent as well as a means of gathering information.

Your sexuality may not feel very comfortable to you at times. Your more serious and traditional Capricorn Sun usually doesn't indulge in casual affairs or one-night stands, but your Sagittarius Mars doesn't recognize any traditions or conventions. Capricorn likes parameters and structure, the very thing Sagittarius abhors. Since these two planets are both a part of your sexual blueprint, your love life may fluctuate wildly from one extreme to another or you may find a happy medium somewhere in the vastness between them.

Or it could be that you and Janis Joplin have more in common than you realize. Joplin found a certain structure through her musical creativity and her entertainment skills and was, by all accounts, a relentless worker even when she was stoned. But sexually, she didn't recognize any boundaries. She did what she wanted, when she wanted, and ultimately paid the price through an overdose of heroin. This doesn't mean that you're going to overdose or die young, but it does indicate that you have the same tendency toward extremes.

With this combination, passion and ambition are doled out in equal doses. Use both to achieve your potential, and don't become a slave to either one.

Best Matches: Venus in Sagittarius or another fire sign, Mars or Venus in an earth sign, the Sun in an earth sign.

Examples: Janis Joplin, Faye Dunaway, Rudyard Kipling, Val Kilmer, William Peter Blatty

MARS IN CAPRICORN♂♑

When your Mars and your Sun are in the same sign, it's known as a conjunction, an aspect that intensifies the qualities of the sign. It shouldn't be any surprise, then, that this combination is one of the most ambitious and focused.

You were probably aware of what you wanted to do by the time you hit kindergarten, and didn't waste time setting your course for the achievement of that goal. Even if you have distractions and minor detours along the way, you rarely lose sight of the endpoint.

Check your natal chart to find out the houses in which your Sun and Mars are placed. If you, like Henri Matisse and Sebastian Junger (*The Perfect Storm*) have the Sun and Mars in Capricorn in the fifth house, then you had better get busy creating something because you've got a lot of creative energy in your favor. Louis Pasteur had his Sun, Mars, and four other planets in Capricorn in the third house. His singular, focused path to success was written in his chart from the moment he drew his first breath.

Any time you have a concentration of planets in one sign and one house, the energy is so highly focused that you are compelled to act in accordance with what the planets and the house represent.

Sexually, you're as ambitious as you are in your career. Sounds odd, but once you set your sights on a particular person or relationship, you're relentless in your pursuit of what you want. This combination can be enormously controlling, though not in the same way that a combination with Scorpio can be and not for the same reasons. But controlling nonetheless, and this makes it difficult for you to sustain a committed relationship. There are double Capricorns who do it successfully, but it takes conscious awareness and work.

In a committed relationship, you seek a partner who is supportive of what you do (often sublimating his or her own ambitions for yours), and who is monogamous, dedicated, and loving. You expect to give the same things in return and when you actually do, things work great. But sooner or later, something else enters the picture (usually ambition) and your promises and expectations are delayed, detoured, or vanish altogether.

Even so, awareness of personality patterns and a willingness to work with them can help any committed relationship succeed.

Best Matches: You would think Venus in Capricorn would be best, but it might be the energy that tips the scale too far into Capricorn's domain. Better to look for a Venus in Taurus, a more sensual match, or even Venus, Mars, or the Sun in a water sign— Pisces or Cancer being the favorites.

Examples: In terms of achievement, this is an impressive group and a rather large group. In addition to Henri Matisse, Louis Pasteur, and Sebastian Junger, there are Nicolas Cage, Marlene Dietrich, Diane Von Fustenberg, Alan Watts, Jimmy Buffet, and dolphin researcher John Lilly

MARS IN AQUARIUS ♂ ♒

Earth and air. Not much going on here either way, no friction, no boost. Maybe just indifference.

But when you look a little deeper, this combination has some fascinating things in its favor. The energy allows you to apply your visionary qualities in a focused, directed way, along a single career path or toward a particular goal or dream. The Aquarius part of the equation also brings in people who support your dream or who are helpful in some way. You attract these individuals through your talent, personality, and drive.

You definitely march to a different drummer and this trait was apparent from the time you were young. You live according to your own rules and beliefs, and at times this is sure to drive your traditional Capricorn Sun half crazy. On good days, when you feel plugged in to the universal mind or the collective soup of humanity or whatever you want to call it, you can shut your eyes, take a few deep breaths, and off you go, tripping the light fantastic. And what you bring back from these magnificent forays are ideas, visions, glimpses of other worlds, perhaps, and they become the fodder for your creative mind.

Professionally, you do best in a career where you are free to pursue your ideals in a creative, innovative way. You don't need a boss breathing down your neck, you don't need parameters, boundaries, rules or restrictions. You have discipline enough to work independently and that's the way you like it. That's the environment in which you flourish.

Aquarius isn't a sign that is usually associated with sexuality, or even sensuality. Everything is intellect. Even in combination with earthy Capricorn, sexuality isn't the first thing you think of. As strange as it sounds, the passion with this combination begins with an idea or an ideal and grows from there. To be seduced, you need that mental stimulation. You don't need a monogamous relationship, you don't need flowers or moonlit beaches. You simply need a partner who both honors and stimulates your mind. Unless that mental connection exists, you just aren't interested in committing to a relationship.

When it does exist, when you find this ideal, your sexuality is set free. It may seem contradictory that someone as independent as you is set free within a relationship that has boundaries and parameters, but there you have it. Until you find it, though, you are actually pretty content to go your own way, listening to that different, inner drumbeat.

Best Matches: Venus in Aquarius or another air sign, Mars in Capricorn or another earth sign, the Sun in Aquarius or another air sign. Sometimes, a fire-sign Sun works out nicely because it inspires your Aquarius Mars.

Examples: Screenwriter Lawrence Kasdan (*Body Heat*), Cuba Gooding, Jr., Jean Dixon, Cary Grant, Rod Stewart

MARS IN PISCES ♂ ♓

This combination is innately psychic. That doesn't mean you necessarily listen to your inner guidance, but the talent is there, lying dormant like some mutant gene, just waiting for an opportunity to exhibit what it can do. You have the ability to pull information from the collective mind, the cosmic kettle, whatever name you want to give it.

Earth and water enjoy each other's company, which facilitates the exchange between your self-expression and your sexual and physical energy. Your imagination is as deep as it is vast and within it lies the answers to many of the questions you will ask throughout your life. Your inner life is a mystery to others, even those who love and know you best.

Mars in Pisces usually doesn't have issues with anger. It's so emotional and sensitive to everything that its challenge lies in establishing boundaries between self and others. There's a crusading element to Mars in this sign and with Capricorn's relentlessness backing, it's entirely possible that crusading may be your calling.

The Pisces Mars-Capricorn Sun potential is rich. Here's how it works:

You're alone in a crowd. Your eyes meet someone else's. A connection is made. You can't define it and the other person probably can't, either. Neither of you act on it until the day that you're in another crowd and you see the same person. Your eyes connect again. And something inside of you shifts. You recognize this connection as important. No, you realize it's damn strange, that it goes well beyond coincidence, that it is part of the ocean in which you live your most private, sacred life. So you act on it. Or the other person does. Or both of you act simultaneously. And your life is never quite the same again.

From the place that you're coming from, it's not unreasonable to want the whole package: body, mind, soul, and whatever else is left over. You want epiphany, bliss, something so special that your life seems blessed. Okay, that's great. But we live in a world that's like an iceberg, where only the tip of what's real and tangible actually shows. You may have to take a leap of faith and dive down deep. Can you do this? Is your faith that large? This question is the essential riddle of your life.

Best Matches: Venus in Pisces or another water sign or Venus in an earth sign. Mars or the Sun in a water or earth sign. A Venus or Mars in Scorpio won't overpower you, but the relationship will feel destined or karmic. A Sun in Pisces or another water sign will soften all that ambition.

Examples: Denzel Washington (those large, expressive eyes are the giveaway of the Mars in Pisces), Anthony Hopkins (also has expressive Piscean eyes), Andy Kaufman, Jack London, Jay McInerney, televangelist Jim Bakker

SENSE-MEMORY EXERCISE FOR SUN IN CAPRICORN

Mars represents our physical senses. Most of us have at least one sense that is stronger than the others or provides information more quickly about our physical environment. Is your hearing really acute? Do you have an exquisite sense of smell? Your strongest sense, whatever it is, provides you with immediate and reliable information about yourself or others, your environment, and your personal world.

In the space below, describe any instance where one of your physical senses played a vital role. Be detailed and specific.

_____
_____
_____
_____
_____

The incident or situation you've just described pertains to the second question you asked in the inventory at the beginning of part two. If the connection isn't immediately apparent, look for the metaphor.

A widow and grandmother of three who was in one of my workshops described a sunrise that she saw while on vacation in the Caribbean. It filled her with such awe that she felt like a cave

woman seeing a sunrise for the first time. Her second question
was whether she should marry a man she had been dating for
about six months. She had met him at the bereavement group
she joined after her husband had died.

She realized from her description that she felt "awed" that she
had met anyone at this stage in her life. She thought it was significant that she'd chosen to describe a sunrise rather than a sunset—the beginning of the day rather than its end—and decided
the answer to her question was yes, she should definitely marry
the man.

13

Sun in Aquarius ☉ ♒

THE INDIVIDUALIST
Fixed Air

"My mind is my castle."

Strengths: Original thinker, experiential, intellectual, values individuality, friends are important, innovative, follows own path, perceptive, altruistic, nonconformist, visionary qualities

Weaknesses: Stubborn, inflexible, emotionally detached, impatient, empty rebellion

Sexual Blueprint: Seduce my mind.

You're the nonconformist of the zodiac, the original thinker who refuses to accept something as true just because someone else tells you so. You have to find out for yourself what is true or not true, real or not real. In some ways, your life is like a Zen koan. *What is the sound of one hand clapping?* You don't have the answer today, but you're determined to find it even if it takes a couple of lifetimes.

Once you've formed an opinion about an issue, situation, or person, you're slow to change your mind. The evidence has to be convincing and even then you may stick to your original assessment. You can be as stubborn as the other two fixed signs, Taurus and Scorpio, and can be even more relentless than those two when you've decided to pursue—or to end—something.

You have a variety of unusual friends, both male and female, who come from a broad spectrum of backgrounds. It isn't unusual for an Aquarius to know a partner first as a friend. Once the relationship becomes more than that, the friendship part of it is integral to the relationship's success. Your partners are often unique or eccentric in some way and if they're smart, they understand that the most direct way to your heart is through your mind. In any romantic or sexual relationship, you demand a great deal of personal freedom and need the space to express your individuality.

SUN IN AQUARIUS AND . . .

MARS IN ARIES ♂ ♈

As the ruler of Aries, Mars is very comfortable in this sign, where it's also quite cozy in combination with Aquarius. These two planets form a 60-degree angle to each other, an aspect called a sextile that facilitates an easy exchange of energy. And because Aquarius is such a mental sign, that energy stimulates your intellect sending it in unconventional directions.

Whatever your profession, you're something of a pioneer, a paradigm-buster who shatters preconceived notions and finds new approaches and methods. Writer Judy Blume, for example, broke new ground in her books about adolescent sexuality that were written for young adults. Her books have been banned periodically over the years, with the most vicious attacks occurring during the Reagan administration and peaking in the mid-nineties.

Mars in Aries adds passion, flair, and impatience to your Aquarian personality. You're the consummate idea person, great at launching projects and campaigns. Usually, though, if your passion wanes, you have trouble finishing what you start. This tendency is diminished when Aries is combined with Aquarius because Aquarians either feel obligated to finish what they start or they simply hate to give up. It's important that whatever niche you fill in the marketplace is one about which you feel great passion and enthusiasm. The happier you are in your work, the happier and healthier you are overall.

Physically, Aquarius rules the ankles, shins, and circulatory system and Aries rules the head. When you're stressed out, you may feel it first in one of those areas. Migraine headaches aren't uncommon for people with this combination.

Your sexuality isn't everyone's cup of tea, but you aren't here to live according to other people's morals and belief systems. You're here to define your own set of rules and are quite comfortable with your sexuality, thank you very much. Words like commitment and monogamy may be foreign to you. For sexual chemistry to exist, your partner has to court you intellectually—seduce your mind—and be able to keep up with you physically. This combination enjoys thrills—rock climbing, white-water kayaking, skydiving—so it's important that your partner enjoys this kind of stuff, too. Thrills like this turn you on.

You're a passionate person for whom sex is just one of many needs integral to your life. You're blunt about your sexuality, and want sex when the spirit moves you. You can be jealous and possessive, even though you won't tolerate a partner who exhibits these same traits. You aren't the easiest person to live with, but when you find the right partner at the right time in your life, a committed relationship brings all your passion and enthusiasm right into the heart of everything you are.

Best Matches: Venus in Aries or another fire sign spells sexual fireworks. Venus or Mars in Aquarius or another air sign means you and your partner communicate well and are on the same wavelength in terms of life goals. A Sun in an air sign works very well, too.

Examples: Judy Blume, Princess Caroline of Monoco, Charles Dickens, Tom Brokaw, Geena Davis, Norman Mailer, Paul Newman, Jack Nicklaus, Molly Ringwald

MARS IN TAURUS ♂ ♉

This double fixed combination is plenty stubborn and rarely yields a personal belief without a convincing argument or a fight. Musical talent is often present with Mars in Taurus, and when Aquarius is tossed into the mix, its expression can be eccentric or radically different from the norm, perhaps even cutting-edge.

Your talents aren't limited to just music. The arts, entertainment, communication, public relations, medicine, or metaphysics are all viable career options. Whatever profession you choose, you're a tireless worker and no one will ever accuse you of being a quitter.

So what is sexuality about with this intellectual air and grounded earth sign as partners? Well, it's a lot more sensual than a double air combination, that's for sure. Since neither Aquarius nor Taurus need boundaries or parameters that fit society's norms, casual affairs are probably just fine with you. Given the condition of your Taurean sensuality and Aquarian need for intellectual excitement, it's likely that your mind is the sensual organ in any sexual relationship, every bit as sensitive as another person's skin.

In terms of seduction, your preferences depend on which planet is in charge in a given situation. If it's Aquarius, then you're best seduced through whatever appeals to your mind—ideas and ideals, books, films, debates, politics. If your Taurus Mars is in charge, then your potential partner had better be a nature lover or a musician or someone with great artistic tastes or perhaps a gourmet cook.

If you're the sort of Aquarius who really is *not* interested in the great outdoors yet that's where your partner takes you, then it doesn't take a psychic to predict the relationship will go exactly nowhere. Make sure you don't give out mixed signals. If you're a woman, then you probably are looking for someone like a Taurus who is grounded, nature-loving, and maybe a great cook to boot. If you're a man, check out the sign of *your* Venus. That will tell you the type of woman you're actually looking for.

Other factors enter into sexual compatibility, and if you're really serious about exploring astrology (as some Aquarians are), then be sure that your Moon (emotions) sign is compatible with the other person's Sun sign or Moon sign.

Best Matches: Venus in Taurus is the most sensual. Venus or Mars in Aquarius or another air sign means great communication in the relationship. The Sun in either Taurus or an air sign either stabilizes (Taurus) or heightens mutual interests.

Examples: Mac Davis, Hal Holbrook, Carole King, Jack Lemmon, Christopher Marlowe, Graham Nash, Antonio Carlos Jobim

MARS IN GEMINI ♂ ♊

These two air brothers see eye to eye on just about everything. They form an angle to each other called a trine, an aspect where the exchange of energy is practically flawless, as smooth-flowing as liquid chocolate. The combination is inherently mental, so your mind isn't just your castle; it's your entire world.

You have a lot of nervous energy; you think and speak rapidly and can tell a good yarn before your first cup of coffee in the morning. You've got the gift of gab down pat. Your facility with language and ideas extends beyond the spoken word. You have talent in writing—fiction, nonfiction, lyrics. You may have musical talent as well if you have a number of planets in water signs in your natal chart.

As for professions, well, anything routine will put you into therapy. You despise restrictions, sameness, the humdrum. Technology fascinates you, and if you aren't already a whiz with computers, you will be. People also intrigue you. You would enjoy anything dealing with the public, as long as the public isn't so demanding that they start bossing you around. Clairvoyance is often evident with this combination—sharp, vivid impressions of situations and events, or strong hunches that force you to sit up and take notice. You probably won't call these impressions clairvoyant, but that's what they are.

Sexually, you're all mind. Even though you're aware of your body (a fact that some people you know will dispute), your body is secondary in importance to your intellect. There can be hubris with this combination, an intellectual snobbery, and yet you're put off by snobs of any kind. Your partners come from every walk of life and must be as smart as you are, as curious, as humanitarian. And they absolutely must give you the personal freedom you demand. Oh, one other thing. These partners had better be talkers as versatile as you are—or good listeners.

Your passion is that of a visionary. When someone ignites your mind, your ideas, your imagination, you are instantly smitten. You are theirs. At least, you are theirs *for this second only*. Tomorrow . . .

hey, who knows? You have causes and issues, and some of these revolve around freedom and rebellion against the status quo.

If you've got this combination, then do yourself a big favor: find a qualified astrologer who can explain your chart to you in depth. You need to know why you're here, why your soul chose these circumstances, this time, this family and circle.

Best Matches: Venus or Mars in an air sign or fire sign. Air enhances everything already present in this combination; fire adds sexual passion, flair, flamboyance. A Sun in either air or fire will work beautifully as well.

Examples: Sixties radical and professor Angela Davis, Mary Todd Lincoln, James Joyce, Franklin D. Roosevelt, Virginia Woolf, Thomas Edison

MARS IN CANCER ♂♋

These two definitely have issues. Aquarius is air, an intellectual, paradigm-buster, and freedom fighter. Cancer is water, a homebody, intuitive and emotional. You can see the problem already.

Yet some eccentric and very talented people have this combination. The Cancer Mars part of you allows you to sink into the collective mind and return to the everyday world with the emotional reality of your vision. You're able to find whatever it is that speaks to other people.

Your approach to just about everything in your life is intuitive, subjective, and fully involved. Aquarius, on the other hand, has a sort of detached emotion. It values individuality, yet embraces humanity. The Cancer part of you keeps it very personal, one-on-one, face-to-face. Aquarius doesn't have any use for society's norms, but Cancer is more conservative in that sense, more traditional. Aquarius gets involved in casual affairs, but Cancer isn't nearly as quick and eager to jump into bed.

Sexually, you may feel uncomfortable. You understand your own needs and desires, you're blunt about them when asked. But you have this inner blueprint called *other*, and until you find the partner who fits that blueprint, you would just as soon do without sex.

As soon as you begin to nurture your ideas, your imagination, and try to understand the real reasons for your rebellion, then you're on your way to incorporating the best of Aquarius and the best of Cancer. It doesn't mean your sex life will be any more clear to you, but other things will be. It doesn't mean your relationships will be perfect, but perhaps your creativity will be. Or your children. Or your ability to make other people feel good about themselves.

Your life and everything in it is a process that you feel compelled to understand. Sometimes the process is intellectual, sometimes it's emotional, and sometimes it's both, with spirituality thrown in as well. And that's really the frustrating thing about it. You want it to be one thing or another. You want black or white, good or bad, no shades of gray, please. You want to enjoy something, like sex, without carrying on endless internal dialogues about the nuances, the things you and your partner thought, felt, and speculated about.

Your best bet? Learn to relax, to take your cues from what's going on in your life. Look for the metaphor, look for the deeper thread.

Best Matches: Venus or Mars in a water sign enhances the intuitive and continual qualities of the relationship. Sun in an air sign brings mutual communication skills to the relationship. Simple, right?

Examples: Gypsy Rose Lee, Toni Morrison, Amadeus Mozart, Farrah Fawcett

MARS IN LEO♂♌

You're a double fixed combination, air and fire, and that means you are stubborn (sometimes more stubborn than Taurus), passionate, and loyal. Your Sun and Mars form an opposition to each other, an aspect of 180 degrees that creates a tension that will never be resolved, but which can nonetheless be used to help you fulfill your potential. *If* you can do the work. *If* you're willing to be introspective. *If* you can divert the focus from yourself long enough.

Big ifs. Leo, by its very nature, is self-centered and focused on self-expression. When combined with visionary Aquarius, the impetus of Leo propels you into new creative areas and modes of expression. You do well in any profession that allows you to flex your creative muscles and to be on center stage. Acting would be a natural fit, but also consider teaching, public relations, business, entertainment, and the arts.

Leo Mars or Mars in any fire sign infuses your Aquarian nature with passion and a dynamic, action-oriented personality. As a result, not everything with you is centered around the mind and intellect. You pursue your causes with an eye on end results and actually foster change in existing paradigms and structures rather than just thinking about change.

You're incredibly inflexible about certain things, however, and when it comes to your sexuality, you have definite parameters that have to be met. Your partner must recognize you for your talents and achievements and must be demonstrative in his or her affection for you. Sex isn't just a physical need for you. It's a kind of creative self-expression. You are direct and honest in your approach to sex and expect nothing less from your partner. Aquarius usually isn't a jealous or possessive sign, but Leo is. *Love me, show me that you love me, make love to me daily, and never ever take me for granted, and never ever look at another man or woman when you're with me.*

These tenets exist whether the relationship is committed or not. If a new or casual partner fulfills them, then he or she passes the test for being worthy of your attention, love, and commitment.

Best Matches: Venus in Leo or another fire sign is sexually passionate. Mars or the Sun in an air sign facilitates communication. Mars in a fire sign is passionate, but results in a conflict of wills.

Examples: Rip Torn, James Dean, Isabel Peron

MARS IN VIRGO ♂ ♍

Air and earth are rather like strangers sitting next to each other on a plane. They may chat, share a few tidbits about their lives, or they may just ignore each other the entire trip. The problem with this analogy, though, is that these two strangers are both a part of you.

Mars in Virgo gives you a discriminating intellect that may drive your Aquarius Sun half crazy. You're a perfectionist in at least one area of your life and are picky about things in your personal environment. You may be fussy about the foods you eat and have sensitivities to dust or other environmental elements. When you're stressed out, it may show up physically as stomach upsets or allergies.

Sometimes with Mars in Virgo, there's a tendency toward self-criticism and criticism of others. When the criticism is directed at others, it isn't done in a way that is consciously malicious. However, the person on the receiving end may take it that way, particularly if that person is a child. When you turn this criticism on yourself, it can undermine your confidence. Themes like *I'm not good enough* or *I don't measure up* then become something against which you struggle all your life.

Your wit and charm attract many friends from varied walks of life. But your closest friends will be people with whom you share a common vision or worldview and those who support your dreams and ambitions. Partners may be people you know first as friends or people you meet in your daily life.

Unless you've got a Scorpio Moon, Scorpio rising, or Scorpio is otherwise prominent in your birth chart, sex doesn't top your list of priorities. But with the right partner, that changes. Your partner, though, has to meet some specific criteria. He (or she) must be independent, must value individuality, and must not be threatened by your vast number of friends and causes. He or she must be able to talk about personal feelings and act on those feelings.

In a committed relationship, that critical streak may rear its ugly head from time to time, alienating you from your partner. If you're aware of it, you can work with it by first asking yourself why you feel compelled to criticize your partner. Quite often, the criticism relates to something you don't like in yourself. Your capacity for intimacy deepens when you find the right partner and takes you to places in the mind and in your creative life that you haven't even imagined yet.

Best Matches: A Venus in Virgo would seem to be the best pairing here, but the relationship may deteriorate into a struggle for perfectionism. Look for a Venus in Taurus instead, which would infuse the relationship with sensuality. Mars in an earth or an air sign would work and so would a Sun in an air sign.

Examples: Alice Cooper, Clark Gable, Barbara Hershey, Kim Novak, Susan Sontag, Oprah Winfrey, and Yoko Ono

MARS IN LIBRA ♂︎ ♎

The focus of this double air combination is on the intellect. The two planets in these signs form a geometric angle to each other called a trine, an aspect that facilitates an easy, flowing exchange of energy. The individuality and vision of your Aquarius Sun is geared toward people and relationships. You have great insight into other people's motives and the forces that move their lives.

A Mars in Libra gives you the ability to balance the many facets of your life. You may not always succeed in achieving *inner* balance in your life, but you excel at multitasking. Professionally, you would do well in the legal field, criminal justice, the arts and entertainment, counseling or mediation, modeling, politics, or public relations. However, your mindset is so unique that you would do well in any field that requires vision and the setting of trends.

You have an innate sense of fairness when it relates to other people's lives, but can be indecisive when it comes to your own life. Aquarius is independent, but Libra is so people-oriented that you experience periodic inner conflict between these two needs. The Aquarian part of you has many causes and ideologies to which you're devoted and the Libra part of you brings an aesthetic sense to these causes.

One woman with this combination is a family court judge who is active in the Girl Scouts of America, an organization that she feels teaches young girls and teenagers the values that foster both individual independence and cooperation within groups. She also collects art, has artistic talent herself, and owns horses, all distinctly Libran pursuits.

Partnerships of all kinds are important to you, but intimate partnerships in particular are your territory. You initiate sex without any hesitation and the initial parameters of the relationship don't have to fit any of society's norms. However, because you're a romantic at heart, you enjoy the courting part of a relationship and are bowled over when your partner sends flowers or a love poem or whisks you off for a romantic weekend in some distant part of the world. Any partner who infuses the relationship with a large dose of romance wins you over easily.

In a committed relationship, you and your partner must be equals for things to work. Thanks to your Mars in Libra, though, you sometimes go to extremes to accommodate your partner's needs and quirks, perhaps at the expense of your own needs. You're a loving partner, usually faithful, but you aren't opposed to looking around or flirting. You generally won't walk away from a relationship unless you already have somewhere else to go.

Best Matches: Venus in Libra results in a pair of lovebirds. Venus or Mars in Aquarius or Gemini is great for communication. A fire sign Venus or Mars infuses passion and sexual chemistry into the relationship.

Examples: Laura Dern, Charles Darwin, psychic investigator and writer Hans Holzer, Abraham Lincoln, Cybill Shepherd, Sonny Bono

MARS IN SCORPIO ♂ ♏

Air and water don't have a whole lot to say to each other. But this combination is also a double fixed-sign pairing and that translates as stubbornness, singular purpose, and the ability to finish whatever you start.

The big challenge with this combination is that Scorpio's emotional intensity is anathema to Aquarius's emotional detachment. You may experience great highs and lows emotionally that cause you to feel as if your life is a seesaw in constant need of adjustment. The planets in these two signs form a 90-degree angle to each other called a square, an aspect that creates friction and resistance, but which also can compel you to action.

If you have your natal chart, check out the house placements for your Sun and Mars, then read the house descriptions for each planet in Chapter 2. This will give you a clearer idea of how the two energies are likely to manifest themselves in your life. If, for example, your Aquarius Sun is in the second house of finances and personal values, and your Mars is in the eleventh house of wishes and dreams, then you experience friction between your earning capacity and what you value and your ability to achieve your dreams. You might feel that the two are constantly in conflict, but one way or another, given the fixed nature of these two signs, you will achieve what you want.

Scorpio is one of the most sexual placements for Mars, which co-rules that sign. It gives you a kind of smoldering sexuality that is often apparent in your intense, piercing eyes even when sex is the last thing on your mind. If you're in the entertainment business or in a business where appearances and first impressions are vital to your success, then this placement is a plus because it gives you great sex appeal. Combined with your visionary Aquarius Sun, it creates a mystique about you, something that intrigues people.

You rarely have any compunction about initiating sex, but the paradox here is that the sex probably interests you less than establishing a profound connection that facilitates communication. It's unlikely that you will divulge long-held personal secrets, though, unless trust is established between you and your partner, but sex allows *you* to understand your partner. Once trust is established, you're a faithful, loving partner with a profound capacity for intimacy. You expect the same dedication and love in return. And if your partner violates that trust, you're gone. It's black or white, no shades of gray.

Best Matches: Venus in Scorpio creates an intensely emotional and sexual relationship. But power issues may surface frequently. If that bothers you, then stick to someone whose Venus or Mars is in Aquarius or one of the other air signs, which enhances communication and mental camaraderie. Also, don't discount a Venus in sensual Taurus, which would get along nicely with your Scorpio Mars, or a Sun in an air sign.

Examples: Helen Gurley Brown, Colette, Christian Dior, Roberta Flack, Ayn Rand, Germaine Greer

MARS IN SAGITTARIUS ♂ ♐

With this air-and-fire combination, you're the life of any party and have a commanding presence that people feel immediately. Sagittarius Mars gives you passion and wit, and feeds your Aquarian individuality in distinctive ways. In these signs, the two planets form a sextile to each other, an aspect that confers an easy exchange of energy. These two rarely disagree and when they do, Sagittarius probably wins.

A lot of creativity is inherent to this combination. You do best in a profession in which your individuality and your visionary qualities can be expressed. You demand creative freedom in your work and also a lot of personal freedom. You aren't the type who can punch a clock, put in eight hours of mindless work, then go home and pretend your life is great and utterly fulfilled. Self-employment would suit you and you would do whatever it takes to make the business successful.

Your causes and humanitarian work get an additional boost from Sagittarius Mars. You're more action-oriented than, say, a double air-sign combination, and aren't satisfied with just thinking about change. You're out there on the front lines, *initiating* change. You have the ability to see the larger picture in whatever you do and, with your Aquarius Sun eager to bust open existing paradigms, that ability often includes a prescience about upcoming trends and events.

There's a spiritual component to this combination that can be tough to pin down. You may develop a spirituality that has nothing to do with the religious beliefs you grew up with or you may go to extremes, perching on your pulpit and pummeling other people with the way, the truth, and the light—according to you.

If your spiritual beliefs don't interfere with your sexuality, then just about anything goes for you, from one-night stands to committed relationships. Given your need for personal freedom, though, your partner had better be someone who needs an equal amount of freedom and doesn't balk when you take off for some exotic port. You aren't the type who craves to be romanced and courted; you would rather cut right to the chase and get on with whatever unfolds. Your bluntness may put off potential partners, but you shrug off those types, who aren't worth your time, anyway.

In a relationship where you and your partner are equals and you honor each other's needs, your sexuality and capacity for intimacy flourish. Your need to rebel against the status quo ceases to play out within relationships, and you channel it into more constructive and universal concerns.

Best Matches: Venus in Sagittarius or another fire sign means passion and a dynamic relationship. Venus or Mars in Aquarius or another air sign indicates mutual interests and good communication. Sun in Sagittarius or Aquarius, or another fire or air sign also work well.

Examples: Jules Verne, John Travolta, Sir Francis Bacon, Fritjov Capra, Lewis Carroll, Geena Davis, Stendahl

MARS IN CAPRICORN♂♑

Ambition, pragmatism, restrictions, parameters, structure: this is what Capricorn Mars is all about. Since the Aquarius Sun is about *none* of that, the dilemma with this combination is obvious. In addition, it's a combination of air and earth, which don't have very much in common.

However, this combination has some very powerful points in its favor. As with any combination that involves a Capricorn Mars, ambition is pronounced. This isn't just naked ambition, either. It's visionary ambition, a need to instigate change in a sweeping, universal way. Change sometimes involves destruction of existing structures, but you simply step in and rebuild. You make your visions practical and useful to others. Whether you're building a family, a novel, a song, or a career, you begin with the vision of what might be and then strategize, plan, and implement.

Your determination and efficiency attract people of like mind who often become your team, individuals who share your vision and are willing to put in long hours and work until they drop to launch a project or realize an ideal. In whatever you do professionally, you're a tireless worker (although sometimes much too serious) and need to be reminded to chill out once in a while, to kick back and enjoy your life.

Thomas Edison is one of the best examples of this combination. He had a vision—the incandescent electric lamp (light bulb)—and then went about bringing the idea into physical reality. He had a team that helped him to achieve the goal. There can be an element of ruthlessness with this combination, which Edison exhibited in his relationship with Nicola Tesla and also in his relationships with his three children by his first wife.

Your sexuality feels uncomfortable sometimes, like a nagging, amorphous ache that you can't relieve because you don't know what's causing it. Your Aquarius Sun wants independence in a relationship, doesn't care about parameters, yet your Capricorn Mars seeks more traditional relationships. As a result, you either swing back and forth between these two extremes or one or the other becomes dominant in your life.

A happier and healthier medium lies in going with the flow in a relationship, whatever its context, and taking things one day at a time rather than projecting into some vague future. If you feel like having sex with someone you've just met, then do it. Don't rationalize what you feel, don't make excuses for it. *Act on the impulse*. This shatters the Aquarian insistence on having things its own way and shatters the Capricorn need for control. You have good instincts, but don't always listen to them when you should.

Best Matches: A Venus in Capricorn could result in a relationship where ambition is king. Go for a softer earth Venus, like sensual Taurus, or for Venus in one of the air signs, which would foster communication. Mars in an air or earth sign would work, too, and so would a Sun in an air sign.

Examples: Mia Farrow, Buzz Aldrin, Thomas Edison, Andrew Greeley, Gene Hackman, Eartha Kitt, Tom Selleck, James Spader

MARS IN AQUARIUS ♂ ≈

This double air, double fixed sign combination is a whammy that spells mind, vision, and stubbornness in the extreme. Your opinions are *your* opinions, and you don't surrender them without a fight or, at the very least, a convincing argument. Your network of friends is vast and crosses cultural, ethnic, and religious boundaries. You simply don't recognize boundaries of any kind. Many of these friends support the same causes that you do, have the same ideals and creative interests, and you are as generous with them as they are with you. All of you, at some level, are united by an ideal vision of how the world could be.

Few combinations are able to bust existing paradigms or belief systems in the way you do, by standing up for your beliefs. A good example was astrologer Evangeline Adams. In 1914, while living in New York, she was accused of fortunetelling and taken to court. She claimed that astrology was a science as exacting as any other and challenged the court to give her the birth data on someone she didn't know so she could demonstrate what she did. The judge rose to the occasion and gave her the date, time, and place of birth of an individual—the judge's son. Her reading was so accurate that the judge dismissed the case. "Adams raises astrology to the dignity of an exact science," the judge concluded.

You're extremely comfortable with your sexuality—even if other people aren't. For you, all sex begins in the mind, with an idea or a word or a conversation that awakens your interest and curiosity. As you get to know the person a little more, the chemistry is sparked—or it isn't. If it isn't, then the person probably becomes a friend and that's it. But if there's chemistry, then you begin to explore things more deeply, finding common interests, passions, and ideas. The other person has to excite your mind, intrigue you with the way he or she thinks, and absolutely must honor your extreme need for personal freedom. Any potential sexual partner has to be able to communicate honestly about what he or she thinks and feels.

Your "must have" list isn't that long, and revolves around two central issues: mental connections and communication. Since Aquarius is ruled by Uranus, the planet of genius and of sudden and unexpected change, many of your relationships will have a Uranian quality to them. They may begin and end suddenly, leap into your life out of nowhere, and bring exciting changes and stimulus. Your ideal partner is highly individualistic, just as you are, and probably attracts eccentric and intriguing people, just as you do.

In a committed relationship, all this can translate into a hectic life with a lot of people constantly coming and going. Your home may be a hub for artists or scientists or psychics. It may be where your office is based. There are sure to be a lot of high-tech gizmos around the house. In the bedroom, sex won't be the heated, intense experience that it is for a double Scorpio, but it will be *your* ideal. And in the end, that's what really matters.

Best Matches: A Venus in Aquarius should be the best match, but it really depends on how many other planets you both have in Aquarius. Too much Aquarius interaction can result in neither person being present in the relationship because they are off saving the rest of the world. A Venus in Libra or Gemini would work well in a day-to-day sense and so would a Venus or Mars in one of the fire signs. An air-sign Sun would be good, too, but even better would be a fire-sign Sun.

Examples: John Belushi, Evangeline Adams, Bill Bixby (*My Favorite Martian*), Garth Brooks, Matt Dillon, Jessica Savitch

MARS IN PISCES ♂ ♓

Air versus water, intellect versus feeling, logic versus imagination, left brain versus right brain: you see immediately where this is going. This is a difficult combination precisely because your head and your heart constantly struggle against each other. These two are like warring clans, but without the bloodshed.

Here's the challenge: Aquarius represents the new millennium and Pisces represents the millennium we are leaving behind. Aquarius is forward-thinking, quick to spot trends, and even quicker to blow apart outmoded structures and belief systems. Pisces can reach the same conclusions that Aquarius does, but the methods differ. Pisces doesn't need to think, rationalize, or intellectualize; Pisces *feels* and *intuits*. Aquarius is ruled by innovative Uranus and Pisces is ruled by amorphous Neptune, the planet that blurs the boundaries between ego and soul. Uranus blows things apart; Neptune simply dissolves them.

When these two planetary energies are part of the same person, it means that what people perceive as you—the bravado, the bluster, the irreverence and wit, the crusader, the visionary, the rebel and individualist—is just the tip of the proverbial iceberg. Hidden beneath it all lies a vast uncertainty, an underground ocean whose waters touch shores so distant that the reasoning mind can barely imagine them. Within this secret place, you strive to understand what you feel. Are your feelings as real as your thoughts? Are your hunches as real as what you see, hear, touch, taste, and smell? Is that guy across the room actually watching you or are you just imagining it? Is your partner having an affair or are you just paranoid?

Sometimes, things work in reverse. Your logical self and detachment go south, the Pisces Mars part of you surfaces, and all that compassion and those profound feelings come pouring out. You cry at the sight of a limping dog, a homeless person on the street, even a movie. You feel as if the boundaries between you and the rest of the world are dissolving.

Your sexuality also reflects this tug-of-war between Aquarius and Pisces. You vacillate between your extreme independence and disinterest in sexual or intimate relationships and a desire for a total connection with a partner, a connection at the emotional, physical, and spiritual levels. The reality usually falls somewhere between these two extremes; the big question is whether something in between interests you. Again, that depends on whether the Aquarius or the Pisces part of you is in charge at the time.

Even when you're involved in a relationship, the tug-of-war continues—not as frequently or as intensely, but it's still there, an underlying theme. So what's the ultimate purpose behind this combination? The answer undoubtedly varies from one person to another, but overall the purpose may be simply to recognize that the deeper layers of life—and of your psyche—have as much if not more validity as the things you perceive on a daily basis.

Best Matches: Venus in Pisces is the obvious choice, but could create some of the same relationship challenges that you face. Venus in Cancer may be too clingy, and Venus in Scorpio too intense. Your best bet may be to stick to Venus or Mars in an air sign or a Sun in either an air or fire sign.

Examples: Somerset Maugham, George Segal, Brad Steiger, Lana Turner

SENSE-MEMORY EXERCISE FOR SUN IN AQUARIUS

Mars represents our physical senses. Most of us have at least one sense that is stronger than the others or provides information more quickly about our physical environment. It might be your hearing or sense of touch. It could be your sense of taste. Your strongest sense, whatever it is, provides you with immediate and reliable information about yourself or others, your environment, and your personal world.

In the space below, describe any instance where one of your physical senses played a vital role. Be detailed and specific.

_____

_____

_____

_____

_____

The incident or situation you've just described pertains to the second question you asked in the inventory at the beginning of part two. If the connection isn't immediately apparent, look for the metaphor.

A young girl, an Aquarius teenager who used to live in our neighborhood, tried this activity one night. She thought and thought and finally shrugged. "I can't think of any experience."

"Nothing?" I asked. "Nothing at all?"

She thought some more and finally said there was one memory, but it didn't fit into any normal context. She believed, in fact, that it originated when her mother was pregnant with her. It was sound—of her mother humming to music—and it filled her with such peace that whenever she feels stressed, she shuts her eyes and is able to conjure that feeling all over again.

Her second question? What was she really looking for in a guy? Someone who made her feel peaceful.

Sometimes, it's just that simple.

14

Sun in Pisces ☉ ♓

THE EMPATH
Mutable Water

"I feel, therefore I am."

Strengths: Compassion, psychic ability, incredible imagination, great creative resources, quiet strength, adaptable, flexible, healing abilities, excellent insight into others

Weaknesses: Too adaptable, too flexible, martyr/savior syndrome, escapism, addiction, struggle between heart and mind

Sexual Blueprint: Love my soul.

Every Sun sign has a particular way in which it explores the world. You do your exploration through your emotions, intuition, and spirituality, swimming through oceans of impressions that would exhaust lesser human beings. In many ways, you're a psychic sponge, absorbing the feelings and psychic residue of other people. This is just one of the reasons that make it vital for you to associate with upbeat, optimistic people.

The other reason is a little less clear, but equally valid. You have such deep compassion for others that it's very easy for you to fall into the martyr/savior syndrome. *He lost his wife, his kids, no wonder he's an alcoholic. I can change all that. I can help him.* No, you can't. You can't change or save anyone else and if you try, you risk becoming a martyr to a lost cause.

Perhaps due to intense empathy and profound emotions, Pisces sometimes has problems with alcohol, drugs, and other forms of addiction, including sex. This tendency exists whether it's a Pisces Sun, Moon, or rising, and is something to be aware of, but don't view it as cast in stone. *You* are the ultimate scriptwriter of your life.

Sexually, you seem mysterious to other people, with an air of utter complexity about you. Often, this sexuality and mystery is centered in your eyes, which tend to be large, with a liquid quality that expresses great emotions. Think Liz Taylor here, a classic Pisces with compelling violet eyes. Your ideal partner is one with whom you have a soul connection. Even though you can fall into that martyr/savior syndrome and even though other people may sometimes figure you for a pushover, you won't stand for dogma or anything didactic that restricts your freedom of expression.

When your energy is used constructively and is highly evolved, you're capable of producing astonishing works of art, literature, music. You really do hear the music of other worlds.

SUN IN PISCES AND . . .

MARS IN ARIES ♂ ♈

Ouch. That's how this water/fire combination feels until you integrate the energies. Everything you are is anathema to Aries and vice versa. Your Sun sign prefers an easy, languid pace, but your Mars is headstrong, impatient, and moves like lightning. Your Sun seeks an intuitive approach to problem-solving, but your Mars believes that might overcomes all, and slams through obstacles.

But an abundance of creative talent accompanies this combination, and quite often it's pioneering stuff, new and exciting, groundbreaking. Your intuitive Pisces Sun taps into the collective mind for inspiration, then your action-oriented Mars brings it forth into the world. And that's how these two signs work best together, in creative collaboration.

This collaboration breaks down in the sexual and romantic arenas. The problem is simple. Aries, never known for subtlety, rushes in, cutting to the sexual chase, then splits just as fast, leaving Pisces behind to pick up the pieces. By then, of course, your heart is breaking because you wanted so desperately to believe that because you had sex with someone, a relationship had been established. Even though the problem is simple, the solution is anything but. The solution is called experience and involves repetition. When this pattern repeats itself enough times and your heart begins to feel like a slab of raw meat, you realize the only way to conduct yourself is to rein in Aries. Or to toughen up Pisces. Or both.

For men with this combination, it's easier to identify with macho Aries. You court, seduce, make love, and flee all in one night. For women, the combination is somewhat more difficult because Pisces is yin, and feels familiar. So women identify more strongly with the Pisces part of their natures rather than Aries. The dilemma is thematic.

Years ago, Mia Farrow and Dustin Hoffman starred in a movie called *John and Mary*, based on a novel by the same name. The plot is simple. Girl meets boy, they spend the night together, and over the course of the weekend, they get to know each other. But they don't exchange names until the very end, when both have reached an unspoken agreement to explore the relationship. The Aries part of their natures wants to get out without having to provide a name, but the Pisces part feels a connection and sticks around.

Here's a nugget to think about. On a deeper, soul level, it may be that you chose this combination because you need impulsiveness and thrills to feel truly alive and yet need that river of feeling moving through you to connect you with everything that is truly eternal.

Best Matches: Okay, Venus in Aries or another fire sign—the sex would be explosive, but the rest of your life together would be nothing but trouble. A Venus in a water sign is preferable. Or Mars in an air sign. Or the Sun in a water sign. You're looking for energy that complements your own.

Examples: Frédéric Chopin, Nat King Cole, Marjorie Merriweather Post, Paula Prentice, Kurt Russell

MARS IN TAURUS ♂ ♉

These two signs form a 60-degree angle to each other, an aspect known as a sextile that facilitates a smooth exchange of energy between your Sun and Mars. It's more physical and artistic than some of the other combinations with Pisces. You bring patience and fortitude to whatever you do, and usually don't quit what you've started. You're in the game for the long haul.

Water nurtures earth, so your Pisces Sun is supportive of your Taurus Mars. This translates as great physical energy and pronounced artistic talents, and also indicates that you're comfortable with your sexuality. The creative talent associated with this combination can be used in virtually any profession, from business to the arts and entertainment.

Your earth Mars confers a certain protection against the very things that make you emotionally vulnerable because Taurus insists that everything be grounded and solid, even emotions. In other words, where your Pisces Sun might take off into flights of imagination that produce paranoia or fear, your Taurus Mars insists on proof. *Where's the evidence of an affair? Where's the evidence that you may get fired?* Taurus doesn't let Pisces get away with anything. Yet at the same time, when it comes to the creative imagination of Pisces, Taurus backs it a hundred percent and is able to bring the ideas into physical reality.

You're a deeply sensual person. You're also so highly imaginative that in sexual relationships, your imagination is a key component to your pleasure, satisfaction, and emotional connection to your partner. Call it fantasy play, call it intuition, call it whatever you want. But unless your imagination is involved, the relationship won't be as rich or meaningful for you.

There're escapist tendencies with the Pisces Sun and sometimes that escapism finds expression through sex and casual affairs. Taurus Mars won't give you any resistance in that regard. If you have your natal chart, check the house placements for your Sun and Mars and read the house descriptions in Chapter 2 to find out how these energies are most likely to find expression in your life. One thing is certain, however. As you get older, your need for stability and spiritual connection in your relationships will become more pronounced, and it's less likely that you'll use sex as an escape.

In a committed relationship, your fear of getting hurt diminishes and your capacity for intimacy deepens. Once you commit, you usually commit for life.

Best Matches: Venus in Taurus or Pisces stabilizes and deepens emotion and romance. Mars or the Sun in an earth or water sign work well, too.

Examples: Robert Altman, Mario Andretti, Erma Brombeck, Peter Fonda, Rex Harrison, Andrew Jackson, Rudolph Nureyev, Sam Peckinpah

MARS IN GEMINI ♂ ♊

Water and air don't have much in common, but this pairing can work pretty well because it's a double mutable combination. You're adaptable and flexible and able to go with the flow most of the time. However, at times you may be so adaptable that you lack a firm opinion or course of action or you bend too far to accommodate other people.

Your intuitive impressions usually find expression through your emotions and register somewhere in your body, perhaps in the solar plexus region. Or you experience classic examples of clairvoyance—mind pictures. Sometimes, it's a combination of these two. It's to your distinct advantage to heed these impressions. If you don't, you usually regret it. In your creative work, these intuitive impressions provide you with information that you need. In your sexual and romantic life, the impressions allow you to immediately assess a person. Sometimes, you can do this simply by closing your eyes, focusing on the person or issue, and altering your breathing slightly so that a shift in consciousness occurs. The information you receive in this way is always useful and illuminating.

The Sun and Mars in these two signs form a 90-degree angle to each other, an aspect called a square that creates friction and resistance between the planets. Squares definitely feel uncomfortable, but they often compel people to achieve and to overcome challenges and obstacles. They can become strengths and assets rather than liabilities. In terms of your daily life, the square between your Sun and your Mars creates friction between your self-expression and your physical and sexual energy. Exactly what form that friction takes depends on the particulars in your life.

Sex may not be a very powerful influence in your life, as it would be for a combination with one of the fire signs. You have certain needs that must be met in any relationship and they revolve around communication (*seduce my mind*, the air signs always say), an honest exchange of feelings, and a spiritual connection. You want all of these, but in the absence of one or the other, you make do with what you have—or you do without, and pour all your energy into your creativity or some other area of your life.

In a committed relationship that has everything you're looking for, you are a caring, loving partner. Even though you may do too much to accommodate your partner's needs, your desire for permanence and stability of some kind makes the tradeoff worth it.

Best Matches: Venus in Gemini or another sign enhances communication. Venus in Scorpio would bring sexual intensity, but might be too powerful and controlling for this double mutable combination. Your Gemini Mars would enjoy a Venus in a fire sign, and your Pisces Sun would relish the embrace of a Cancer Sun.

Examples: Harry Belafonte, Fabio, Pat Nixon, George Plimpton, Mike Wallace

MARS IN CANCER ♂♋

In this double water combination, everything about Pisces is emphasized and heightened—emotions, intuition, sensitivity, compassion. Everything you experience is viewed through a highly subjective lens. This trait is especially true if both your Sun and Mars are found in houses one through six, beneath the horizon (the bottom half of your birth chart).

If, for example, your Cancer Mars falls in the third house, then your communication abilities are exceptionally intuitive. If it falls in the sixth house, then your approach to your daily work and your health will be intuitive, and any health problems you have possess a strong emotional component.

In these signs, the Sun and Mars form a 120-degree angle to each other, an aspect known as a trine that facilitates a smooth exchange of energies. Your self-expression and your physical and sexual energy are in complete agreement with each other. You may prefer to live near water or you find comfort and solace when you're around water or you enjoy water sports. Occasionally, I have run across people with this combination who don't feel anything one way or another about water or who are terrified of swimming, but they are the exception.

Your hunches and gut feelings should be unusually strong and frequent. This combination seems to lend itself to meeting up with people you have known in past lives and with whom you have unfinished business. You may have a particularly strong need for domesticity, a home, children, and family. You have a gift for real-estate investments and may end up owning several properties that you rent out.

Professional opportunities are many and varied for you, but to maximize your potential, get into a line of work where you can use your intuition and innate compassion. Possibilities might be medicine, hospice work, arts and entertainment, scientific research, or writing. The business world also might suit you. Two of the biggest names in business have this combination—Rupert Murdoch and Simon Newcomb.

You're very comfortable in your own skin, with a sexuality that is, like everything else in your life, intuitive, emotional, and spiritual. You generally aren't interested in casual sex. Your relationships tend to be deeper and more encompassing than just the satisfaction of physical desire. Your ideal partner is someone who is as aware as you are of higher forces in life and whose values about family and home are similar to your own.

This combination isn't a sexual powerhouse, as a combination with a fire sign or with Scorpio would be. But it *is* an emotional powerhouse and those emotions fuel your sexuality, your already deep capacity for intimacy, and your sensuality. In an established relationship, you're apt to be loyal, loving, nurturing, and somewhat protective of your partner.

Best Matches: A Venus in Scorpio would add sexual chemistry to the relationship, and a Venus in sensual Taurus would add sensuality and stability. A Venus in Cancer might be too clingy, even for you. A Mars or Sun in a water sign would work, too.

Examples: Liza Minnelli, Rupert Murdoch, Simon Newcomb, Karen Silkwood, Natalie Wood, Anne Morrow Lindbergh

MARS IN LEO ♂ ♌

Water and fire have no great love for each other. But because Leo is ruled by the Sun, your Pisces Sun may be energized by this combination. Or the passion and flamboyance of your Leo Mars may be considerably dampened by your Pisces Sun. It can work both ways or work one way some of the time and another way the rest of the time. It depends on other elements in your natal chart and on the house placements of both planets.

The Leo Mars pushes you to achieve and receive recognition for your achievements. Helen Keller is probably one of the best examples of how this combination works in terms of achievement. This sign for Mars also puts you in the spotlight more than your Pisces Sun may like. On the other hand, your Pisces Sun may enjoy the spotlight.

Pisces, like Gemini, is represented by two of something—a pair of fish swimming in opposite directions—so it's not surprising that there are usually two sides of an issue for you or two sides to how you feel about something or someone. Emotionally, you're often torn between one thing and another and may have trouble making decisions. However, with your Mars in the fixed sign of Leo, that won't be as big an issue as it would be with Mars in another mutable sign, like Gemini or Sagittarius.

Your sexuality feels uncomfortable at times. Very uncomfortable. You want to be loved, you enjoy sex, and you're forthright about what you want. But the Pisces in you is more reticent and shy and may feel tense and uncertain about being so frank about sex. Where your Leo Mars prefers a flamboyant show of affection from a partner—expensive bouquets of flowers that arrive unexpectedly, surprise tickets to a concert, a trip around the world—your Pisces Sun just wants to be hugged in private. Leo Mars has a fiery sexuality; Pisces Sun is softer, more receptive, more emotionally fluid. Leo roars and struts around and likes to be seen. Pisces dives into the ocean and swims away.

To successfully integrate these two energies requires self-awareness and conscious work to sharpen the qualities of one and soften the qualities of the other. This isn't a simple process, but can be accomplished through developing your intuitive and creative abilities. It's as if the energies, when directed toward specific goals, come together in a kind of uneasy alliance so that the job, whatever it is, can be accomplished.

Best Matches: Venus in Leo or a fire sign is sure to create plenty of sexual excitement and chemistry. Venus or Mars in Pisces or another water sign provides an easy emotional and intuitive exchange. The Sun in a water sign would also work.

Examples: Grover Cleveland, Jennifer O'Neill, Mary McCarthy, Neil Simon, Helen Keller, Nelson Rockefeller, Ringo Starr

MARS IN VIRGO♂♍

Pisces and Virgo form a 180-degree angle to each other, an aspect known as an opposition. This aspect creates a fundamental challenge in that the energies of the opposing planets won't ever be fully integrated, although you can learn to balance them and use them as a kind of fulcrum. All oppositions involve compatible elements, and with this combination—water and earth—Virgo grounds and roots the emotional fluidity of Pisces.

You're a perfectionist in some area of your life—an area best described by the house placement for your Mars. Your ability with details helps your Pisces Sun, which hates details. In turn, the imagination of your Pisces Sun helps your Virgo Mars see the larger world.

You're health-oriented or, at the very least, aware of your own health and health issues. This is especially true if your Mars falls in the sixth house. This combination is great for gathering knowledge and information, so professions like medical and scientific research are favored. Pisces has such wonderful emotional depth and imagination that acting and art are excellent career choices. Other good possibilities are writing and communication, business, veterinary science, and the health industry in general.

As a double mutable sign, you tend to bend way too much in relationships, regardless of whether these are sexual, business, friendship, or intimate partnerships. It's as if you're afraid that if you don't bend, the other person simply won't be interested. This pattern reflects your feeling that you don't measure up in some way, that you aren't good enough or attractive enough or smart enough. Mars in Virgo can be extremely self-critical and that only feeds the insecurities of the Pisces Sun. It's a vicious cycle that actually has more to do with habit. Break the habit and watch your life change.

Relationships provide the ideal way to break the habit. Instead of surrendering to a partner's needs or demands when you feel it isn't right or you just plain don't want to, stand up for yourself and your opinions. Insist on equal say. Doing this will also diminish the likelihood of the martyr/savior syndrome in your life.

In the right relationship, with a partner who values you the way you value him or her, your sexuality flourishes, as does your capacity for intimacy and trust.

Best Matches: Venus in Virgo would seem to be the best match, but probably isn't. It might create conditions in which you and your partner pick too much at each other or criticize each other. A Venus or Mars in Taurus would be more sensual. Venus in Scorpio would be intensely sexual, but Scorpio's energy might overwhelm your Pisces Sun. A Sun in Scorpio or Cancer would be a nice blend, too.

Examples: Researcher and Nobel Prize winner Linus Pauling, Philip Roth, Mickey Spillane, Quincy Jones, science-fiction writer Theodore Sturgeon

MARS IN LIBRA ♂ ♎

Water and air exist quite separately from one another. They neither support nor defy each other. In this combination of the Sun and Mars, the natural empathic qualities of Pisces find expression through the people skills and artistic sensibilities of Libra.

Professionally, you do well in the arts and entertainment, in investigating and researching whatever is strange and mysterious, in counseling, therapy, publicity, advertising, and in the health field. In whatever profession you choose, you must be able to use your intuition, empathy, and the deeper aspects of your personality.

One of the intriguing aspects of Libra Mars, particularly when paired with Pisces, is a tendency to view sex as an art form. This sometimes comes about because of a trauma early in life that leaves an emotional void that begs to be filled. Writer Anaïs Nin, for instance, was abandoned by her father when she was eleven. She spent most of the next twenty years trying to fill that void both through psychoanalysis and through sexual affairs with artists and writers—Henry Miller and his wife June, Laurence Durrell, psychoanalyst Otto Rank, and others. Then she wrote endlessly about it in her diaries, drawing numerous analogies between sex and art.

Your sex drive is powerful, but it's never just about sex. It's about communication and connection at deeper levels with yourself and with your partner. Your approach to sex is intuitive, emotional, and perhaps artistic as well, at least in that sex often awakens the artistic side of your personality. You probably have a mystical quality about you or are fascinated by the mystical, and sex may enhance this quality and interest in some way. It may be that sex for you is a mystical experience or that you're looking for sex that brings about a mystical experience.

You don't need a committed relationship to enjoy sex. In fact, your sexual relationships are apt to be unconventional and sometimes eccentric. If and when you do commit, you aren't necessarily the most monogamous partner. Mars in Libra is always on the alert for other interesting prospects. You may not act on every prospect, but you sure do enjoy looking around.

Best Matches: Venus in Libra or in Pisces, Mars in an air sign or water sign, and the Sun in an air sign. One word of caution: any combination with Scorpio will intensify the relationship sexually and may overwhelm your intrinsically gentle Piscean personality.

Examples: Karen Carpenter, Anaïs Nin, psychic investigator Andrija Puharich, James Redfield

MARS IN SCORPIO ♂ ♏

This double water combination is all about intense experiences—sexual, emotional, psychic, and spiritual. The dramatic and the profound are your territory.

Such an excess of emotion accompanies this combination that escapism is always a distinct possibility. If it's artistic escapism, then at least your emotionalism has a constructive channel. If it's escapism to lose yourself, the results can be heartbreaking.

Kurt Cobain, who started the punk band Nirvana, is one of the more tragic examples. He was not only a heroin addict, but ended as a suicide. Then there are people like Boris Pasternak, who wrote *Dr. Zhivago*, a love story that spanned the tempestuous years of the Russian revolution. The difference seems to lie not only in the obvious things like family, environment, and the time period into which you are born, but in self-awareness, in becoming conscious of both the demons and the gods that live inside you and choosing which one is going to run your life.

Professionally, your options are wide open. Music is a big draw for this combination, perhaps because of your emotional depth. Enrico Caruso is one of the best examples. You would do well in the arts, entertainment, business, communication, research and investigation, medicine—any career in which your emotions and intuition can be used in a positive, constructive way.

Your sexuality is a dominant force in your life and there's nothing passive about it. Even though you're extremely private and secretive, a part of you craves involvement and anticipates the strange wonder of intimate relationships. Casual sex and casual affairs don't hold much interest for you, however. You want the intense connections, the dramatic and emotional highs and lows, the magnificence of glimpsing another person's soul. You want nothing less than the stuff of great romantic literature!

When your emotions are stirred through sex and intimate relationships, you feel more alive, more present, more artistic and psychic, and, well, *inspired*. Many experiences in your life will take place against dramatic backdrops, like *Dr. Zhivago* does, and even though these backdrops may not be national revolutions, they nonetheless will be revolutions to you. Your entire psyche will shift, opening new areas for you to explore, new possibilities, new opportunities.

You have a kind, cynical wit that emerges in intimate relationships and through your creative endeavors. Actor Tony Randall is probably best remembered for playing the nitpicky guy in *The Odd Couple*. Hank Ketchum created *Dennis the Menace*. The cynicism, like all moments of understanding for you, is often born of astute observation and of digging around in yourself for the absolute bottom line. *Now I get it*. Lights go on, the echoes of drum rolls fill your head. Illumination has just happened.

In the end, illumination is really what you're looking for. And the more you discover about yourself, the more enlightened you are.

Best Matches: A Venus in Scorpio is the best, but will also be the most sexually and emotionally intense. A Venus in Pisces may be passive, but you'll invariably agree on creative and spiritual issues. The other option? A Sun in a water sign.

Examples: Enrico Caruso, Kurt Cobain, Hank Ketchum, Boris Pasternak, Tony Randall, Pierre-August Renoir, George Washington

MARS IN SAGITTARIUS♂ ♐

Water and fire: we're back to elementary science. Even though the elements in this combination avoid each other, both Pisces and Sagittarius are mutable signs. That's good. It gives them some basis for communication.

Mars in Sagittarius is a major plus for the Pisces Sun, who experiences wide mood fluctuations. It's tough to be depressed or to look on the negative side of any experience when you have Sagittarius in your court. Even if you experience a blue funk now and then, Sagittarius Mars should snap you right back into a more optimistic and positive frame of mind.

You have a knack for seeing the big picture of anything you're involved in, whether it's a project or a relationship. What your Sagittarius Mars can't grasp in the bigger picture, your Pisces Sun can supply by going within, plumbing the depth of that collective sea where you live. You excel in any profession or career where you can use your prescient vision, your imagination and intuition, and your natural ability with people. You have the gift of gab and the ability to learn easily. You benefit through travel, foreign countries and foreign-born individuals, publishing, and spirituality.

These two signs, Pisces and Sagittarius, form a 90-degree angle to each other known as a square, an aspect that creates friction and resistance between your self-expression and your sexuality. As a result, your sexuality may be intensely uncomfortable at times. Your Sagittarius Mars is up-front and bluntly direct about sex, is often the aggressor in a relationship, and holds nothing back. Your Pisces Sun is shyer, less confident, and generally not aggressive in sexual situations. How you reconcile these differences depends on which planetary energy is in charge at a given time.

Some people live out the archetype of their Sun sign to the nth degree; others live out the archetype of their Mars sign or of some other planetary placement. But none of us is composed of just the Sun or Mars or any single other planet. As complex beings, we are represented by our entire birth chart. But here's one possible way to shed light on the Sun/Mars square. Look at the sign and house placement of your natal Venus. The planet (Sun or Mars) that is most compatible with the element of the sign Venus is in the planet through which the tension can be navigated, if not resolved. If your Venus is in earth sign Taurus, for example, then you work out your tension through your sun sign, because Pisces (water) is more compatible with earth Taurus.

Wanderlust is a major theme with Sagittarius Mars. For author Jack Kerouac, travel became not only a lifestyle, but the creative fodder for his books. The wanderlust isn't always about physical travel. It can be the journey of creative process, or travel through uncharted regions in the mind. Any partner to whom you commit should share or at least support the way in which *your* wanderlust is expressed.

Best Matches: A Venus in Aries would be way too selfish and independent for your Pisces Sun. But there would be plenty of sexual fireworks. Ditto for Venus in Sagittarius or Leo. A Mars in a fire sign might lead to ego conflicts, so stick to Mars or a Sun in either Pisces or Cancer.

Examples: Lesley-Anne Down, George Frederic Handel, Jack Kerouac, Patty Hearst, Ron Howard, Henrik Ibsen, Edna St. Vincent Millay

MARS IN CAPRICORN ♂ ♑

This combination works very smoothly. Water and earth feed and nurture each other. In this instance, your Pisces Sun supports the ambitions of your Capricorn Mars and provides greater imagination and intuition than Capricorn usually has.

You tend to be somewhat serious about life and single-minded when you want something. You plan, strategize, set your course, and then work tirelessly to attain your goal. You have a surprising reservoir of humor that gets you through challenges; if you're in the entertainment business, that humor may be your ticket to fame and recognition.

This combination favors a profession in which your Pisces Sun can reach within and your Capricorn Mars can then build your career brick by brick, achievement by achievement. This seems to have been what happened with Edgar Cayce, probably the greatest psychic of the twentieth century. He spent a large part of his adult life in trance, doing readings for people he'd never met, undoubtedly grounded by his Mars in Capricorn, which also gave him the perseverance to build his reputation.

The mystical qualities of this combination can't be underestimated. It may be that you are able to reach so far within that you tap into the universal mind, what Carl Jung called the collective unconscious. And it may be this very thing that you're looking for in your sexual relationships. In the right relationship, your passion can tap into that deeper Piscean part of you to access levels beyond physical connection—and take you somewhere else altogether.

You like to be courted, but it doesn't have to be especially romantic or anything else. You simply enjoy being appreciated for who you are. Gestures of appreciation are great, but they don't make or break the relationship. The martyr/savior syndrome that plagues Pisces is far less likely in this combination. Capricorn is just too busy, too ambitious, and too focused to nurture an alcoholic into sobriety or a drug addict into kicking the habit.

Best Matches: Venus in Taurus infuses a relationship with

sensuality. Venus in Capricorn would work well, too, but wouldn't be as sensual. A Mars or Sun in an earth or water sign would work nicely, too.

Examples: Prince Andrew, Prince Albert, Drew Barrymore, Edgar Cayce, Albert Einstein, George Harrison, L. Ron Hubbard

MARS IN AQUARIUS ♂ ≈

Despite the lack of compatibility between Pisces and Aquarius, this combination has the same visionary quality to it that any combination with Aquarius does. However, the rebellious streak that is so prevalent in Aquarius may offend Pisces, who usually doesn't seek to overturn existing modes of thought, behavior, or belief. If anything, Pisces simply escapes into its own world. The result is that you may feel a strange, inner tension at times and not be sure what causes it.

You're idealistic, something on which both your Sun and Mars agree, and you seek to act on those ideals. If an ideal appeals to the Pisces in you, then your imagination, intuition, and emotions kick in to help. If Pisces doesn't feel anything about the ideal one way or another, then chances are that it remains as nothing more than an intellectual exercise for you.

This isn't to imply that you're schizophrenic (just in case you're getting that impression), only that part of your challenge is to find a way to make these two energies work together. After all, an ideal that has passion behind it is much more likely to be realized than one backed only by the mind.

You might not be very comfortable with your sexuality. From the viewpoint of your Pisces Sun, it's Mars's fault. *How can she say that?* Pisces moans. Or: *How can I possibly do this?* But from the viewpoint of your Mars in Aquarius, it's the Sun's fault. *Oh, please, let's get out there and do something about it!* Mars gripes. *Get off your duff.* Aquarius Mars has to be seduced by ideas; your Pisces Sun needs the emotional connections. Aquarius doesn't need a conventional relationship, but Pisces may prefer convention.

The challenge is to learn how to merge these two energies so that you fulfill your potential rather than scatter it, so that you enjoy your sexuality rather than avoid it. One way of doing this is through your creative abilities and by recognizing synchronicities that may be pointing you in new directions, toward new opportunities and new people.

Best Matches: A Venus in Aquarius or another air sign would work well, but to infuse the relationship with more sexuality, you might want a Venus in a fire sign—Sagittarius or Leo would be great. A Mars or Sun in an air sign or water sign would work, too, although you may want to think twice about a Scorpio Sun.

Examples: Jon Bon Jovi, Bobby Fischer, Gabriel Garcia Marquez, Edward James Olmos, Tom Wolfe

MARS IN PISCES ♂ ♓

When a planet—any planet—is in the same sign as your Sun, the qualities of your Sun are enhanced and the two energies are mutually supportive. In an actual natal chart, the two planets couldn't be separated by more than five degrees to be truly conjunct. But for the purposes of this book, we're looking primarily at the signs. And with this conjunction, your imagination is as vast as the Pacific Ocean, your compassion is profound, and your ideals are large.

Professionally, you're a natural for the arts and entertainment, communication, research, politics, and anything that deals with liquids and beauty. You also work well behind the scenes, within institutional settings where your compassion finds full expression—hospices, prisons, mental institutions; medicine, podiatry, pediatrics, nursing.

Liz Taylor is the quintessential double Pisces. First, as previously mentioned, there are her exquisite eyes, a Piscean trait. Then, the addictions to alcohol and pills. Then, there are eight marriages, two of them to Richard Burton. And then there's her charity work, through which she has raised millions for AIDS.

The multiple marriages aren't necessarily a given if you're a double Pisces, but it's likely and has to do with your inability to make up your mind in the romance department. Even if you do make up your mind and commit to a relationship, you may discover that you were caught up in the whirlwind of the romance and that the person to whom you committed isn't a suitable partner for you. Your compassion as a double Pisces often results in an intense need to dedicate yourself to a particular cause.

You undoubtedly have great intuitive insight into other people, but may fall short on insight when it comes to yourself and your life. It's difficult for you to detach emotionally and to view yourself or your life in an objective way. And when it comes to sex and love, it's nearly impossible for you to be objective. As a double Pisces, you run the risk of the martyr/savior syndrome precisely because a deep part of you longs to heal the person you love. There's considerable healing ability with the double Pisces combination, but when it gets tangled up in your emotions, it spells big trouble.

Best Matches: Venus in Pisces is a natural, but don't discount the sensual (and earthy) Taurus Venus. Venus or Mars in Scorpio would mean a sexually and emotionally intense relationship, but the other person's sexual energy could overwhelm you. A Sun in a water sign, or even an earth sign like Taurus or your mutable sibling, Virgo, might work well, too.

Examples: Elizabeth Taylor, Elizabeth Barrett Browning, Anthony Burgess, Johnny Cash, Glenn Close, John Connolly, Adelle Davis, Sybil Leek, Sam Donaldson

SENSE-MEMORY EXERCISE FOR SUN IN PISCES

Mars represents our physical senses. Most of us have at least one sense that is stronger than the others or provides information more quickly about our physical environment. It might be your hearing or sense of touch. It could be your sense of taste. Your strongest sense, whatever it is, provides you with immediate and reliable information about yourself or others, your environment, and your personal world.

In the space below, describe any instance where one of your physical senses played a vital role. Be detailed and specific.

_____

_____

_____

_____

_____

The incident or situation you've just described pertains to the second question you asked in the inventory at the beginning of part two. If the connection isn't immediately apparent, look for the metaphor.

A Pisces woman who is an interior designer described an experience she'd had when she was just a child in which she was physically abused by a neighbor. There was no one specific physical sense in the description, just a horrifying feeling of hopelessness. Her second question asked why her marriage had really broken up. What was the underlying reason behind it?

Her description, in light of the question, was an eye-opener. Despite her intuitive abilities, she couldn't step back enough from her own life to connect the childhood experience with the failure of her marriage.

PART THREE

Venus

"What's love got to do with it?"

— TINA TURNER

ROMANTIC INVENTORY

$\mathcal{B}$efore you read the Venus descriptions, go through this list of statements and check the ones that apply to you most of the time.

1. I'm fiercely passionate.
2. I'm a true romantic.
3. I believe that love is everything.
4. I leap into relationships.
5. I'm fascinated by the inner person.
6. I want a partner who is as committed to his or her ideals as I am to mine.
7. I want a partner who is creative.
8. I am often critical of my partner.
9. I'm interested in transformative relationships, romances from which I learn something.
10. I want harmony and balance in romance.
11. I want thrills in a relationship—risk, drama.
12. I want a partner who can communicate his or her feelings, thoughts, and ideas.
13. I need intuitive and spiritual connections to my partner.
14. Sensuality is vital in my intimate relationships.
15. I need and expect a lot of freedom in my romantic relationships.
16. Don't tie me down.

17. Show me how much you love me.
18. My partner has to share my beliefs and worldview.
19. Balance is vital in my romantic relationships.
20. Sex has got to be great in my romances; that's first.

A Romantic Experience

Describe a romantic experience you've had. It can be from any phase of your life, a childhood experience or something more recent. The point here is to capture your feelings about this experience.

_____

_____

_____

_____

_____

_____

_____

_____

You've just answered the first question you asked in the inventory at the beginning of part two. As with the exercise that addressed the second question, it may take some interpretation on your part to understand your answer.

15

Venus, the Babe

She was known to the ancient Greeks as Aphrodite and has always been associated with love, romance, and pleasure. There are two versions of her birth, so take your pick. In the first, reported by Homer, she was the daughter of Zeus and Dione. End of story. This version was never popular, perhaps because it was too normal for an Olympian, and eventually another version came into being. In this second, more violent version, Aphrodite rose out of ocean foam when Cronus castrated his father, Uranus, and threw his genitals into the ocean. Hardly something to write home about.

In this version, she was transported across the sea to Cythera and then to Cyprus, by the god of the west wind, Zephyrus. There, Aphrodite was welcomed by the Themis's daughters Horae, who fancied her up with nice clothes and precious jewels and took her to Olympus. She was so incomparably beautiful that all the male gods wanted to marry her. Zeus was afraid she would create violence among the gods (too much testosterone?) so he married her off to Hephaestus (Vulcan), the god of fire, who was both lame and ugly.

Aphrodite wasn't faithful to him for very long. She fell in love with Ares (Mars) and had two sons, Deimos and Phobos, and a daughter, Harmonia. Helios, the god who saw everything, told Hephaestus that Aphrodite was cheating on him with Ares. So Hephaestus forged an invisible net, spread it over his wife's bed, and the next time his wife and Ares were together, he closed the net, trapping them inside. Hephaestus called all the Olympian gods to witness Aphrodite's infidelity. Poseidon had to intervene before Hephaestus would free the lovers. Aphrodite, humiliated by what had happened, left for Cyprus, and Ares for Thrace.

She had numerous lovers among both gods and mortals, and bore many children. To say she had major problems with monogamy is an understatement. She wasn't much of a mother, either. In our time, she would be investigated by Child Protective Services and her kids probably would be taken away from her. Yet she surpassed all the other goddesses in beauty and eventually received the prize for beauty (Miss Universe?) from Paris, which started the Trojan Wars.

There were many cults devoted to Aphrodite in both Athens and Rome, and eventually she became known as the goddess of love, beauty, and sensuality. She had the power to confer beauty and irresistible charm on others. She was known to get even with people who went against her and to protect those who were faithful to her. Her mythological history is typical for the Olympians, but sure doesn't do much to support what she has become in astrological circles.

VENUS IN ASTROLOGY

Since many of the astrological meanings of the planets come from mythology, it isn't surprising that Venus is associated with love and romance. Interestingly, despite the fact that Aphrodite was so promiscuous, she's not associated with that in astrology. Instead, she has rulership over the rosy part of love and romance and also rules harmony, refinement, money and possessions, aesthetic and artistic tastes, friendships and sociability, attraction, and marriage and other partnerships. Venus embodies *relationships*, and rules both Taurus and Libra.

Astrologer Robert Hand has one of the best descriptions of the Venus/Mars connections that I've ever run across. "Whereas Venus is a planet of merging, Mars helps one establish one's separate identity," he writes in *Horoscope Symbols*. "Unless you have established yourself as an individual, Venus cannot operate properly in your life. You have to express yourself, be what you really are, before you can love or be truly loved."

Even though Aphrodite wasn't exactly a model mom, in astrology she is associated, along with the Moon, with what Hand refers to as "the mother complex of symbols." By this, he means that Venus symbolizes the unconditional love of a parent for a child.

In terms of your sexuality and birth chart, Venus symbolizes the romantic side of your personality. For a woman, Venus describes the image she projects both romantically and sexually, as well as the way in which she wants to be loved. Madonna, for instance, has a Venus in Leo. On the negative side, this is the sign of the showoff, the woman who *must* be noticed regardless, and who has difficulties separating her genuine self from her public self. On the positive side, it suggests a woman who is warm, affectionate, and enormously generous with a partner. The partner should be physically attractive, which makes her look good, and must be supportive of her goals and applaud her achievements.

In a man's chart, Venus describes the kind of woman and intimate relationship he's seeking and also tells a great deal about his animus, the yin or receptive side of his personality. Actor and producer Michael Douglas, for example, has a Venus in Libra, indicating that he looks for a partner who is attractive and artistic, enjoys harmony and beauty, has a kind, sympathetic nature, and shares his values. His Sun and Mars are also in Libra. His wife, Catherine Zeta-Jones, is a Libra born on the same day as Douglas, but many years later, so there's a Venus/Sun contact, and she also has four other planets in Libra. Douglas's Venus placement indicates that he is most receptive and intuitive when it comes to relationships and to his creativity.

Venus/Mars, Venus/Sun, and Venus/Venus contacts usually result in immediate attraction. Also significant are contacts from any of these three planets to the Ascendant. Other significant contacts are Venus/Neptune, Moon/Moon, Sun/Moon, Venus/Moon, and Mars/Moon. These last five are beyond the scope of this book, but are worth noting in the event that you're comparing your chart to someone else's. In all of these contacts, the closer the aspect between them, the greater the attraction. The most powerful is the conjunction, when two planets lie not only in the same sign, but also in the same degree. Perhaps your Sun is at 10-degrees Libra and your significant other has Venus at 10-degrees Libra. This connection would result in immediate attraction.

In your birth chart, look for the sign Venus is in and the house placement. If Venus is in the same sign as another planet, combine the meanings of the two planets by using the keywords for the planets in the table in Chapter 2. If Venus is in the same sign or house as your Sun or Mars, then it enhances the qualities of that planet.

An Example

I debated about which chart to use as an example for this section. Someone famous? Someone weird and famous? Someone weird and infamous? I finally selected the chart of a teenage girl. Her chart illustrates the potential that lies within any birth horoscope, and illustrates some interesting points about the placements and signs of Venus, Mars, and the Sun.

The teenager has the Sun ☉ and Moon ☾ in Virgo, in the sixth house. Her Mars ♂ is also in Virgo, within one degree of the seventh house cusp. In the seventh house, she has Venus ♀ and Mercury ☿ in Libra and a point called the Vertex Vtx in Virgo.

The Vertex is a point that's considered to have a destined or fated texture about it. In a natal chart, it indicates a fated encounter with someone who has that sign prevalent in their charts. Any time your Vertex is in the same sign or degree (within two degrees on either side) as one of your partner's planets, pay attention. It indicates an agreement you made with that person before you were born. The nature of that agreement depends on the nature of the planets and the houses involved.

The teenager's rising sign is Pisces; since Neptune ♆ rules Pisces, Neptune is said to rule her chart. But because Jupiter is the co-ruler of Pisces, its sign and placement are also important in the astrological scheme of things. Also in her sixth house, but in the sign of Leo, is the South Node of the Moon ☋. Its opposite, the North Node ☊, is in the twelfth house in Aquarius. The South Node describes that which is familiar and habitual for us and relates to past-life patterns. The North Node represents the direction in which we should move to evolve spiritually in *this* life and to fulfill the potential of our birth chart.

The focus of the teen's chart lies in the sixth and seventh houses. Five out of ten planets fall in those two houses, along with the South Node and the Vertex. This means that her health and daily work routine and relationships are her focus. The three planets in her tenth house of profession and career are also important—Neptune ♆ (the ruler of the chart), Saturn ♄, and

VENUS

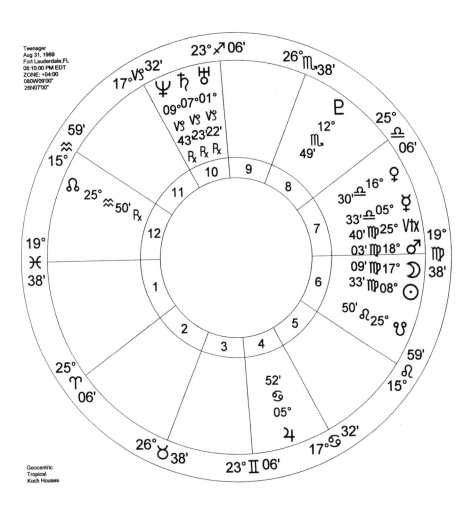

Teenager
Aug 31, 1989
Fort Lauderdale, FL
08:10:00 PM EDT
ZONE: +04:00
080W09'00"
26N07'00"

Geocentric
Tropical
Koch Houses

©1994 Matrix Software Big Rapids, MI

Uranus ♅, all of them retrograde. But since we're talking about the Sun, Mars, and Venus, let's concentrate on those planets.

Venus and Mars don't form any major aspects to each other, so the house placements become even more important. Since she's not an adult yet, the seventh house relates to friendships and the sixth house, in addition to health, relates to her daily life—i.e., school. With both Venus and Mercury (conscious thought) in Libra, the sign of relationships, friendships are the focus of the teen's life. Yes, this can be said of any teenager's life. But with these particular signs and placements, friendships are everything.

With Venus in Libra, she will bend over backward to accommodate the needs of her friends. With Mars in Virgo so close to the seventh house cusp, she is precise (Virgo) and often contentious (Mars) when it comes to friendships. When her friends don't measure up, they hear about it even if they don't want to hear about it. She also isn't the least bit timid about standing up for herself, unless that Libra Venus kicks in; then she flips back into the energy of keeping peace at any cost.

Mars is within a one-degree conjunction of her Moon, significant because the Moon symbolizes our emotions and inner life, as well as our ability to nurture and how we are nurtured. This aspect indicates that the full expression of her emotions is vital to her well-being and health. Individuals born in the latter part of the Virgo cycle will play important roles in her life (the Vertex). Her best romantic match will be someone with a Libra Sun or Mars, or someone whose Sun is in Pisces (her rising), or even another Virgo, because she has her Sun, Moon, Mars, and the cusp of her seventh house in Virgo. As she matures, she will favor partners whose personalities are a blend of Virgo and Libra energies, but who have the imaginative and mystical qualities of Pisces (her rising).

Her closest friend is the boy next door, a Pisces with a Capri-

corn Moon (which fits nicely with her Virgo earth Moon) and a
Leo rising (her South Node). This may be a past-life relationship
here.

In a birth chart, there are four critical angles: the ascendant or
rising, which is the cusp of the first house; and the cusps of the
fourth, seventh, and tenth houses. Any planets that fall in these
houses are especially important. We've already looked at the
teen's ascendant and seventh house cusp and house, so let's look
at her fourth and tenth houses.

The sign on the cusp of the fourth house is Gemini $\mathrm{I\!I}$, and the
only planet in that house is Jupiter in Cancer $\mathrm{2\!\!\downarrow\,69}$. The fourth
house describes our fundamental being, early childhood, our
home life, the nurturing parent—which changes over the years—
and the last twenty years or so of life. With Gemini on the cusp,
communication is a focal point in her childhood (true). She is
surrounded by books (true) and both of her parents are writers,
which also fits the sign. She enjoys movies, another form of communication, and there's a lot of activity in her home (true).
Information and travel are also important (true). Her mother's
Sun sign is Gemini, the sign on the cusp of the fourth house,
which sometimes represents the mother.

I've found that quite often a mother's Sun sign appears on the
cusp of the fourth house of her first-born child. My mother, for instance, was a Capricorn, the sign on the cusp of my fourth house.

Jupiter in Cancer here is a positive placement, indicating that
she has a lot of emotional support from her parents and that her
home is comfortable and pleasant (true). It gives her an expan-
sive foundation from which the rest of her life can evolve. Jupiter
here also suggests that the latter part of her life will be comfortable and that she will die peacefully, at a ripe old age, and probably owning quite a bit of real estate, also represented by the
fourth house.

The cusp of her tenth house is in Sagittarius ♐, with three planets in Capricorn in that house. Uranus and Neptune move much more slowly than the other planets, so they impact large numbers of people. Everyone born between February 15, 1988 and May 27, 1988, and December 3, 1988 and April 1, 1995, have Uranus and Neptune in Capricorn, somewhere in their charts. Saturn, which takes about two and a half years to go through a sign, was in Capricorn between February 14, 1988 and June 10, 1988, and November 12, 1988 and February 7, 1991.

The fact that these three planets are in Capricorn indicates that the teenager—and her contemporaries—will have conflicts with the established way of doing things. The changes they make in existing paradigms and structures will be practical and far-reaching and will impact the larger society in which they live. With Uranus so close to her Midheaven (tenth-house cusp), she won't do well with a boss breathing down her neck. Self-employment is likely to give her the most freedom, which she will definitely need in her professional life.

Since Uranus rules sudden and unexpected change—as well as astrology, the Internet, the Aquarian Age, television and the media, and a host of other areas—it's likely that she will have more than one profession. The teenager and her dad have coauthored a book on astrology for teens.

Saturn here in Capricorn, the sign that it rules, suggests that within her profession, she will seek significant achievements. Neptune in Capricorn is a tough one. Neptune is so ephemeral and filled with illusions that when it's in Capricorn, it's as if it's in chains. Practical principles won't interest her; she'll strive to be more intuitive in her career. The fact that all three are retrograde suggests that the energies of the planets are turned inward. These children assimilate their experiences, but don't express them until the planets turn direct by progression or are triggered by transits.

The sign on the teen's tenth-house cusp (Midheaven) is Sagittarius, symbolized by the centaur, the mythological creature that is half human, half horse. Given the areas that Sagittarius rules, it's possible that she will work overseas or in publishing or for a foreign company or individuals born in a foreign country. It's possible that animals, particularly horses, will figure into her professional life.

Already, part of this is evolving. When the teenager was in third grade, she began horseback riding lessons. After that first lesson, her teacher remarked that she had never seen a child who took to horses like this girl did, as if she had been riding since she was born. This is all the more unusual because neither of her parents ride.

In terms of animals, her family has a menagerie of pets—three cats, a dog, a bird, and a mouse. They have also owned hamsters, nursed wounded ducks and doves, lizards and mice, and any number of other creatures in need of a temporary refuge.

The Pluto in Scorpio in the eighth house is less obvious, but beginning to unfold. If you refer to the description of the eighth house in Chapter 2, you'll realize that it boils down to metaphysics, sex, and to things like insurance, trusts, taxes, and shared resources. The teen is interested in things that go bump in the night and embraces spiritual ideas that lie outside of mainstream religion. For three years, her grandfather lived with the family, a sharing of resources in the familial sense.

Pluto compels us to seek the absolute bottom line in whatever we tackle, according to sign and house placement, and will become more prominent and active in her chart as she matures.

Even though I've provided only the bare minimum about her chart, it gives you some idea of just how much information a chart can yield in just a pared-down version. I used this particular chart because I am absolutely sure about the teen's time of birth and about the accuracy of the information. She's my daughter. When I asked Megan if I could use her chart as an example, her response was typical for a double Virgo: "Sure. But what are you trying to illustrate, anyway?" In other words, *Spell it out for me, Mom . . . and then let me read what you've written.*

16

Venus in the Signs and Houses

Even though Venus relates primarily to love and romance, it's also connected to our creative ability, so I've included examples of individuals under each sign.

VENUS IN . . .

Aries ♀♈: Your nature is passionate, all-consuming, and as a result, you are impetuous and impulsive in romantic relationships. You're aggressive in the pursuit of sex and romance (and everything else, too), and when you fall in love, you fall hard. But even when you're madly in love, you can't tolerate restraints of any kind. You expect your partner to be as independent and competitive as you are.

You also tend to insist on having your own way—not some of the time, but all of the time—so you're not the easiest person to live with. You are usually the dominant partner unless your partner has Mars in a fire sign—or a lot of other planets in fire signs. You have great warmth, an affectionate nature, and a certain magnetism, so you never lack for partners. The challenge with

Venus in Aries is to develop more consideration for and aware-ness of your partner.

Examples: Charlotte Brontë, Julie Christie, Robert Frost, Pierre-Auguste Renoir, Bob Marley, Drew Carey

Taurus ♀ ♉: This is one of the signs that Venus rules; that means the planet is extremely comfortable here. You're sensual, creative, and hard-working. You're also practical, except where your expensive tastes are concerned. This doesn't necessarily mean you run out and buy expensive items just to buy them. You may be the type who collects certain things—books, for instance, or rare manuscripts or art. An element of financial luck accompa-nies this sign for Venus.

In romance, you usually go one of two ways either you grow into love and the relationship or the attraction is immediate, vis-ceral. Sex is important to you and in any relationship it can be the factor that determines the course of a relationship. If it's good, then it enhances and deepens the relationship emotionally. If it's only mediocre, then chances are very good that the rest of the relationship is mediocre as well.

In all romantic relationships, you value loyalty, stability, and creativity, and look for a partner who shares those values.

Examples: Nancy Reagan, Bertrand Russell, James Taylor, Jacques Cousteau, Billy Crystal, Salvador Dali

Gemini ♀ ♊: You're the social butterfly, all charm and wit and movement. It's hard to pin you down about romance and love be-cause you don't stay in one place long enough to think about it. You thrive on variety and change and when you look for roman-tic partners, they have to be people who stimulate your intellect and curiosity.

Even though you're certainly capable of falling deeply in love, it won't be the passionate, overwhelming emotion of Venus in a fire sign. Your love will be more detached emotionally, but with a deeper mental connection. You probably won't be the dominant partner; you're much too adaptable for that. But you will guide the relationship in terms of creativity, intellectual stimulation, communication, and social activities. In short, you'll be the social director.

Examples: Uma Thurman, Giorgio Armani, Cat Stevens, Malcolm X, Courtney Love, Henry David Thoreau

Cancer ♀♋: You enter every relationship through your heart. Superficial relationships rarely interest you (unless you've got Mars in Aries). As a result, your most intimate relationships may lack balance. Sex is important to you in any intimate relationship, but not nearly as important as the emotional connection and what you sense intuitively about your karmic history with this person.

There's a strong urge to nurture and care for when Venus is in Cancer. If you identify strongly with this facet of your personality, then you run the risk of nurturing your partners, especially those who have mother issues. But if your nurturing can find another outlet—creativity, animals, activism—then you're better able to use the full potential of this placement for Venus.

Examples: Clint Eastwood, Angelina Jolie, Herman Hesse, Alex Haley, Carl Jung, Nicola Tesla

Leo ♀♌: You love to be loved and love to be shown that you are loved. You're fun-loving, warm, generous, and charismatic when it comes to romance, love, and sex. When you're in love, your heart opens up and embraces every part of the relationship and everything about your partner. Even if you see the person's flaws, you tend to overlook them as long as your partner makes you the center of attention.

The challenge with Venus in Leo is that you have to stop looking to others for validation of your opinions and creative abilities.

Examples: Madonna, Raymond Chandler, Thomas Wolfe, David Copperfield

Virgo ♀♍: This can be a difficult placement for Venus. Virgo, by its very nature, is focused on details and perfection. All too often you can be critical of your partners or, just as bad, feel that you aren't worthy of a fulfilling and romantic relationship. One of the best ways to deal with this quality in yourself is through a relationship in which you and your partner are involved in a joint creative profession.

The real challenge for you is to understand that perfection is an abstract ideal. We live in an imperfect world that has moments of perfection and it's those moments that we strive to achieve or to maintain, not the abstract ideal.

Examples: Carrie Fisher, Robert Redford, Sylvia Plath, Linda Ronstadt, John Lennon

Libra ♀♎: As this is one of the signs that Venus rules, the planet is comfortable here. You have grace, charm, and considerable creative talent. Relationships are your domain. You're a true romantic who luxuriates in moonlit strolls on beaches, candlelit dinners, and all the other typically romantic scenarios and gestures. You're in love with love, as long as that love is balanced and harmonious.

The ideal romantic relationship for you is one in which you and your partner are involved in something creative together. Then all of the artistic sensibilities of this Venus placement unfold with often astonishing results.

Example: Stephen King, Margaret Mitchell, Picasso, Michael Crichton, Lauren Hutton, Christopher Reeve

Scorpio ♀♏: Your focus in all romantic relationships is emotional, spiritual, psychic, and, in the really intimate relationships, karmic. Your energy is directed inward, to the absolute bottom line of your partner's personality and how it meshes (or doesn't mesh) with your own. You probably aren't interested in idle social chatter unless you have a Sun or Mars in one of the air signs. Your intensity in romance can be difficult for your partner, unless he or she is similar in disposition.

You're quite independent and can get along just fine without being in a relationship. However, your search for depth and your insight into the human psyche compel you to get involved. The challenge with this placement for Venus is to learn that relationships function on many different levels. Just because you're looking for the deepest levels doesn't mean that everyone else is. Loosen up, chill out, and try to embrace the many levels of romantic relationships.

Examples: H.G. Wells, B.B. King, Goldie Hawn, Odetta, Dan Rather, Eugene O'Neill, Harold Pinter

Sagittarius ♀♐: Like Venus in other fire signs, this placement isn't really about personal relationships. Its focus is on freedom and expansion and a quest for truth. You require an enormous amount of personal freedom in your romantic relationships—*there, but not there*, as one woman so aptly put it—which doesn't exactly make for a lot of romance, much less a stable relationship. However, if your partner values the same type of freedom, then there shouldn't be a problem. But there often is because you expect your partner to take a lot on faith. Words, especially the three that count, *I love you*, have to be backed up by action.

The challenge with this placement is to learn that love isn't just the power that makes everything else happen, it's at the heart of all that is spiritual.

Examples: Rod Serling, Gene Hackman, Jimi Hendrix, Rudyard Kipling, James Michener, Claude Monet

Capricorn ♀♑: You tend to reduce love and romance to an equation that has more to do with materialism and status than it does with emotion. You're always aware of how your partner reflects on you. If he or she doesn't look or act in the way that you think is proper or doesn't earn enough money in the "right" profession (whatever that may be for you), then you may lose interest or not get involved to begin with.

However, in a relationship where you have successfully separated your materialism from your emotions, you are a loving partner who seeks to build a foundation for the relationship to evolve and grow throughout your time together.

Examples: Dale Carnegie, Faye Dunaway, Sinclair Lewis, A.A. Milne, Robert Kennedy, Louis Pasteur

Aquarius ♀♒: You aren't an emotional person, unless you have the Moon and Mars in fire signs. You're attached to ideals and are more comfortable working with groups who share those ideals. In romance and love, you're independent and it's as difficult for your partner as it is for you to pin down what you feel in any given moment about the relationship. You have such strong visionary qualities that your love life becomes extremely difficult when the reality doesn't match the vision.

Generally, your relationships are atypical and don't fit into the consensus reality of society. But that's fine with you. If your partner supports and shares your ideals, then the relationship becomes much more viable and you're better able to understand that it's possible to live your ideals through your most intimate partnerships.

Examples: Hal Holbrook, Janis Joplin, Margaret Mead, Jack London, Nostradamus, Yoko Ono

Pisces ♀ ♓: Venus is considered to be exalted in Pisces, which means its energy is comfortable in this sign, so this is a wonderful placement. Here, Venus's love of beauty and harmony finds an ideal balance with the spirituality and emotionalism of Pisces. It's through people, beauty, and emotions that you relate to the larger world and to the cosmos. In romance, the ideal partner is one with whom you feel a spiritual connection and who shares your feelings about beauty, creativity, and emotional expression. You're the type of person who, when confronted with something that you consider to be beautiful—art, music, a book, or the perfect sunset—is moved to tears.

You're an inherently gentle person, and can be easily hurt but are loathe to show it. You embody the poetic language of the soul.

Examples: Edith Wharton, Ron Howard, Martin Luther King, Charles Lindbergh, Harper Lee, Carl Sandburg

VENUS IN THE HOUSES

First House: The Self

Your nature is deeply sensual, and this sensuality permeates everything you do. You're also physically attractive, charming, and friendly, and all of these attributes contribute to your sensuality.

You're a refined person with an inherent appreciation for art, literature, poetry, opera, and beautiful surroundings. Venus in the first house usually bodes well for good fortune, but squares and oppositions to Venus here can indicate laziness and vanity.

The signs in parentheses are for Venus.

Examples: Ellen Burstyn (Sagittarius), Albert Camus (Libra), Uri Geller (Scorpio), Abraham Lincoln (Aries)

Second House: Finances and Personal Values

Lucky you. Venus here usually indicates financial comfort and sometimes even wealth. You place great importance on your personal possessions. You're a big spender, but for quality, usually expensive things. Your sensuality is deeply ingrained in your value system and you enjoy partners who appreciate that—and your artistic tastes.

The more planets you have in this house, the greater the chances that you're a workaholic. With Mars and/or the Sun here, a lot of your energy goes into making money—and spending it.

Examples: Mario Andretti (Aries), Russell Banks (Taurus), Margaret Bourke-White (Gemini), Francis Ford Coppola (Pisces)

Third House: Communication and Siblings

In love and romance, your emphasis is on communication with your partner. A lively exchange of ideas and philosophies is integral to the success of any romantic relationship you have. If your partner enjoys books, music, and the arts, so much the better, since that's where your interests lie. And your partner better enjoy your parents and siblings, too, because you're close to them.

This is a very social position for Venus. You know everyone in your neighborhood, and they know you.

Examples: F. Lee Bailey (Cancer), Tom Brokaw (Pisces), Rita Mae Brown (Capricorn), Aretha Franklin (Aquarius), Sue Grafton (Gemini), Peter Jennings (Virgo)

Fourth House: The Home and the Nurturing Parent

Your emotional bonds with your birthplace and your birth family are strong. Your childhood was happy and your memories of that part of your life are good. You gain through your parents, property, houses, and real estate.

In your adult home, you seek harmony and go to great lengths to maintain it. Your family and children are vital to your happiness and your home life generally is content. If you're single, you need an intuitive and spiritual connection to a partner and what you're seeking is patterned on your experience of your parents and early home life.

Examples: Louisa May Alcott (Capricorn), Dean Martin (Gemini), Colleen McCullough (Aries), Joni Mitchell (Virgo)

Fifth House: Creativity, Children, and Pleasure

A great placement for happy love affairs and artistic creativity. You have numerous romances, find great pleasure in sex, and gain financially and otherwise through your romantic partners. You're very direct about sex, romance, and what you feel, and you're looking for a partner who responds in kind.

You gain through speculation and investments and, since the fifth house represents children, particularly the first-born, your kids are dream children: beautiful, talented, and gifted in some way.

Examples: Tina Turner (Sagittarius), Bruce Springsteen (Scorpio), Robert Silverberg (Aquarius), Dolly Parton (Capricorn), and Mick Jagger (Virgo)

Sixth House: Health and Work

You find enormous pleasure in your work and have pleasant working conditions, coworkers, and bosses. You're fortunate with jobs—often in the right place at the right time—and are lucky in that you usually get the job you want. It's quite possible that you meet your romantic partners through work or through health-related events or experiences.

This placement cautions against excessive use of alcohol and drugs.

Examples: Antonio Banderas (Virgo), Dustin Hoffman (Cancer), Charles Dickens (Pisces), Bob Dylan (Gemini), Sigmund Freud (Aries), Whitney Houston (Leo)

Seventh House: Partnerships and Marriage

Venus here promises a happy marriage and profitable business and personal partnerships. It's possible that you and your partner work together professionally, and if Venus is in Taurus or Libra, a creative partnership of some kind is indicated. Sometimes with this house placement for Venus, there's a strong past-life connection. When you meet your partner, one or both of you recognizes the other's soul.

You're at ease in social situations and when you're at your charismatic best, act like a magnet that attracts the right contacts and situations for financial affairs. Your finances probably improve considerably after marriage.

Examples: Glenn Close (Aquarius), Edgar Degas (Virgo), John Glenn (Gemini), Sugar Ray Leonard (Cancer), David Sanborn (Taurus)

Eighth House: Sex and Shared Resources

You gain financially through inheritances, joint finances, marriage, and partnerships. You're intrigued by metaphysical topics—life after death, mediumship, astrology, death and dying, the survival of the soul. You may meet romantic partners through groups that deal with metaphysical topics or through situations that deal with insurance, taxes, trust law, death and bereavement, or inheritances.

Venus's sign for this house placement is important. A Scorpio Venus, for example, might view sexuality in a mystical way. A Leo Venus is likely to share her resources with others in a way that puts her in the spotlight.

Examples: Catherine Deneuve (Virgo), Mel Gibson (Libra), Coco Chanel (Leo), Angelica Huston (Virgo), Tina Brown (Scorpio)

Ninth House: Higher Mind

Your most memorable romances will occur overseas or with a foreign-born individual. Your significant other or spouse may be from another country, be an academic or work in publishing or law, or be spiritually oriented. Your artistic and spiritual interests reflect a heightened awareness of the cosmic unity in life. The closer Venus is to the Midheaven or tenth house cusp, the stronger its influence in your chart.

When Venus is within a degree or so of your Midheaven, either in the ninth or tenth house, honors, recognition, and success are indicated.

Examples: David Bowie (Sagittarius), Marsha Mason (Libra), Jim Morrison (Scorpio), Sydney Omarr (Cancer), Ram Dass (Pisces), Edgar Cayce (Pisces)

Tenth House: Profession and Career

Your romances tend to cluster around your profession and career. You meet partners through your work before the public or may even work with your partner in some professional capacity. Your sensuality may play an important role in your profession.

You tend to be very fortunate in your own career. In fact, Venus here is a great placement for writers, artists, entertainers, diplomats and actors, and people who work in finance. The sign of Venus is important. If it's in Capricorn, for example, then your ambition finds smooth and easy expression. In Sagittarius, a profession that involves spirituality, publishing, the law, travel, or higher education would be naturals.

Examples: Drew Barrymore (Pisces), Kathy Bates (Cancer), Pierre Cardin (Leo), Johnny Depp (Taurus)

Eleventh House: Wishes and Dreams, Group Associations

Your friends and group associations are important to you. It's possible that you meet many of your romantic partners (or your significant other) through a group that you attend. This group is most likely to be one that supports your interests, passions, and causes—a writing or book group, a bridge group, or a musical or theater group. Through these groups, and through any romantic partners that you meet through them, some wish, hope, or dream that you have is expanded or fulfilled.

Pay attention to the sign of your Venus when it's in the eleventh house. It will tell you a great deal about the types of romantic and sexual experiences you have through groups.

Examples: Philip K. Dick (Aquarius), Betty Hill (Leo), Billy Joel (Taurus), Kurt Russell (Aries)

Twelfth House: Personal Unconscious, Institutions, Karma

Everything that happens in this house feels fated. With Venus here, you're prone to secret love affairs and romantic intrigues. And some of the people with whom you get involved are individuals you have known in past lives. You'll sense the connection. It's psychic, spiritual, and often strange, like a prolonged déjà vu. You may even dream about the past lives in which you have known these people. Your sensuality can be excessive at times, but just how excessive depends on Venus's sign. You have a special love for adventure and mystery.

The creative element with Venus here can produce astonishing results because you are pushed deeply into yourself, so deep that you discover past-life talents and abilities and now are able to bring them forward.

Examples: George Gershwin (Scorpio), Ben Affleck (Cancer), T.S. Eliot (Libra), Andy Gibbs (Aquarius)

DREAMING WITH VENUS

This activity involves a technique called dream incubation. It's a fancy term for a simple process. Before you fall asleep at night, give yourself a suggestion that you will have a dream that concerns the third question you asked in the inventory at the beginning of part two. Be sure to request that you will remember the dream and will awaken as soon as it's finished so that you can record it.

Some people are able to do this on the first attempt. For others, it may take several nights or a week or a month. But if you persist, you'll get the dream. Our unconscious is incredibly attentive and when we bring our intent and desire to a process, it delivers.

Try to recall as many details about the dream as you can and record them. Sometimes, dream details begin slipping away as soon as you open your eyes and you have to coax the minutiae into your conscious awareness. You may have to shut your eyes and fall back into the dream for a few minutes. Or you may have to engage in a dialogue with it. But sooner or later, you'll have the dream recorded. Then you have to interpret it. What do the symbols suggest? What are the metaphors? Make associations. If the dream was in color, note that.

Generic dream dictionaries are okay if you're trying to make associations, but they usually are so general—or so far out there— that they aren't of much use. Discover your own symbolic language.

Not long after I met my husband, I requested a dream that would address any past-life connections that we had that related to this life. I knew on an intuitive level and from a comparison of our birth charts that the connections existed. It took a couple of weeks, but I finally had a series of dreams.

I was a woman, in prison, and it felt like the middle ages. He was a prison guard and used to bring me food and stories about the outside world. There was a student/teacher relationship first because I was in prison for practicing a metaphysical craft and he was curious about what I knew. We became friends, then lovers. I was eventually executed.

In another dream, we were married and he went off to war and never came back. That dream had no historical context, but the feeling of abandonment and grief were genuinely tangible.

In a third dream, I knew him in Edinburgh, Scotland, around the 1700s. We were both writers and renegades. The details were murky, but the setting was vivid.

There have been other dreams over the years. It's almost as if once you request the information, a channel is opened. But those first dreams remain the most startling because of their resonance and their odd parallels in *this* life.

For instance, I worked as a librarian and Spanish teacher in a medium-security prison, and left shortly before I met Rob.

When his lottery number came up during the Vietnam War, he refused to go, was arrested for draft evasion, sentenced to community service, and was eventually pardoned.

Years before we met, we both traveled in Scotland. We later figured out that we were in Edinburgh the same week in 1975. During my time there, I felt as if I had come home.

We are both writers this time around. We are both fascinated by the metaphysical aspects of life. We met when I was teaching English to Cuban refugees, a job that had 500 other applicants (many far better qualified than I was), and he was a reporter covering the education beat in a South Florida town. He still isn't sure how he got that job. He applied for it when he was living in

Minnesota; someone else had been hired, and then couldn't take
the job, so he was contacted.

The skeptic in me, of course, continues to nag, reminding me
that I write fiction and all of this might just be some fantastic scenario my dreaming self has tossed my way, fodder for a future
novel. After all, we live in a time when we are taught to distrust
our intuition, when we are told that our subjective experiences
have no validity. And yet, I still recall the evening that Rob—a
reporter reporting for an interview—walked into the center
where I taught, and I glanced up and thought, *Holy shit, I know
this guy.* The shock of recognition: I finally understood what that
phrase meant.

Now, twenty years after my shock, I have come to believe that
our most significant relationships—those that shape who we are
creatively, sexually, emotionally, and spiritually—are past-life connections. Before we are born, we agree to explore certain conditions, situations, events, dramas, and challenges with these
individuals. Whether we keep those agreements, of course, is another matter entirely, and always rests with our free will.

I would love to hear *your* stories. Contact me at:
www.booktalk.com/tjmacgregor

Appendix

Ephemeres for Mars and Venus

To look up the signs for your Mars and Venus on the day you were born, locate the dates closest to your birthday. SR after an entry means stationary retrograde, that the planet was about to reverse motion; SD means stationary direct, that the planet was about to turn direct again.

In the Mars ephemeris, for example, on February 12, 1950, Mars in Libra is listed at SR. The retrograde period—indicated by the SD after that entry—lasted until May 3, 1950, when it began to move direct again. If you were born under a retrograde of either Mars or Venus, remember that it simply means the energy of the planet is directed inward.

All entries are for noon, eastern standard time, and should be accurate unless you were born on the other side of the international dateline or to the extreme south or north. Then the entries are off by about a day.

The abbreviations for the signs are:

Aries —Ar	Leo — Le	Sagittarius — Sa
Taurus — Ta	Virgo — Vi	Capricorn — Cp
Gemini — Ge	Libra — Li	Aquarius — Aq
Cancer — Ca	Scorpio — Sc	Pisces — Pi

MARS

1940–1949					
01-03-1940	Ma	Ar	03-24-1945	Ma	Pi
02-16-1940	Ma	Ta	05-02-1945	Ma	Ar
04-01-1940	Ma	Ge	06-11-1945	Ma	Ta
05-17-1940	Ma	Ca	07-23-1945	Ma	Ge
07-03-1940	Ma	Le	09-07-1945	Ma	Ca
08-19-1940	Ma	Vi	11-11-1945	Ma	Le
10-05-1940	Ma	Li	12-04-1945	Ma	SR
11-20-1940	Ma	Sc	12-26-1945	Ma	Le
01-04-1941	Ma	Sg	02-21-1946	Ma	SD
02-17-1941	Ma	Cp	04-22-1946	Ma	Le
04-02-1941	Ma	Aq	06-20-1946	Ma	Vi
05-16-1941	Ma	Pi	08-09-1946	Ma	Li
07-02-1941	Ma	Ar	09-24-1946	Ma	Sc
09-06-1941	Ma	SR	11-06-1946	Ma	Sg
11-10-1941	Ma	SD	12-17-1946	Ma	Cp
01-11-1942	Ma	Ta	01-25-1947	Ma	Aq
03-07-1942	Ma	Ge	03-04-1947	Ma	Pi
04-26-1942	Ma	Ca	04-11-1947	Ma	Ar
06-13-1942	Ma	Le	05-20-1947	Ma	Ta
08-01-1942	Ma	Vi	06-30-1947	Ma	Ge
09-17-1942	Ma	Li	08-13-1947	Ma	Ca
11-01-1942	Ma	Sc	09-30-1947	Ma	Le
12-15-1942	Ma	Sg	12-01-1947	Ma	Vi
01-26-1943	Ma	Cp	01-08-1948	Ma	SR
03-08-1943	Ma	Aq	02-12-1948	Ma	Vi
04-17-1943	Ma	Pi	03-29-1948	Ma	SD
05-27-1943	Ma	Ar	05-18-1948	Ma	Vi
07-07-1943	Ma	Ta	07-17-1948	Ma	Li
08-23-1943	Ma	Ge	09-03-1948	Ma	Sc
10-28-1943	Ma	SR	10-17-1948	Ma	Sg
01-09-1944	Ma	SD	11-26-1948	Ma	Cp
03-28-1944	Ma	Ca	01-04-1949	Ma	Aq
05-22-1944	Ma	Le	02-11-1949	Ma	Pi
07-11-1944	Ma	Vi	03-21-1949	Ma	Ar
08-28-1944	Ma	Li	04-29-1949	Ma	Ta
10-13-1944	Ma	Sc	06-09-1949	Ma	Ge
11-25-1944	Ma	Sg	07-23-1949	Ma	Ca
01-05-1945	Ma	Cp	09-06-1949	Ma	Le
02-14-1945	Ma	Aq	10-26-1949	Ma	Vi
			12-26-1949	Ma	Li

1950–1959

02-12-1950	Ma	SR
03-28-1950	Ma	Li
05-03-1950	Ma	SD
06-11-1950	Ma	Li
08-10-1950	Ma	Sc
09-25-1950	Ma	Sg
11-06-1950	Ma	Cp
12-15-1950	Ma	Aq
01-22-1951	Ma	Pi
03-01-1951	Ma	Ar
04-10-1951	Ma	Ta
05-21-1951	Ma	Ge
07-03-1951	Ma	Ca
08-18-1951	Ma	Le
10-04-1951	Ma	Vi
11-24-1951	Na	Li
01-19-1952	Ma	Sc
03-25-1952	Ma	SR
06-09-1952	Ma	SD
08-27-1952	Ma	Sg
10-11-1952	Ma	Cp
11-21-1952	Ma	Aq
12-30-1952	Ma	Pi
02-07-1953	Ma	Ar
03-20-1953	Ma	Ta
05-01-1953	Ma	Ge
06-13-1953	Ma	Ca
07-29-1953	Ma	Le
09-14-1953	Ma	Vi
11-01-1953	Ma	Li
12-20-1953	Ma	Sc
02-09-1954	Ma	Sg
04-12-1954	Ma	Cp
05-23-1954	Ma	SR
07-03-1954	Ma	Cp
07-29-1954	Ma	SD
08-24-1954	Ma	Cp
10-21-1954	Ma	Aq
12-04-1954	Ma	Pi
01-14-1955	Ma	Ar
02-26-1955	Ma	Ta

04-10-1955	Ma	Ge
05-25-1955	Ma	Ca
07-11-1955	Ma	Le
08-27-1955	Ma	Vi
10-13-1955	Ma	Li
11-28-1955	Ma	Sc
01-13-1956	Ma	Sg
02-28-1956	Ma	Cp
04-14-1956	Ma	Aq
06-03-1956	Ma	Pi
08-10-1956	Ma	SR
10-10-1956	Ma	SD
12-06-1956	Ma	Ar
01-28-1957	Ma	Ta
03-17-1957	Ma	Ge
05-04-1957	Ma	Ca
06-21-1957	Ma	Le
08-08-1957	Ma	Vi
09-23-1957	Ma	Li
11-08-1957	Ma	Sc
12-22-1957	Ma	Sg
02-03-1958	Ma	Cp
03-17-1958	Ma	Aq
04-26-1958	Ma	Pi
06-07-1958	Ma	Ar
07-21-1958	Ma	Ta
09-21-1958	Ma	Ge
10-10-1958	Ma	SR
10-28-1958	Ma	Ge
12-20-1958	Ma	SD
02-10-1959	Ma	Ge
04-10-1959	Ma	Ca
05-31-1959	Ma	Le
07-20-1959	Ma	Vi
09-05-1959	Ma	Li
10-21-1959	Ma	Sc
12-03-1959	Ma	Sg

1960–1969

01-13-1960	Ma	Cp
02-22-1960	Ma	Aq
04-02-1960	Ma	Pi

05-11-1960	Ma	Ar		12-23-1965	Ma	Aq
06-20-1960	Ma	Ta		01-30-1966	Ma	Pi
08-01-1960	Ma	Ge		03-09-1966	Ma	Ar
09-20-1960	Ma	Ca		04-17-1966	Ma	Ta
11-20-1960	Ma	SR		05-28-1966	Ma	Ge
02-04-1961	Ma	Ca		07-10-1966	Ma	Ca
02-05-1961	Ma	SD		08-25-1966	Ma	Le
02-07-1961	Ma	Ca		10-12-1966	Ma	Vi
05-05-1961	Ma	Le		12-03-1966	Ma	Li
06-28-1961	Ma	Vi		02-12-1967	Ma	Sc
08-16-1961	Ma	Li		03-08-1967	Ma	SR
10-01-1961	Ma	Sc		03-31-1967	Ma	Sc
11-13-1961	Ma	Sg		05-26-1967	Ma	SD
12-24-1961	Ma	Cp		07-19-1967	Ma	Sc
02-01-1962	Ma	Aq		09-09-1967	Ma	Sg
03-12-1962	Ma	Pi		10-22-1967	Ma	Cp
04-19-1962	Ma	Ar		12-01-1967	Ma	Aq
05-28-1962	Ma	Ta		01-09-1968	Ma	Pi
07-08-1962	Ma	Ge		02-16-1968	Ma	Ar
08-22-1962	Ma	Ca		03-27-1968	Ma	Ta
10-11-1962	Ma	Le		05-08-1968	Ma	Ge
12-26-1962	Ma	SR		06-21-1968	Ma	Ca
03-16-1963	Ma	SD		08-05-1968	Ma	Le
06-03-1963	Ma	Vi		09-21-1968	Ma	Vi
07-26-1963	Ma	Li		11-09-1968	Ma	Li
09-12-1963	Ma	Sc		12-29-1968	Ma	Sc
10-25-1963	Ma	Sg		02-25-1969	Ma	Sg
12-05-1963	Ma	Cp		04-27-1969	Ma	SR
01-13-1964	Ma	Aq		07-08-1969	Ma	SD
02-20-1964	Ma	Pi		09-21-1969	Ma	Cp
03-29-1964	Ma	Ar		11-04-1969	Ma	Aq
05-07-1964	Ma	Ta		12-15-1969	Ma	Pi
06-17-1964	Ma	Ge				
07-30-1964	Ma	Ca		**1970–1979**		
09-15-1964	Ma	Le		01-24-1970	Ma	Ar
11-05-1964	Ma	Vi		03-06-1970	Ma	Ta
01-28-1965	Ma	SR		04-18-1970	Ma	Ge
04-19-1965	Ma	SD		06-02-1970	Ma	Ca
06-28-1965	Ma	Li		07-18-1970	Ma	Le
08-20-1965	Ma	Sc		09-02-1970	Ma	Vi
10-04-1965	Ma	Sg		10-20-1970	Ma	Li
11-14-1965	Ma	Cp		12-06-1970	Ma	Sc

01-22-1971	Ma	Sg
03-12-1971	Ma	Cp
05-03-1971	Ma	Aq
07-11-1971	Ma	SR
09-09-1971	Ma	SD
11-06-1971	Ma	Pi
12-26-1971	Ma	Ar
02-10-1972	Ma	Ta
03-26-1972	Ma	Ge
05-12-1972	Ma	Ca
06-28-1972	Ma	Le
08-14-1972	Ma	Vi
09-30-1972	Ma	Li
11-15-1972	Ma	Sc
12-30-1972	Ma	Sg
02-12-1973	Ma	Cp
03-26-1973	Ma	Aq
05-07-1973	Ma	Pi
06-20-1973	Ma	Ar
08-12-1973	Ma	Ta
09-19-1973	Ma	SR
10-29-1973	Ma	Ta
11-25-1973	Ma	SD
12-24-1973	Ma	Ta
02-27-1974	Ma	Ge
04-20-1974	Ma	Ca
06-08-1974	Ma	Le
07-27-1974	Ma	Vi
09-12-1974	Ma	Li
10-28-1974	Ma	Sc
12-10-1974	Ma	Sg
01-21-1975	Ma	Cp
03-03-1975	Ma	Aq
04-11-1975	Ma	Pi
05-21-1975	Ma	Ar
06-30-1975	Ma	Ta
08-14-1975	Ma	Ge
10-17-1975	Ma	Ca
11-06-1975	Ma	SR
11-25-1975	Ma	Ca
01-20-1976	Ma	SD
03-18-1976	Ma	Ca

05-16-1976	Ma	Le
07-06-1976	Ma	Vi
08-24-1976	Ma	Li
10-08-1976	Ma	Sc
11-20-1976	Ma	Sg
12-31-1976	Ma	Cp
02-09-1977	Ma	Aq
03-19-1977	Ma	Pi
04-27-1977	Ma	Ar
06-05-1977	Ma	Ta
07-17-1977	Ma	Ge
08-31-1977	Ma	Ca
10-26-1977	Ma	Le
12-12-1977	Ma	SR
01-25-1978	Ma	Le
03-02-1978	Ma	SD
04-10-1978	Ma	Le
06-13-1978	Ma	Vi
08-04-1978	Ma	Li
09-19-1978	Ma	Sc
11-01-1978	Ma	Sg
12-12-1978	Ma	Cp
01-20-1979	Ma	Aq
02-27-1979	Ma	Pi
04-06-1979	Ma	Ar
05-15-1979	Ma	Ta
06-25-1979	Ma	Ge
08-08-1979	Ma	Ca
09-24-1979	Ma	Le
11-19-1979	Ma	Vi

1980–1989

01-16-1980	Ma	SR
03-11-1980	Ma	Vi
04-06-1980	Ma	SD
05-03-1980	Ma	Vi
07-10-1980	Ma	Li
08-29-1980	Ma	Sc
10-12-1980	Ma	Sg
11-21-1980	Ma	Cp
12-30-1980	Ma	Aq

02-06-1981	Ma	Pi		11-25-1986	Ma	Pi
03-16-1981	Ma	Ar		01-08-1987	Ma	Ar
04-25-1981	Ma	Ta		02-20-1987	Ma	Ta
06-05-1981	Ma	Ge		04-05-1987	Ma	Ge
07-18-1981	Ma	Ca		05-20-1987	Ma	Ca
09-01-1981	Ma	Le		07-06-1987	Ma	Le
10-20-1981	Ma	Vi		08-22-1987	Ma	Vi
12-15-1981	Ma	Li		10-08-1987	Ma	Li
02-20-1982	Ma	SR		11-23-1987	Ma	Sc
05-11-1982	Ma	SD		01-08-1988	Ma	Sg
08-03-1982	Ma	Sc		02-22-1988	Ma	Cp
09-19-1982	Ma	Sg		04-06-1988	Ma	Aq
10-31-1982	Ma	Cp		05-22-1988	Ma	Pi
12-10-1982	Ma	Aq		07-13-1988	Ma	Ar
01-17-1983	Ma	Pi		08-26-1988	Ma	SR
02-24-1983	Ma	Ar		10-23-1988	Ma	Ar
04-05-1983	Ma	Ta		10-28-1988	Ma	SD
05-16-1983	Ma	Ge		11-01-1988	Ma	Ar
06-29-1983	Ma	Ca		01-19-1989	Ma	Ta
08-13-1983	Ma	Le		03-11-1989	Ma	Ge
09-29-1983	Ma	Vi		04-28-1989	Ma	Ca
11-18-1983	Ma	Li		06-16-1989	Ma	Le
01-10-1984	Ma	Sc		08-03-1989	Ma	Vi
04-05-1984	Ma	SR		09-19-1989	Ma	Li
06-19-1984	Ma	SD		11-04-1989	Ma	Sc
08-17-1984	Ma	Sg		12-17-1989	Ma	Sg
10-05-1984	Ma	Cp				
11-15-1984	Ma	Aq		**1990–1999**		
12-25-1984	Ma	Pi		01-29-1990	Ma	Cp
02-02-1985	Ma	Ar		03-11-1990	Ma	Aq
03-15-1985	Ma	Ta		04-20-1990	Ma	Pi
04-26-1985	Ma	Ge		05-31-1990	Ma	Ar
06-09-1985	Ma	Ca		07-12-1990	Ma	Ta
07-24-1985	Ma	Le		08-31-1990	Ma	Ge
09-09-1985	Ma	Vi		10-20-1990	Ma	SR
10-27-1985	Ma	Li		12-14-1990	Ma	Ge
12-14-1985	Ma	Sc		01-01-1991	Ma	SD
02-02-1986	Ma	Sg		01-20-1991	Ma	Ge
03-27-1986	Ma	Cp		04-02-1991	Ma	Ca
06-08-1986	Ma	SR		05-26-1991	Ma	Le
08-12-1986	Ma	SD		07-15-1991	Ma	Vi
10-08-1986	Ma	Aq		09-01-1991	Ma	Li

10-16-1991	Ma	Sc		02-05-1997	Ma	SR
11-28-1991	Ma	Sg		03-08-1997	Ma	Li
01-09-1992	Ma	Cp		04-27-1997	Ma	SD
02-17-1992	Ma	Aq		06-19-1997	Ma	Li
03-27-1992	Ma	Pi		08-14-1997	Ma	Sc
05-05-1992	Ma	Ar		09-28-1997	Ma	Sg
06-14-1992	Ma	Ta		11-09-1997	Ma	Cp
07-26-1992	Ma	Ge		12-18-1997	Ma	Aq
09-12-1992	Ma	Ca		01-25-1998	Ma	Pi
11-28-1992	Ma	SR		03-04-1998	Ma	Ar
02-15-1993	Ma	SD		04-12-1998	Ma	Ta
04-27-1993	Ma	Le		05-23-1998	Ma	Ge
06-23-1993	Ma	Vi		07-06-1998	Ma	Ca
08-11-1993	Ma	Li		08-20-1998	Ma	Le
09-26-1993	Ma	Sc		10-07-1998	Ma	Vi
11-09-1993	Ma	Sg		11-27-1998	Ma	Li
12-19-1993	Ma	Cp		01-26-1999	Ma	Sc
01-27-1994	Ma	Aq		03-18-1999	Ma	SR
03-07-1994	Ma	Pi		05-05-1999	Ma	Sc
04-14-1994	Ma	Ar		06-04-1999	Ma	SD
05-23-1994	Ma	Ta		07-04-1999	Ma	Sc
07-03-1994	Ma	Ge		09-02-1999	Ma	Sg
08-16-1994	Ma	Ca		10-16-1999	Ma	Cp
10-04-1994	Ma	Le		11-26-1999	Ma	Aq
12-12-1994	Ma	Vi				
01-02-1995	Ma	SR		**2000–2009**		
01-22-1995	Ma	Vi		01-03-2000	Ma	Pi
03-24-1995	Ma	SD		02-11-2000	Ma	Ar
05-25-1995	Ma	Vi		03-22-2000	Ma	Ta
07-21-1995	Ma	Li		05-03-2000	Ma	Ge
09-07-1995	Ma	Sc		06-16-2000	Ma	Ca
10-20-1995	Ma	Sg		07-31-2000	Ma	Le
11-30-1995	Ma	Cp		09-16-2000	Ma	Vi
01-08-1996	Ma	Aq		11-03-2000	Ma	Li
02-15-1996	Ma	Pi		12-23-2000	Ma	Sc
03-24-1996	Ma	Ar		02-14-2001	Ma	Sg
05-02-1996	Ma	Ta		05-11-2001	Ma	SR
06-12-1996	Ma	Ge		07-19-2001	Ma	SD
07-25-1996	Ma	Ca		09-08-2001	Ma	Cp
09-09-1996	Ma	Le		10-27-2001	Ma	Aq
10-30-1996	Ma	Vi		12-08-2001	Ma	Pi
01-03-1997	Ma	Li		01-18-2002	Ma	Ar

03-01-2002	Ma	Ta		06-03-2006	Ma	Le
04-13-2002	Ma	Ge		07-22-2006	Ma	Vi
05-28-2002	Ma	Ca		09-07-2006	Ma	Li
07-13-2002	Ma	Le		10-23-2006	Ma	Sc
08-29-2002	Ma	Vi		12-05-2006	Ma	Sg
10-15-2002	Ma	Li		01-16-2007	Ma	Cp
12-01-2002	Ma	Sc		02-25-2007	Ma	Aq
01-16-2003	Ma	Sg		04-06-2007	Ma	Pi
03-04-2003	Ma	Cp		05-15-2007	Ma	Ar
04-21-2003	Ma	Aq		06-24-2007	Ma	Ta
06-16-2003	Ma	Pi		08-07-2007	Ma	Ge
07-29-2003	Ma	SR		09-28-2007	Ma	Ca
09-27-2003	Ma	SD		11-15-2007	Ma	SR
12-16-2003	Ma	Ar		12-31-2007	Ma	Ca
02-03-2004	Ma	Ta		01-30-2008	Ma	SD
03-21-2004	Ma	Ge		03-04-2008	Ma	Ca
05-07-2004	Ma	Ca		05-09-2008	Ma	Le
06-23-2004	Ma	Le		07-01-2008	Ma	Vi
08-10-2004	Ma	Vi		08-19-2008	Ma	Li
09-26-2004	Ma	Li		10-03-2008	Ma	Sc
11-11-2004	Ma	Sc		11-16-2008	Ma	Sg
12-25-2004	Ma	Sg		12-27-2008	Ma	Cp
02-06-2005	Ma	Cp		02-04-2009	Ma	Aq
03-20-2005	Ma	Aq		03-14-2009	Ma	Pi
04-30-2005	Ma	Pi		04-22-2009	Ma	Ar
06-11-2005	Ma	Ar		05-31-2009	Ma	Ta
07-28-2005	Ma	Ta		07-11-2009	Ma	Ge
10-01-2005	Ma	SR		08-25-2009	Ma	Ca
12-09-2005	Ma	SD		10-16-2009	Ma	Le
02-17-2006	Ma	Ge		12-20-2009	Ma	SR
04-13-2006	Ma	Ca				

VENUS

1940–1949

				07-31-1940	Ve	Ca
01-18-1940	Ve	Pi		09-08-1940	Ve	Le
02-12-1940	Ve	Ar		10-06-1940	Ve	Vi
03-08-1940	Ve	Ta		11-01-1940	Ve	Li
04-04-1940	Ve	Ge		11-26-1940	Ve	Sc
05-06-1940	Ve	Ca		12-20-1940	Ve	Sg
06-05-1940	Ve	SR		01-13-1941	Ve	Cp
07-05-1940	Ve	Ca		02-06-1941	Ve	Aq
07-18-1940	Ve	SD		03-02-1941	Ve	Pi

03-26-1941	Ve	Ar		05-29-1944	Ve	Ge
04-20-1941	Ve	Ta		06-22-1944	Ve	Ca
05-14-1941	Ve	Ge		07-16-1944	Ve	Le
06-07-1941	Ve	Ca		08-10-1944	Ve	Vi
07-02-1941	Ve	Le		09-03-1944	Ve	Li
07-26-1941	Ve	Vi		09-28-1944	Ve	Sc
08-20-1941	Ve	Li		10-22-1944	Ve	Sg
09-14-1941	Ve	Sc		11-16-1944	Ve	Cp
10-10-1941	Ve	Sg		12-10-1944	Ve	Aq
11-06-1941	Ve	Cp		01-05-1945	Ve	Pi
12-05-1941	Ve	Aq		02-02-1945	Ve	Ar
01-12-1942	Ve	SR		03-11-1945	Ve	Ta
02-23-1942	Ve	SD		03-25-1945	Ve	SR
04-06-1942	Ve	Pi		04-07-1945	Ve	Ta
05-05-1942	Ve	Ar		05-06-1945	Ve	SD
06-01-1942	Ve	Ta		06-04-1945	Ve	Ta
06-27-1942	Ve	Ge		07-07-1945	Ve	Ge
07-23-1942	Ve	Ca		08-04-1945	Ve	Ca
08-16-1942	Ve	Le		08-30-1945	Ve	Le
09-10-1942	Ve	Vi		09-24-1945	Ve	Vi
10-04-1942	Ve	Li		10-18-1945	Ve	Li
10-28-1942	Ve	Sc		11-12-1945	Ve	Sc
11-21-1942	Ve	Sg		12-06-1945	Ve	Sg
12-15-1942	Ve	Cp		12-29-1945	Ve	Cp
01-08-1943	Ve	Aq		01-22-1946	Ve	Aq
02-01-1943	Ve	Pi		02-15-1946	Ve	Pi
02-25-1943	Ve	Ar		03-11-1946	Ve	Ar
03-21-1943	Ve	Ta		04-04-1946	Ve	Ta
04-15-1943	Ve	Ge		04-29-1946	Ve	Ge
05-11-1943	Ve	Ca		05-23-1946	Ve	Ca
06-07-1943	Ve	Le		06-18-1946	Ve	Le
07-07-1943	Ve	Vi		07-13-1946	Ve	Vi
08-15-1943	Ve	SR		08-09-1946	Ve	Li
09-27-1943	Ve	SD		09-06-1946	Ve	Sc
11-09-1943	Ve	Li		10-16-1946	Ve	Sg
12-08-1943	Ve	Sc		10-27-1946	Ve	SR
01-02-1944	Ve	Sg		11-08-1946	Ve	Sg
01-27-1944	Ve	Cp		12-08-1946	Ve	SD
02-21-1944	Ve	Aq		01-05-1947	Ve	Sg
03-16-1944	Ve	Pi		02-06-1947	Ve	Cp
04-10-1944	Ve	Ar		03-05-1947	Ve	Aq
05-04-1944	Ve	Ta		03-30-1947	Ve	Pi

04-24-1947	Ve	Ar		04-06-1950	Ve	Pi
05-19-1947	Ve	Ta		05-05-1950	Ve	Ar
06-13-1947	Ve	Ge		06-01-1950	Ve	Ta
07-08-1947	Ve	Ca		06-27-1950	Ve	Ge
08-01-1947	Ve	Le		07-22-1950	Ve	Ca
08-26-1947	Ve	Vi		08-16-1950	Ve	Le
09-19-1947	Ve	Li		09-09-1950	Ve	Vi
10-13-1947	Ve	Sc		10-04-1950	Ve	Li
11-06-1947	Ve	Sg		10-28-1950	Ve	Sc
11-30-1947	Ve	Cp		11-20-1950	Ve	Sg
12-24-1947	Ve	Aq		12-14-1950	Ve	Cp
01-17-1948	Ve	Pi		01-07-1951	Ve	Aq
02-11-1948	Ve	Ar		01-31-1951	Ve	Pi
03-08-1948	Ve	Ta		02-24-1951	Ve	Ar
04-04-1948	Ve	Ge		03-21-1951	Ve	Ta
05-07-1948	Ve	Ca		04-15-1951	Ve	Ge
06-02-1948	Ve	SR		05-10-1951	Ve	Ca
06-29-1948	Ve	Ca		06-07-1951	Ve	Le
07-16-1948	Ve	SD		07-07-1951	Ve	Vi
08-02-1948	Ve	Ca		08-13-1951	Ve	SR
09-08-1948	Ve	Le		09-24-1951	Ve	SD
10-06-1948	Ve	Vi		11-09-1951	Ve	Li
11-01-1948	Ve	Li		12-07-1951	Ve	Sc
11-25-1948	Ve	Sc		01-02-1952	Ve	Sg
12-20-1948	Ve	Sg		01-27-1952	Ve	Cp
01-13-1949	Ve	Cp		02-20-1952	Ve	Aq
02-06-1949	Ve	Aq		03-16-1952	Ve	Pi
03-02-1949	Ve	Pi		04-09-1952	Ve	Ar
03-26-1949	Ve	Ar		05-04-1952	Ve	Ta
04-19-1949	Ve	Ta		05-28-1952	Ve	Ge
05-13-1949	Ve	Ge		06-22-1952	Ve	Ca
06-07-1949	Ve	Ca		07-16-1952	Ve	Le
07-01-1949	Ve	Le		08-09-1952	Ve	Vi
07-26-1949	Ve	Vi		09-03-1952	Ve	Li
08-20-1949	Ve	Li		09-27-1952	Ve	Sc
09-14-1949	Ve	Sc		10-22-1952	Ve	Sg
10-10-1949	Ve	Sg		11-15-1952	Ve	Cp
11-05-1949	Ve	Cp		12-10-1952	Ve	Aq
12-06-1949	Ve	Aq		01-05-1953	Ve	Pi
				02-02-1953	Ve	Ar
1950–1959				03-14-1953	Ve	Ta
01-10-1950	Ve	SR		03-22-1953	Ve	SR
02-20-1950	Ve	SD		03-31-1953	Ve	Ta

05-04-1953	Ve	SD		05-07-1956	Ve	Ca
06-05-1953	Ve	Ta		05-31-1956	Ve	SR
07-07-1953	Ve	Ge		06-23-1956	Ve	Ca
08-03-1953	Ve	Ca		07-13-1956	Ve	SD
08-29-1953	Ve	Le		08-04-1956	Ve	Ca
09-23-1953	Ve	Vi		09-08-1956	Ve	Le
10-18-1953	Ve	Li		10-05-1956	Ve	Vi
11-11-1953	Ve	Sc		10-31-1956	Ve	Li
12-05-1953	Ve	Sg		11-25-1956	Ve	Sc
12-29-1953	Ve	Cp		12-19-1956	Ve	Sg
01-22-1954	Ve	Aq		01-12-1957	Ve	Cp
02-15-1954	Ve	Pi		02-05-1957	Ve	Aq
03-11-1954	Ve	Ar		03-01-1957	Ve	Pi
04-04-1954	Ve	Ta		03-25-1957	Ve	Ar
04-28-1954	Ve	Ge		04-18-1957	Ve	Ta
05-23-1954	Ve	Ca		05-13-1957	Ve	Ge
06-17-1954	Ve	Le		06-06-1957	Ve	Ca
07-13-1954	Ve	Vi		07-01-1957	Ve	Le
08-08-1954	Ve	Li		07-25-1957	Ve	Vi
09-06-1954	Ve	Sc		08-19-1957	Ve	Li
10-23-1954	Ve	Sg		09-14-1957	Ve	Sc
10-25-1954	Ve	SR		10-09-1957	Ve	Sg
10-27-1954	Ve	Sg		11-05-1957	Ve	Cp
12-05-1954	Ve	SD		12-06-1957	Ve	Aq
01-06-1955	Ve	Sg		01-07-1958	Ve	SR
02-05-1955	Ve	Cp		02-18-1958	Ve	SD
03-04-1955	Ve	Aq		04-06-1958	Ve	Pi
03-30-1955	Ve	Pi		05-05-1958	Ve	Ar
04-24-1955	Ve	Ar		05-31-1958	Ve	Ta
05-19-1955	Ve	Ta		06-26-1958	Ve	Ge
06-13-1955	Ve	Ge		07-22-1958	Ve	Ca
07-07-1955	Ve	Ca		08-15-1958	Ve	Le
08-01-1955	Ve	Le		09-09-1958	Ve	Vi
08-25-1955	Ve	Vi		10-03-1958	Ve	Li
09-18-1955	Ve	Li		10-27-1958	Ve	Sc
10-12-1955	Ve	Sc		11-20-1958	Ve	Sg
11-05-1955	Ve	Sg		12-14-1958	Ve	Cp
11-29-1955	Ve	Cp		01-07-1959	Ve	Aq
12-24-1955	Ve	Aq		01-31-1959	Ve	Pi
01-17-1956	Ve	Pi		02-24-1959	Ve	Ar
02-11-1956	Ve	Ar		03-20-1959	Ve	Ta
03-07-1956	Ve	Ta		04-14-1959	Ve	Ge
04-04-1956	Ve	Ge		05-10-1959	Ve	Ca

06-06-1959	Ve	Le		05-22-1962	Ve	Ca
07-08-1959	Ve	Vi		06-17-1962	Ve	Le
08-10-1959	Ve	SR		07-12-1962	Ve	Vi
09-19-1959	Ve	Vi		08-08-1962	Ve	Li
09-22-1959	Ve	SD		09-06-1962	Ve	Sc
09-25-1959	Ve	Vi		10-22-1962	Ve	SR
11-09-1959	Ve	Li		12-03-1962	Ve	SD
12-07-1959	Ve	Sc		01-06-1963	Ve	Sg
				02-05-1963	Ve	Cp

1960–1969

				03-04-1963	Ve	Aq
01-02-1960	Ve	Sg		03-29-1963	Ve	Pi
01-26-1960	Ve	Cp		04-23-1963	Ve	Ar
02-20-1960	Ve	Aq		05-18-1963	Ve	Ta
03-15-1960	Ve	Pi		06-12-1963	Ve	Ge
04-09-1960	Ve	Ar		07-07-1963	Ve	Ca
05-03-1960	Ve	Ta		07-31-1963	Ve	Le
05-28-1960	Ve	Ge		08-25-1963	Ve	Vi
06-21-1960	Ve	Ca		09-18-1963	Ve	Li
07-15-1960	Ve	Le		10-12-1963	Ve	Sc
08-09-1960	Ve	Vi		11-05-1963	Ve	Sg
09-02-1960	Ve	Li		11-29-1963	Ve	Cp
09-27-1960	Ve	Sc		12-23-1963	Ve	Aq
10-21-1960	Ve	Sg		01-16-1964	Ve	Pi
11-15-1960	Ve	Cp		02-10-1964	Ve	Ar
12-10-1960	Ve	Aq		03-07-1964	Ve	Ta
01-04-1961	Ve	Pi		04-03-1964	Ve	Ge
02-01-1961	Ve	Ar		05-08-1964	Ve	Ca
03-20-1961	Ve	SR		05-29-1964	Ve	SR
05-01-1961	Ve	SD		06-17-1964	Ve	Ca
06-05-1961	Ve	Ta		07-11-1964	Ve	SD
07-06-1961	Ve	Ge		08-05-1964	Ve	Ca
08-03-1961	Ve	Ca		09-07-1964	Ve	Le
08-29-1961	Ve	Le		10-05-1964	Ve	Vi
09-23-1961	Ve	Vi		10-31-1964	Ve	Li
10-17-1961	Ve	Li		11-24-1964	Ve	Sc
11-11-1961	Ve	Sc		12-19-1964	Ve	Sg
12-04-1961	Ve	Sg		01-12-1965	Ve	Cp
12-28-1961	Ve	Cp		02-05-1965	Ve	Aq
01-21-1962	Ve	Aq		03-01-1965	Ve	Pi
02-14-1962	Ve	Pi		03-25-1965	Ve	Ar
03-10-1962	Ve	Ar		04-18-1965	Ve	Ta
04-03-1962	Ve	Ta		05-12-1965	Ve	Ge
04-28-1962	Ve	Ge		06-06-1965	Ve	Ca

06-30-1965	Ve	Le		06-20-1968	Ve	Ca
07-25-1965	Ve	Vi		07-15-1968	Ve	Le
08-19-1965	Ve	Li		08-08-1968	Ve	Vi
09-13-1965	Ve	Sc		09-02-1968	Ve	Li
10-09-1965	Ve	Sg		09-26-1968	Ve	Sc
11-05-1965	Ve	Cp		10-21-1968	Ve	Sg
12-06-1965	Ve	Aq		11-14-1968	Ve	Cp
01-05-1966	Ve	SR		12-09-1968	Ve	Aq
02-06-1966	Ve	Aq		01-04-1969	Ve	Pi
02-15-1966	Ve	SD		02-01-1969	Ve	Ar
02-25-1966	Ve	Aq		03-18-1969	Ve	SR
04-06-1966	Ve	Pi		04-29-1969	Ve	SD
05-04-1966	Ve	Ar		06-05-1969	Ve	Ta
05-31-1966	Ve	Ta		07-06-1965	Ve	Ge
06-26-1966	Ve	Ge		08-03-1969	Ve	Ca
07-21-1966	Ve	Ca		08-28-1969	Ve	Le
08-15-1966	Ve	Le		09-22-1969	Ve	Vi
09-08-1966	Ve	Vi		10-17-1969	Ve	Li
10-02-1966	Ve	Li		11-10-1969	Ve	Sc
10-26-1966	Ve	Sc		12-04-1969	Ve	Sg
11-19-1966	Ve	Sg		12-28-1969	Ve	Cp
12-13-1966	Ve	Cp				
01-06-1967	Ve	Aq		**1970–1979**		
01-30-1967	Ve	Pi		01-21-1970	Ve	Aq
02-23-1967	Ve	Ar		02-14-1970	Ve	Pi
03-20-1967	Ve	Ta		03-10-1970	Ve	Ar
04-14-1967	Ve	Ge		04-03-1970	Ve	Ta
05-10-1967	Ve	Ca		04-27-1970	Ve	Ge
06-06-1967	Ve	Le		05-22-1970	Ve	Ca
07-08-1967	Ve	Vi		06-16-1970	Ve	Le
08-80-1967	Ve	SR		07-12-1970	Ve	Vi
09-09-1967	Ve	Vi		08-08-1970	Ve	Li
09-20-1967	Ve	SD		09-06-1970	Ve	Sc
10-01-1967	Ve	Vi		10-20-1970	Ve	SR
11-09-1967	Ve	Li		11-30-1970	Ve	SD
12-07-1967	Ve	Sc		01-06-1971	Ve	Sg
01-01-1968	Ve	Sg		02-05-1971	Ve	Cp
01-26-1968	Ve	Cp		03-03-1971	Ve	Aq
02-19-1968	Ve	Aq		03-29-1971	Ve	Pi
03-15-1968	Ve	Pi		04-23-1971	Ve	Ar
04-08-1968	Ve	Ar		05-18-1971	Ve	Ta
05-03-1968	Ve	Ta		06-12-1971	Ve	Ge
05-27-1968	Ve	Ge		07-06-1971	Ve	Ca

07-31-1971	Ve	Le	07-20-1974	Ve	Ca
08-24-1971	Ve	Vi	08-14-1974	Ve	Le
09-17-1971	Ve	Li	09-08-1974	Ve	Vi
10-11-1971	Ve	Sc	10-02-1974	Ve	Li
11-04-1971	Ve	Sg	10-26-1974	Ve	Sc
11-28-1971	Ve	Cp	11-19-1974	Ve	Sg
12-23-1971	Ve	Aq	12-13-1974	Ve	Cp
01-16-1972	Ve	Pi	01-06-1975	Ve	Aq
02-10-1972	Ve	Ar	01-30-1975	Ve	Pi
03-06-1972	Ve	Ta	02-23-1975	Ve	Ar
04-03-1972	Ve	Ge	03-19-1975	Ve	Ta
05-10-1972	Ve	Ca	04-13-1975	Ve	Ge
05-26-1972	Ve	SR	05-09-1975	Ve	Ca
06-11-1972	Ve	Ca	06-06-1975	Ve	Le
07-08-1972	Ve	SD	07-09-1975	Ve	Vi
08-05-1972	Ve	Ca	08-06-1975	Ve	SR
09-07-1972	Ve	Le	09-02-1975	Ve	Vi
10-05-1972	Ve	Vi	09-17-1975	Ve	SD
10-30-1972	Ve	Li	10-04-1975	Ve	Vi
11-24-1972	Ve	Sc	11-09-1975	Ve	Li
12-18-1972	Ve	Sg	12-06-1975	Ve	Sc
01-11-1973	Ve	Cp	01-01-1976	Ve	Sg
02-04-1973	Ve	Aq	01-26-1976	Ve	Cp
02-28-1973	Ve	Pi	02-19-1976	Ve	Aq
03-24-1973	Ve	Ar	03-14-1976	Ve	Pi
04-17-1973	Ve	Ta	04-08-1976	Ve	Ar
05-12-1973	Ve	Ge	05-02-1976	Ve	Ta
06-05-1973	Ve	Ca	05-26-1976	Ve	Ge
06-30-1973	Ve	Le	06-20-1976	Ve	Ca
07-24-1973	Ve	Vi	07-14-1976	Ve	Le
08-18-1973	Ve	Li	08-08-1976	Ve	Vi
09-13-1973	Ve	Sc	09-01-1976	Ve	Li
10-09-1973	Ve	Sg	09-25-1976	Ve	Sc
11-05-1973	Ve	Cp	10-20-1976	Ve	Sg
12-07-1973	Ve	Aq	11-14-1976	Ve	Cp
01-03-1974	Ve	SR	12-09-1976	Ve	Aq
01-29-1974	Ve	Aq	01-04-1977	Ve	Pi
02-13-1974	Ve	SD	02-02-1977	Ve	Ar
02-28-1974	Ve	Aq	03-15-1977	Ve	SR
04-06-1974	Ve	Pi	04-27-1977	Ve	SD
05-04-1974	Ve	Ar	06-06-1977	Ve	Ta
05-31-1974	Ve	Ta	07-06-1977	Ve	Ge
06-25-1974	Ve	Ge	08-02-1977	Ve	Ca

08-28-1977	Ve	Le		08-06-1980	Ve	Ca
09-22-1977	Ve	Vi		09-07-1980	Ve	Le
10-16-1977	Ve	Li		10-04-1980	Ve	Vi
11-09-1977	Ve	Sc		10-30-1980	Ve	Li
12-03-1977	Ve	Sg		11-23-1980	Ve	Sc
12-27-1977	Ve	Cp		12-18-1980	Ve	Sg
01-20-1978	Ve	Aq		01-11-1981	Ve	Cp
02-13-1978	Ve	Pi		02-04-1981	Ve	Aq
03-09-1978	Ve	Ar		02-28-1981	Ve	Pi
04-02-1978	Ve	Ta		03-24-1981	Ve	Ar
04-27-1978	Ve	Ge		04-17-1981	Ve	Ta
05-21-1978	Ve	Ca		05-11-1981	Ve	Ge
06-16-1978	Ve	Le		06-05-1981	Ve	Ca
07-11-1978	Ve	Vi		06-29-1981	Ve	Le
08-07-1978	Ve	Li		07-24-1981	Ve	Vi
09-07-1978	Ve	Sc		08-18-1981	Ve	Li
10-17-1978	Ve	SR		09-12-1981	Ve	Sc
11-28-1978	Ve	SD		10-08-1981	Ve	Sg
01-07-1979	Ve	Sg		11-05-1981	Ve	Cp
02-05-1979	Ve	Cp		12-08-1981	Ve	Aq
03-03-1979	Ve	Aq		12-31-1981	Ve	SR
03-28-1979	Ve	Pi		01-22-1982	Ve	Aq
04-22-1979	Ve	Ar		02-10-1982	Ve	SD
05-17-1979	Ve	Ta		03-02-1982	Ve	Aq
06-11-1979	Ve	Ge		04-06-1982	Ve	Pi
07-06-1979	Ve	Ca		05-04-1982	Ve	Ar
07-30-1979	Ve	Le		05-30-1982	Ve	Ta
08-23-1979	Ve	Vi		06-25-1982	Ve	Ge
09-17-1979	Ve	Li		07-20-1982	Ve	Ca
10-11-1979	Ve	Sc		08-14-1982	Ve	Le
11-04-1979	Ve	Sg		09-07-1982	Ve	Vi
11-28-1979	Ve	Cp		10-01-1982	Ve	Li
12-22-1979	Ve	Aq		10-25-1982	Ve	Sc
				11-18-1982	Ve	Sg
1980–1989				12-12-1982	Ve	Cp
01-15-1980	Ve	Pi		01-05-1983	Ve	Aq
02-09-1980	Ve	Ar		01-29-1983	Ve	Pi
03-06-1980	Ve	Ta		02-22-1983	Ve	Ar
04-03-1980	Ve	Ge		03-19-1983	Ve	Ta
05-12-1980	Ve	Ca		04-13-1983	Ve	Ge
05-24-1980	Ve	SR		05-09-1983	Ve	Ca
06-05-1980	Ve	Ca		06-06-1983	Ve	Le
07-06-1980	Ve	SD		07-10-1983	Ve	Vi

08-03-1983	Ve	SR		09-07-1986	Ve	Sc
08-27-1983	Ve	Vi		10-15-1986	Ve	SR
09-15-1983	Ve	SD		11-25-1986	Ve	SD
10-05-1983	Ve	Vi		01-07-1987	Ve	Sg
11-09-1983	Ve	Li		02-04-1987	Ve	Cp
12-06-1983	Ve	Sc		03-03-1987	Ve	Aq
12-31-1983	Ve	Sg		03-28-1987	Ve	Pi
01-25-1984	Ve	Cp		04-22-1987	Ve	Ar
02-18-1984	Ve	Aq		05-17-1987	Ve	Ta
03-14-1984	Ve	Pi		06-11-1987	Ve	Ge
04-07-1984	Ve	Ar		07-05-1987	Ve	Ca
05-01-1984	Ve	Ta		07-30-1987	Ve	Le
05-26-1984	Ve	Ge		08-23-1987	Ve	Vi
06-19-1984	Ve	Ca		09-16-1987	Ve	Li
07-14-1984	Ve	Le		10-10-1987	Ve	Sc
08-07-1984	Ve	Vi		11-03-1987	Ve	Sg
09-01-1984	Ve	Li		11-27-1987	Ve	Cp
09-25-1984	Ve	Sc		12-22-1987	Ve	Aq
10-20-1984	Ve	Sg		01-15-1988	Ve	Pi
11-13-1984	Ve	Cp		02-09-1988	Ve	Ar
12-08-1984	Ve	Aq		03-06-1988	Ve	Ta
01-04-1985	Ve	Pi		04-03-1988	Ve	Ge
02-02-1985	Ve	Ar		05-17-1988	Ve	Ca
03-13-1985	Ve	SR		05-22-1988	Ve	SR
04-24-1985	Ve	SD		05-27-1988	Ve	Ca
06-06-1985	Ve	Ta		07-04-1988	Ve	SD
07-06-1985	Ve	Ge		08-06-1988	Ve	Ca
08-02-1985	Ve	Ca		09-07-1988	Ve	Le
08-27-1985	Ve	Le		10-04-1988	Ve	Vi
09-21-1985	Ve	Vi		10-29-1988	Ve	Li
10-16-1985	Ve	Li		11-23-1988	Ve	Sc
11-09-1985	Ve	Sc		12-17-1988	Ve	Sg
12-03-1985	Ve	Sg		01-10-1989	Ve	Cp
12-27-1985	Ve	Cp		02-03-1989	Ve	Aq
01-20-1986	Ve	Aq		02-27-1989	Ve	Pi
02-12-1986	Ve	Pi		03-23-1989	Ve	Ar
03-08-1986	Ve	Ar		04-16-1989	Ve	Ta
04-02-1986	Ve	Ta		05-11-1989	Ve	Ge
04-26-1986	Ve	Ge		06-04-1989	Ve	Ca
05-21-1986	Ve	Ca		06-29-1989	Ve	Le
06-15-1986	Ve	Le		07-23-1989	Ve	Vi
07-11-1986	Ve	Vi		08-17-1989	Ve	Li
08-07-1986	Ve	Li		09-12-1989	Ve	Sc

10-08-1989	Ve	Sg		08-07-1992	Ve	Vi
11-05-1989	Ve	Cp		08-31-1992	Ve	Li
12-09-1989	Ve	Aq		09-24-1992	Ve	Sc
12-29-1989	Ve	SR		10-19-1992	Ve	Sg
				11-13-1992	Ve	Cp
1990–1999				12-08-1992	Ve	Aq
01-16-1990	Ve	Aq		01-03-1993	Ve	Pi
02-08-1990	Ve	SD		02-02-1993	Ve	Ar
03-03-1990	Ve	Aq		03-11-1993	Ve	SR
04-06-1990	Ve	Pi		04-22-1993	Ve	SD
05-03-1990	Ve	Ar		06-06-1993	Ve	Ta
05-30-1990	Ve	Ta		07-05-1993	Ve	Ge
06-24-1990	Ve	Ge		08-01-1993	Ve	Ca
07-19-1990	Ve	Ca		08-27-1993	Ve	Le
08-13-1990	Ve	Le		09-21-1993	Ve	Vi
09-07-1990	Ve	Vi		10-15-1993	Ve	Li
10-01-1990	Ve	Li		11-08-1993	Ve	Sc
10-25-1990	Ve	Sc		12-02-1993	Ve	Sg
11-18-1990	Ve	Sg		12-26-1993	Ve	Cp
12-12-1990	Ve	Cp		01-19-1994	Ve	Aq
01-05-1991	Ve	Aq		02-12-1994	Ve	Pi
01-28-1991	Ve	Pi		03-08-1994	Ve	Ar
02-22-1991	Ve	Ar		04-01-1994	Ve	Ta
03-18-1991	Ve	Ta		04-26-1994	Ve	Ge
04-12-1991	Ve	Ge		05-20-1994	Ve	Ca
05-08-1991	Ve	Ca		06-15-1994	Ve	Le
06-05-1991	Ve	Le		07-11-1994	Ve	Vi
07-11-1991	Ve	Vi		08-07-1994	Ve	Li
08-01-1991	Ve	SR		09-07-1994	Ve	Sc
08-21-1991	Ve	Vi		10-13-1994	Ve	SR
09-13-1991	Ve	SD		11-23-1994	Ve	SD
10-06-1991	Ve	Vi		01-07-1995	Ve	Sg
11-09-1991	Ve	Li		02-04-1995	Ve	Cp
12-06-1991	Ve	Sc		03-02-1995	Ve	Aq
12-31-1991	Ve	Sg		03-28-1995	Ve	Pi
01-25-1992	Ve	Cp		04-21-1995	Ve	Ar
02-18-1992	Ve	Aq		05-16-1995	Ve	Ta
03-13-1992	Ve	Pi		06-10-1995	Ve	Ge
04-07-1992	Ve	Ar		07-05-1995	Ve	Ca
05-01-1992	Ve	Ta		07-29-1995	Ve	Le
05-25-1992	Ve	Ge		08-22-1995	Ve	Vi
06-19-1992	Ve	Ca		09-16-1995	Ve	Li
07-13-1992	Ve	Le		10-10-1995	Ve	Sc

11-03-1995	Ve	Sg		12-11-1998	Ve	Cp
11-27-1995	Ve	Cp		01-04-1999	Ve	Aq
12-21-1995	Ve	Aq		01-28-1999	Ve	Pi
01-14-1996	Ve	Pi		02-21-1999	Ve	Ar
02-08-1996	Ve	Ar		03-18-1999	Ve	Ta
03-05-1996	Ve	Ta		04-12-1999	Ve	Ge
04-03-1996	Ve	Ge		05-08-1999	Ve	Ca
05-20-1996	Ve	SR		06-05-1999	Ve	Le
07-02-1996	Ve	SD		07-12-1999	Ve	Vi
08-07-1996	Ve	Ca		07-29-1999	Ve	SR
09-07-1996	Ve	Le		08-15-1999	Ve	Vi
10-03-1996	Ve	Vi		09-10-1999	Ve	SD
10-29-1996	Ve	Li		10-07-1999	Ve	Vi
11-22-1996	Ve	Sc		11-08-1999	Ve	Li
12-17-1996	Ve	Sg		12-05-1999	Ve	Sc
01-10-1997	Ve	Cp		12-30-1999	Ve	Sg
02-02-1997	Ve	Aq				
02-26-1997	Ve	Pi		**2000-2010**		
03-23-1997	Ve	Ar		01-24-2000	Ve	Cp
04-16-1997	Ve	Ta		02-17-2000	Ve	Aq
05-10-1997	Ve	Ge		03-13-2000	Ve	Pi
06-03-1997	Ve	Ca		04-06-2000	Ve	Ar
06-28-1997	Ve	Le		04-30-2000	Ve	Ta
07-23-1997	Ve	Vi		05-25-2000	Ve	Ge
08-17-1997	Ve	Li		06-18-2000	Ve	Ca
09-11-1997	Ve	Sc		07-13-2000	Ve	Le
10-08-1997	Ve	Sg		08-06-2000	Ve	Vi
11-05-1997	Ve	Cp		08-30-2000	Ve	Li
12-11-1997	Ve	Aq		09-24-2000	Ve	Sc
12-26-1997	Ve	SR		10-19-2000	Ve	Sg
01-09-1998	Ve	Aq		11-12-2000	Ve	Cp
02-05-1998	Ve	SD		12-08-2000	Ve	Aq
03-04-1998	Ve	Aq		01-03-2001	Ve	Pi
04-06-1998	Ve	Pi		02-02-2001	Ve	Ar
05-03-1998	Ve	Ar		03-08-2001	Ve	SR
05-29-1998	Ve	Ta		04-19-2001	Ve	SD
06-24-1998	Ve	Ge		06-06-2001	Ve	Ta
07-19-1998	Ve	Ca		07-05-2001	Ve	Ge
08-13-1998	Ve	Le		08-01-2001	Ve	Ca
09-06-1998	Ve	Vi		08-26-2001	Ve	Le
09-30-1998	Ve	Li		09-20-2001	Ve	Vi
10-24-1998	Ve	Sc		10-15-2001	Ve	Li
11-17-1998	Ve	Sg		11-08-2001	Ve	Sc

12-02-2001	Ve	Sg	02-26-2005	Ve	Pi
12-26-2001	Ve	Cp	03-22-2005	Ve	Ar
01-18-2002	Ve	Aq	04-15-2005	Ve	Ta
02-11-2002	Ve	Pi	05-09-2005	Ve	Ge
03-07-2002	Ve	Ar	06-03-2005	Ve	Ca
04-01-2002	Ve	Ta	06-28-2005	Ve	Le
04-25-2002	Ve	Ge	07-22-2005	Ve	Vi
05-20-2002	Ve	Ca	08-16-2005	Ve	Li
06-14-2002	Ve	Le	09-11-2005	Ve	Sc
07-10-2002	Ve	Vi	10-07-2005	Ve	Sg
08-07-2002	Ve	Li	11-05-2005	Ve	Cp
09-07-2002	Ve	Sc	12-15-2005	Ve	Aq
10-10-2002	Ve	SR	12-24-2005	Ve	SR
11-21-2002	Ve	SD	01-01-2006	Ve	Aq
01-07-2003	Ve	Sg	02-03-2006	Ve	SD
02-04-2003	Ve	Cp	03-05-2006	Ve	Aq
03-02-2003	Ve	Aq	04-05-2006	Ve	Pi
03-27-2003	Ve	Pi	05-03-2006	Ve	Ar
04-21-2003	Ve	Ar	05-29-2006	Ve	Ta
05-16-2003	Ve	Ta	06-23-2006	Ve	Ge
06-09-2003	Ve	Ge	07-18-2006	Ve	Ca
07-04-2003	Ve	Ca	08-12-2006	Ve	Le
07-28-2003	Ve	Le	09-06-2006	Ve	Vi
08-22-2003	Ve	Vi	09-30-2006	Ve	Li
09-15-2003	Ve	Li	10-24-2006	Ve	Sc
10-09-2003	Ve	Sc	11-17-2006	Ve	Sg
11-02-2003	Ve	Sg	12-11-2006	Ve	Cp
11-26-2003	Ve	Cp	01-03-2007	Ve	Aq
12-21-2003	Ve	Aq	01-27-2007	Ve	Pi
01-14-2004	Ve	Pi	02-21-2007	Ve	Ar
02-08-2004	Ve	Ar	03-17-2007	Ve	Ta
03-05-2004	Ve	Ta	04-11-2007	Ve	Ge
04-03-2004	Ve	Ge	05-08-2007	Ve	Ca
05-17-2004	Ve	SR	06-05-2007	Ve	Le
06-29-2004	Ve	SD	07-14-2007	Ve	Vi
08-07-2004	Ve	Ca	07-27-2007	Ve	SR
09-06-2004	Ve	Le	08-08-2007	Ve	Vi
10-03-2004	Ve	Vi	09-08-2007	Ve	SD
10-28-2004	Ve	Li	10-08-2007	Ve	Vi
11-22-2004	Ve	Sc	11-08-2007	Ve	Li
12-16-2004	Ve	Sg	12-05-2007	Ve	Sc
01-09-2005	Ve	Cp	12-30-2007	Ve	Sg
02-02-2005	Ve	Aq	01-24-2008	Ve	Cp

02-17-2008	Ve	Aq		02-02-2009	Ve	Ar
03-12-2008	Ve	Pi		03-06-2009	Ve	SR
04-06-2008	Ve	Ar		04-11-2009	Ve	Ar
04-30-2008	Ve	Ta		04-17-2009	Ve	SD
05-24-2008	Ve	Ge		04-24-2009	Ve	Ar
06-18-2008	Ve	Ca		06-06-2009	Ve	Ta
07-12-2008	Ve	Le		07-05-2009	Ve	Ge
08-05-2008	Ve	Vi		07-31-2009	Ve	Ca
08-30-2008	Ve	Li		08-26-2009	Ve	Le
09-23-2008	Ve	Sc		09-20-2009	Ve	Vi
10-18-2008	Ve	Sg		10-14-2009	Ve	Li
11-12-2008	Ve	Cp		11-07-2009	Ve	Sc
12-07-2008	Ve	Aq		12-01-2009	Ve	Sg
01-03-2009	Ve	Pi		12-25-2009	Ve	Cp